Love him or hate him, John McEnroe is undoubtedly one of the greatest tennis players of all time. He is proud of his achievements but, an innately shy man, he is also desperately uncomfortable with the trappings of stardom that go hand in hand with success.

Richard Evans, a personal friend, explores the McEnroe enigma. With McEnroe's co-operation he describes his middle-class New York Irish upbringing, his spectacular rise as a tennis star and the riches it has brought, the slump in his career and his fight back to the top.

He also examines McEnroe's notorious on-court behaviour, his stormy relationship with the press, marriage and fatherhood, and includes Tatum O'Neal on her life with John and their young family.

McENROE
taming the talent

RICHARD EVANS

BLOOMSBURY

First published in 1990 by
Bloomsbury Publishing Limited,
2 Soho Square, London W1V 5DE

This paperback edition published 1991

Front cover pjotograph by Ch. Guibbaud
Back cover photograph by Colorsport, and
Bill Summer for Nike

British Library Cataloguing in Publication Data

A CIP record for this book is available from the British Library

ISBN 0 7475 0872 0

10   9   8   7   6   5   4   3   2   1

Typeset by Rowland Phototypesetting Limited,
Bury St Edmunds, Suffolk
Printed in Great Britain by
Cox & Wyman Ltd., Reading

CONTENTS

PREFACE

John McEnroe has never quite forgiven Björn Borg for retiring. 'Nothing has ever replaced the feeling I had when playing Björn,' McEnroe admitted recently. 'For a while Connors came close and now I hope to play well enough to have some really competitive matches against Becker who I find extraordinary. But Björn was special and if people remember that tie-break in the 1980 Wimbledon final as the greatest piece of tennis they ever saw, then I must admit it stands out for me as well, even though I lost the match!'

But that was a decade ago and it is now eight years since I wrote the first book on John McEnroe, *A Rage for Perfection*. Eight years of triumph and tumult, of on-court mayhem as only McEnroe knows how to create it and off-court introspection that has made him one of the most fascinating sporting stars of this or any other generation.

Despite the crisis of confidence in himself as a human being as much as a tennis player which hit him in 1985, and again a year later, there was never any danger of McEnroe walking away from his sport as Borg had done. His commitment was too strong and even if he finally acknowledged that perfection was an impossible dream, he set himself another, almost equally difficult task, that of learning to compete effectively in a manner that did not preclude enjoyment and happiness.

'I don't want to be like I used to be any more,' he told me as his youngest son, Sean, played on his knee. 'I was too tough on myself and everyone else. I have to learn to enjoy myself more and if that means I cannot be No. 1 again, I am just going to have to accept that.'

The irony of his default at the 1990 Australian Open was that, to a considerable degree, he had been successful in learning how to tame his talent, at least to levels that were acceptable not only to himself and his public but to that other all-important person in his life, Tatum.

How long he will continue is anybody's guess, but already the remarkable way in which he has spanned a decade, beginning it at No. 2 in the world, rising to No. 1 and ending it at No. 4, has ensured that he will be remembered as one of the most controversial, successful and surprisingly durable athletes of all time.

The story is not over but so much has happened in the life and times of John Patrick McEnroe these last eight years that I felt it was time to bring everything up to date. Part of the material from the earlier publication of *A Rage for Perfection* is retained because nothing, of course, has happened to alter the account of his early years which remain crucial to the understanding of the man we know today.

Once again I would like to thank John, his parents and his brothers for their co-operation, and particularly to thank Tatum for the time she took to talk to me. Few people know, or understand, John better than his one-time mixed doubles partner Mary Carillo, who now brightens up the screens of CBS and ESPN television with her incisive commentaries on the game, or his Italian agent Sergio Palmieri who survives the thrills and spills of travelling with McEnroe week by week when he is on the road. To them, too, I would like to record my thanks. Our conversations are never less than stimulating!

At Bloomsbury, Nigel Newton's staff seem to take working against stringent deadlines in their stride but that in no way lessens my appreciation of the professionalism of Kathy Rooney and her editors who seem to have come to terms with an author who moves too fast for his own good and certainly for theirs.

The same, I suppose, could be said for John McEnroe but neither of us has quite found an answer to the obvious question, 'What do I do when I stop?'

1

A Day in the Life . . .

Let me tell you about a day in the life of John McEnroe; a life in which he admits there is rarely a dull day. The day in question was during the semi-finals in 1989, not in June but October, not at the French Open, which is played outdoors on clay at Stade Roland Garros on the green western fringe of the city, but at the Paris Open, an indoor event played inside the cavernous Omnipalais which tries to be all things to all sports amidst the cubic concrete of that reconstructed eastern end of Paris. Pissarro, were he to try to paint the Quai de Bercy today, would drop his brush and run.

The contrasts did not stop there. McEnroe was due to play Boris Becker, a man with whom he shared a birthplace – West Germany – and an uncommon intelligence, but little else. One the artist, the other the warrior, McEnroe and Becker are startlingly contrasting people.

McEnroe is, above all, a complicated man – complicated to a degree far in excess of the public's comprehension of just how complicated a human being can be. Becker, while many-layered in his personality, would never want to be as complicated as McEnroe. Despite a sensitivity which belies his burly, big-boned features, Boris is not wholly un-German. He likes an element of order and calm in his life. McEnroe may like the idea of such a notion, but he never comes close to attaining it. Never a dull day.

It is quite normal that these two very different people should respect each other. Mediocrity, as Arthur Conan Doyle wrote, knows nothing higher than itself, but talent instantly recognizes genius. Becker is the huge, all-powerful talent; McEnroe the wispy, waspish genius. You don't need Dr Watson to work that out.

But the respect and recognition is not straightforward. How could it be? Becker is often baffled by his immediate predecessor as Wimbledon Champion and McEnroe is frankly in awe of someone who can hit the ball so hard and so accurately on the points that matter.

Both, however, are professionals, paid to win, paid to beat each other, now as much for their pride as for their pockets. All sentiment is left at courtside. In the competitive arena anything goes, within the laws of the game. Inevitably, some laws have fuzzy edges, and McEnroe tends to interpret them differently from many people. Those who insist on depicting McEnroe as a villain maintain everything he does on court is a premeditated act to disrupt his opponent's concentration. They think he cheats. Others, who know him better, realize ninety-five per cent of the tirades McEnroe unleashes on court are spontaneous outbursts over which he still does not have total control. In that respect McEnroe has a serious problem — a subject to which we shall return.

In McEnroe's eyes linesmen and umpires create the problems by calling balls out that were in, and opponents cause problems by using something other than their rackets to win matches. McEnroe, searching manically for some method of denting the Becker armour, had decided that Boris was now using unfair methods on court. By coughing.

The grunters, led by Jimmy Connors, had been with us for some time. But Becker had developed chest problems a few years before and the resulting dry cough had stayed with him, becoming a recurring punctuation during interviews and, later on, in matches. In that the cough became most evident in moments of stress, it seemed to have psychosomatic roots. You do not need to be as intelligent as McEnroe to realize that. But in times of his own stress, McEnroe's intelligence slips its leash and races off as if suddenly embodied in a dog of war. Dangerous rationales are let loose.

On this particular undull day McEnroe did, indeed, plot a premeditated act of psychological warfare against his opponent and, in his own mind, felt perfectly justified in doing so. On court, early in the match, he made an issue of the cough. He started, in Ilie Nastase style, by imitating it. Just as Becker would cough seconds before throwing the ball up to serve, so McEnroe started spluttering down his end of the court.

The crowd, all 15,000 of them packed into every available seat of the Omnipalais, started to titter. Like all French crowds in recent years, they were wholly committed McEnroe fans and were prepared to tolerate their hero's indiscretions – up to a point. But it soon became evident that Becker was being severely embarrassed and he called across the net to McEnroe, saying, 'I have a cough. I can't help it.'

'You've had a cough for three years,' McEnroe retorted. 'Are you ill?'

By now McEnroe was losing some support. It takes a very special kind of personality to turn adoration into abuse, but the New Yorker has always been capable of achieving that in a thrice – another of his special talents.

And so the conflict started within him. Some people see only the snarling face and the petulant gestures of a spoiled brat when McEnroe loses his temper. Others realize the turmoil and conflict that is raging inside – the bull-headed belief that he is right clashing with the deeply sensitive, hopelessly aware human being who knows where this rage is leading; knows it, fears it, hates it and is helpless in the face of it.

I had seen proof of that just a couple of days before when he had blown up briefly against the tenacious and unsettling Austrian Horst Skoff. Richard Ings, the young Australian umpire who had taken a tough line with McEnroe frequently in the past, gave him a code of conduct warning and immediately McEnroe simmered down, grabbed a hold of himself and got back to work. But the fact that McEnroe, playing some of his best tennis beat Skoff appeared to be of little consolation when I dropped by the locker room after the match. McEnroe was livid with himself.

'There go my good intentions for the week,' he muttered morosely. 'I told myself I wasn't going to get involved here this year. It's tough enough to concentrate out there with all the people whistling and carrying on. But at least they are on my side. I don't need all the other shit. Why do I let it happen?'

The answer hung in the air. Mark Woodforde, McEnroe's

doubles partner for the week, looked at me and shrugged. McEnroe's Italian agent Sergio Palmieri, who had heard it all a thousand times before, stared into space. We could all have offered opinions but none of us knew the answer. The real problem was, neither did McEnroe.

Now, playing against Becker, the hurt was boiling up inside him again. He felt he was right in calling Becker's bluff over the cough. It was disturbing, a concentration-breaker — not just for him but for other players as well. They had talked about it. Now McEnroe was trying to do something about it. Didn't anyone realize he was simply trying to right a wrong? Of course not, and even those who did would have challenged his methods. So all hell was breaking loose again and what had been developing into a glorious tennis match was now marred with outbursts of increasing antagonism.

Inevitably there had to be an explosion and Ings, who usually chooses the right moment to intervene but got it wrong this time, triggered it. While spectators, especially those high up in the dark recesses of the huge arena, took their time to settle into something approaching silence, Becker bounced the ball in preparation to serve and McEnroe just stood there. Not crouching forward in his customary receiving stance but just standing there, immobile, with that expression he has mastered of arrogant boredom. Boredom with the pin out. McEnroe-type boredom.

The explosion came when Ings, having counted the seconds ticking away, gave McEnroe a conduct warning for time-wasting. 'You were not in your receiving stance and Mr Becker was ready to serve,' Ings told him as McEnroe stormed forward with that prancing stride he develops whenever the juices are flowing; McEnroe storming the citadel of authority, looking up, hating the need to look up physically to his judge and juror, hating the shackles that were being placed around him; screaming out for the freedom to try and play this magical game to his own level of perfection, without the hindrance of errors and stupidities from fools with rules who didn't know how to implement them.

Much of that was racing through McEnroe's head as he refused to accept Ings' ruling and demanded the Grand Prix Supervisor. Ed Hardisty, a tall Scot who used to referee the tournament in Hong

Kong before he joined the tour, came loping out to face the kind of scene that wakes tennis officials in the night. Unlike the incident against Skoff, Ings had come down on McEnroe when the player had the possibility of mounting an argument in his defence. Fatal. As he had been standing in the right place to receive serve, he could argue that he was ready even if it didn't look like it. And that was what he did ... argue. The place had erupted into bedlam in the meantime and it was a full five minutes before order was restored. By then McEnroe had been docked a penalty point – which cost him the game – and the tennis was allowed to continue.

For a couple of minutes we had seen a flashback to the Real Terror, the bad old McEnroe of which we had seen less and less in the previous couple of years. The conscious effort he had been making to clean up his act in his new role of husband and father really had improved his behaviour, even if you would not have known it from reading the tabloid press where every sniff and dirty look was translated into screaming headlines every bit as over the top as the player's former outbursts.

Nevertheless, the loss of a penalty point doused the ire like a cold shower and, with another throwback to his unruly but brilliantly successful youth, he immediately started to produce his best tennis of the match, even of the year. By the end it was probably as good a spell of tennis as McEnroe had managed since the beginning of 1985 and, with Becker still battling him at every turn, the second set unlocked a treasure chest of jewels that cascaded over the court, dazzling us, taking our breath away.

From a courtside seat, one was able to appreciate the extraordinary levels of skill, speed and power being displayed. Having won the first set on the tie-break, Becker's first serve faltered momentarily in the second set and, once the arguments were over, McEnroe pounced. Just as he had against Ivan Lendl in his heyday five years before, McEnroe revealed his incredible ability to move forward into the mouth of the cannon and use an opponent's power for his own devilish devices. For months he had been haunted by the spectre of Becker's power; a power increased by as much as thirty per cent above that which was possible with the rackets McEnroe remembers so fondly – the Dunlop Maxplys and the

Kramer Wilsons, wood rackets lovingly constructed by artisans for artists.

Now, for the first time, he was finding himself capable of dealing with that power. No longer was he cowed by it; no longer did he feel impotent in the face of the ground strokes that a more consistent and confident Becker was firing from the back court. With these magical hands, he could loosen the wrist, turn the racket head and start guiding the ball about at will before unleashing a little power of his own when the opening appeared. Only on the backhand when he is well set does McEnroe exhibit a sweeping, classic shot. For the most part it is all little jabs and stabs, a touch here and a flick there, even a prod on the volley while lunging for a wide return.

In that respect Camille Pissarro, had he still been painting out-of-doors, could have done things with McEnroe as an artist. Pissarro, apart from being a leading Impressionist, was also the first of that group to join the school of Pointillism fathered by Georges Seurat. Pointillism was so named because Seurat used only the very tip of his brush to juxtapose little points or dots of different colours on the canvas. Tiny jabs of colour executed with the deft touch of a true artist. McEnroe, surely, is a Pointillist tennis player.

As McEnroe worked his way into the match, puncturing Becker's defences with winning volleys launched by a first serve plucked from the halcyon years or a sudden, jabbing approach shot, the crowd was in ferment. So, too, judging from the comments I heard later from people watching on ESPN sports network (in the States) or Eurosport, were many armchair viewers at home. This was McEnroe back on the world stage, reaching into his past to prove that it was not a closed book. The standard of his tennis as he broke serve to close the second set 6–3 was better than he had produced in beating Lendl on his way to winning the WCT Dallas Finals back in April; better than his display against Mats Wilander in the Wimbledon quarter-finals. The sting in the first serve was reappearing, the deterioration in speed barely noticeable now that the body had been fine-tuned again to proper fitness; the touch on the volley as breathtaking as ever.

But was he as good as before? Almost inevitably not. In a game

6

that demands such split-second reflexes and steely nerve, a tennis player of thirty is not going to be as good as he was at twenty-five. Having said that, McEnroe in the second set of the Paris Open of 1989 was playing tennis that would have swept him on to victory against any opponent he could have come up against in 1984. But tennis is not snooker or golf or bowls, where a strong mind can block out the fact that Steve Davis or Nick Faldo is standing at your elbow and thus allow you to play to the maximum level of your physical capability. While not for a moment wishing to underestimate the amount of mental pressure a Faldo can exert on an opponent, it is still not the same as having a Becker blasting balls at you across a net. In tennis an opponent can physically destroy your game with his own power. There was no Becker in 1984 but now, once again, McEnroe was about to be forcibly reminded of what the post-Orwellian years had brought to tennis. Power, power and more power. But, in Becker's case, it was not just the power derived from bulging muscles and a large, tautly-strung graphite racket. It was strength in the mind, too; a mind so set for combat that it actually enjoyed being forced one step back so that it could experience the thrill of taking two steps forward. Gonzales, Hoad, Laver, Rosewall, Newcombe, Connors, Borg, to speak only of the post-war generation: all knew how to claw their way out of a tight corner. But no one, in the history of the game, has bounced off the ropes with such gusto and relish as this big German.

'A big point comes and I just feel good about it,' Becker has said. 'I just think, now I can play my best tennis.'

What a priceless gift! Some of the most beautiful strikers of a tennis ball I have ever seen have been destroyed by the desperate inability to play the one point that matters without their arm turning to jelly.

At one set all against McEnroe in this mood, Becker knew that every point would be big, every shot crucial. Becker's cough had subsided along with McEnroe's temper. All the extraneous rubbish had been cast aside. Both men's concentration was now focused and locked. The baying of the crowd no longer pierced the fragile veil behind which public performers compete at the highest level. They were totally single-minded and utterly oblivious to everything around them except each other's serve; each other's next volley; each other's every look, every move.

Physically, McEnroe started to feel the brunt of Becker's strength again; feeling the force of the ball on his racket. As Becker's first service percentage started to rise, McEnroe found himself back in the guessing game.

'To some extent you have to guess,' he told me later. 'With Boris's first delivery, waiting to read it is too late. It's passed you before you move. You have to read his mind and make your move as he throws the ball up to give yourself any chance at all.'

Sometimes McEnroe guessed right, but the bombs kept on detonating on his side of the court and only occasionally could he return them in equal measure. Once he lunged on the backhand volley to pop over one of those Pointillist volleys, a little blob of red on Becker's canvas. But drawing blood was becoming increasingly difficult. When Becker broke serve with some of those backhand returns that had destroyed Stefan Edberg in that summer's Wimbledon final, McEnroe felt the match slipping away from him. Becker, whose form had been patchy earlier in the week when Wally Masur had come within two points of victory, was shaking off the aftereffects of injury to regain the fluency of movement he needs to play his best tennis.

But even as defeat became inevitable, with Becker wrapping it up 6–3 in the third set, McEnroe felt an inner satisfaction that is usually incompatible with defeat. As he strode forward to shake Boris by the hand and put an arm around the victor's shoulder – just to show the crowd they did not really hate each other – McEnroe knew he had taken an important step forward.

'For the first time I felt I could handle the power,' said McEnroe. 'I began to get into a rhythm against it and could do what I wanted with the ball instead of always being on the defensive. He had to play really well to beat me.'

McEnroe was back in the locker room, trying to come down from the high he had been on out there on court. A packed, animated stadium; a great opponent; an ability to play your best tennis – no drug has yet been concocted that can give the true performer a bigger high than that. But for McEnroe there is no such thing as the straightforward thrill. By the time he walked off the court, leaving behind a cacophony of noise, he was shot through with enough conflicting emotions to blow the psychiatric fuse. Elated at having played so well; disappointed at having lost; thrilled to have been part of a great sporting spectacle; angry at Ings for the penalty point – and, somewhere inside, nagged by an as yet unresolved feeling that he had handled the coughing business badly. Just *how* badly he was to discover later.

Right at this minute the man was on the point of nervous exhaustion, a state with which he was well acquainted. The adrenalin pumped for a little longer, getting him through the press conference and halfway back to the Royal Monceau Hotel near the Etoile, a half-hour drive to the other side of Paris. Then it drained out of him like blood from a wound. He just felt the energy level collapse – a perfectly familiar feeling for McEnroe, who is constantly at the mercy of his own energy levels. Anyone watching him closely over a period of time can gauge those levels. On court, it's the walk; the narrowing of the eyes; the angle of the head; the amount of pulling and plucking at clothing and racket. In press conferences, not only the tone of voice and the body language change but the sentence structure, too. Although some sentences may not finish, as thoughts pour through his brain, those that do are loaded with a more forceful word usage and a more acute intellectual content. When the energy level is up, McEnroe is a formidable human specimen, physically and mentally.

But before the tournament driver swung the car into that avenue of light leading up to the Etoile, McEnroe's wattage was a great deal dimmer than anything on the Champs Elysées. And what was awaiting him? A soothing welcome for the defeated hero and a quiet, candle-lit dinner with his loving wife?

'Tatum screamed at me as soon as I walked through the door,' McEnroe confided later. 'She told me what I had done to Boris was disgusting and that I ought to be ashamed of myself. I went through hell that night and it was her birthday, too.'

Jerked out of his lethargy by this new attack, McEnroe could have been excused for wondering how many others he would have to fend off before the day was done. Becker, Ings, the crowd . . . and now Tatum, who had been watching the match on television, staying away from the Omnipalais that week in a deliberate attempt to remain one pace removed from the mayhem that so often surrounds her husband's tennis — all had assailed McEnroe one way or another.

'It wasn't an easy evening, I can tell you,' he continued. 'I was trying to sort out in my own mind where I had gone wrong, and there was Tatum telling me I was a shit and little Kevin starting to get upset and . . . I don't know, it was just tough, man. But Tatum was right, of course. My attitude has to change. I have to stop trying to change the world and right every wrong.

'But, basically, I'm a maniac when I play. I can see myself saying anything to anyone out there. It's the Jekyll and Hyde syndrome and I'm still trying to learn how to handle it.'

By the time McEnroe fell onto the pillow that night, the notion of 'never a dull day' had possibly taken on a new meaning even by his standards. But the turmoil his emotions had been put through was, as usual, largely of his own doing. He chooses to lead his life on the knife-edge of hysteria. He chose a wife who takes him on with the same reformist zeal with which he berates an umpire for a bad decision. By and large, he is the instigator of the bedlam that surrounds so much of his life. It is not simply a question of wanting it that way, but of needing it that way. What else to do with all that swirling emotion and pent-up energy? How else to calm Dr Jekyll if not to give vent to Mr Hyde?

It is a question he has yet to answer fully, despite the considerable progress that has been made over the past few years. But progress there is, and it was much in evidence the following day when none other than Boris Becker himself joined John, Tatum and Sergio Palmieri for dinner at a Mexican restaurant. Becker and McEnroe dining together twenty-four hours after they had yelled at each other across the net? The public perception is often a very long way from reality.

'We needed to talk things out,' said McEnroe. 'I was impatient to get it out in the open and put it behind us. We can talk because we both understand what goes on out there. It's an elite, special feeling the top players have. With some it's more difficult to strike up a rapport after something happens on court. But Boris is too mature not to be able to handle it. But you know what? Tatum was pissed off that he wasn't pissed off!'

McEnroe laughed, but there is always a cloud of confusion that hangs over McEnroe's humour as if he knows deep down that laughter, like happiness, success and life itself never comes cheap and that, sooner or later, something is going to happen to make the simple things complicated again. For John McEnroe, as he still learns to exist like a genie in the cauldron of his own making, it is all part of never knowing a dull day.

2

A Reassessment

'What we have here is a hard man; destined to be misunderstood; unable to compromise; driven by an inner rage for perfection the ordinary man cannot comprehend. It is no use, therefore, asking of him the ordinary and the commonplace. For John Patrick McEnroe Jnr is an original. There has never been a tennis player like him and, in a nomadic career that has brought me into contact with all manner of champions and achievers, I cannot think of anyone who encompasses his strange mix of qualities and faults.'

It is now eight years since I wrote these words – and they still fit. Though it would be wholly wrong to suggest that neither the inner man nor the public image has changed, John McEnroe remains, in essence, a hard-driven original blessed with exceptional gifts and socially unacceptable faults.

The faults and, to a much lesser extent, the gifts have dimmed with the passing years, but if there is one thing that we have learned about this quite extraordinary human being in the latter half of the decade just ended it is that both McEnroe's will and his talent are far stronger and more durable than most people imagined.

Although he still believes there is room for improvement – he will not allow himself to think otherwise – he has surprised himself by heading into the nineties as a rock-solid, undisputed No. 4 in the world. People who do not understand what is required to hold down the No. 4 spot on the ATP computerized ranking still come up to me and say, with a knowing look, 'McEnroe's finished, eh? Never win big again, will he?'

There he is: statistically, the fourth best person at his profession in the entire world and, artistically, even higher than that – and the talk is of his being finished. Partially, this is a case of his critics – the real died-in-the-wool McEnroe haters – being unable to stomach the fact that he has confounded us all by fighting his way out of a personal abyss in 1986, when his finger was wavering not so very far from the self-destruct button, to reclaim at least a measure of his former glory.

But, more generally, he is the classic victim of his own excellence and notoriety. It would be hard to refute the notion that John McEnroe has been the most celebrated, talked about and argued over performer in sports throughout the eighties. Only a few superstars in rock music and the performing arts can match the longevity of his notoriety and, in purely athletic terms, it is a rare achievement to enter a decade on the verge of becoming No. 1 in the most demanding of individual sports and to leave it at No. 4.

All this and the attendant headlines, writ ever large, propel people to a rush to judgement over McEnroe. There seems to be an urge to make definitive statements about an indefinite subject. Uneasy with complexity on such a vast scale, they search desperately for some way of stripping him down to the bare bones of a normal man, refusing to understand that there are no simple conclusions to be reached when analysing such a volatile and contradictory character. Tender and tough; money-hungry and philanthropic; self-centred and concerned about his fellows – the contradictions pile on top of one another. No wonder any attempt at pinning labels on this subject leaves the analyst astride Vesuvius. Soon bits of the McEnroe personality will be flying around him like volcanic ash.

Nothing pinpoints the absurdity of trying to pigeonhole this strange bird better than the manner in which McEnroe conducts himself on court, in the cockpit of competition, and his record as a public figure off it. For people who view him only from afar, as he rants at umpires and stomps about the tennis court in a fit of supercharged hysteria, McEnroe must seem, in all his Irishness, like a cross between Peter O'Toole, Brendan Behan and Richard Harris, with a heavy dose of his very own father-in-law, Ryan O'Neal, thrown in for good measure. Booze, broads and the odd bare-knuckle swipe at those who arouse the Celtic ire would seem to be the natural extension to the life of the personality McEnroe portrays during one of his tantrums. Yet, off court, only Tatum sees the tantrum and, even then, it is almost always contained within the four walls of some hotel suite, or the beach house in Malibu where the Pacific rollers tend to drown the worst excesses of what are, usually, evenly matched contests.

Of course McEnroe has snarled at photographers and flung the odd four-letter insult in the direction of someone who insists on invading his privacy. But a brawl? Some form of physical alter-cation with any of these people who resent him so deeply? With the lone exception of the instance in the lobby of the Regency Hotel in Melbourne, when he pushed a photographer backwards into the comfort of a large armchair, McEnroe has never laid a finger on a soul; nor has anyone got as far as throwing a punch at him. I find this remarkable.

I find it even more remarkable when one considers that, despite the obvious improvement in his on-court behaviour since his mar-riage, McEnroe remains the first name on anyone's lips when the talk turns to violent, immature, unsportsmanlike conduct. No matter that McEnroe's violence is all verbal. The old 'sticks and stones' theory seems to have fallen victim to society's current attitude towards violence. If we take consideration of McEnroe's reputation to its logical conclusion, we can only assume that words are now deemed more potent than punches. How else to explain that few remember the name of the Olympic boxer who laid into the referee in Seoul? And how about the All Black who foot-stomped the head of an opponent lying on the ground, or any of the other perpetrators of real physical savagery in that lout's game that is supposed to be played by gentlemen, rugby football? Or, if soccer is the gentleman's game played by louts, who can name a lout who is as celebrated for his loutishness as McEnroe?

Fists, feet, knees and elbows fly everywhere when some of these thugs get to work, but McEnroe's only weapon is his tongue. The excuse that boxing and rugby are physical contact sports simply won't wash. And anyone who wants to convince me that McEnroe poses as big a threat to civilized behaviour in sports as the foot-in-the-face rugby player needs only to answer one question. Would he rather have McEnroe verbally abuse him for three minutes or have an All Black in rugby boots stomp on his head for the same length of time? Only if he chooses the latter will I accept his argument.

None of this is an attempt to defend the worst excesses of McEnroe's behaviour. Umpires should have been far stricter from Day One with the scraggly-haired youth who burst, untamed, on to the world stage. But good umpires were a rare breed back in the late seventies and it was the fault of the game's administrators, just as much as the players, that tennis started to get a deservedly bad name for the conduct of some of its competitors.

Thanks largely to the programmes implemented by Marshall Happer, the North Carolina lawyer who became executive director of the Men's Tennis Council in 1981, today's professionally trained and professionally paid umpires have set new standards of officiating and, in so doing, have gained the respect of the vast majority of the players.

Even McEnroe decided a couple of years ago that it was useless, and just a little daft, to go on pretending that umpires were not members of the human race, and now he even calls them by their first names in the middle of some high-pitched complaint.

Once, in Milan, McEnroe found himself just ahead of Richard Ings in the taxi queue outside their hotel. Ings, who likes to make the most of the opportunities world wide travel offers, happened to be escorting an Italian girl to dinner that night and, never knowing quite what to expect from McEnroe, must have been mildly apprehensive when the two came into close proximity.

On this occasion he need not have worried. Just as John got into the taxi, he turned to Richard's date and, laying a hand on her shoulder, said to the startled girl, 'Now you look after young Richard. He's one of the family.'

Dumbstruck, Ings watched McEnroe's taxi disappear into the night, but if he realized that the gesture would not prevent the player from venting his ire next time a dubious decision was made on court, he was absolutely right.

Nevertheless the attempt to put Ings at his ease was symptomatic of the twin promises McEnroe made to himself when he returned to the circuit after his seven-month sabbatical in 1986 – namely, to enjoy his tennis more and offer a better image of himself in his new role as husband and father. If you happen to have been born with a temperament like Stefan Edberg, concealing a competitive spirit and a will of iron behind a soft Swedish smile, it is relatively easy. For McEnroe it is well-nigh impossible. Given the level of intensity he needs to perform at his best, it is hardly surprising that the twin promises have been difficult to keep.

To suggest, however, that McEnroe is as bad as he used to be is absurd. Just as absurd, in fact, as some of the headlines that maintain an image that is as out of date now as his headband and wooden racket. The knee-jerk reaction of many sports editors to the chance of running a 'McEnroe Misbehaves' headline is quite astonishing. Judging by the report in the sober *Sunday Correspondent* on the very last day of the eighties, McEnroe's run-in with British umpire Jane Tabor while playing for the United States against Italy's Paolo Cane in the Hopman Cup in Perth may have been a decibel or two higher than normal by his current standards. But did the incident deserve to take up seventy per cent of the report? Would the story have been given such prominence on the back page had McEnroe not misbehaved?

It is, of course, a question of news judgement. News, if you will excuse a masterly statement of the obvious, is supposed to be new. What on earth is new about McEnroe throwing a fit on a tennis court? Should it be reported at all? In passing, yes, if it had some discernible effect on the outcome of the match, rather than reflecting a reporter's need to find an 'angle' exciting enough to interest his sports editor.

Amongst the *bona fide* tennis writers, however, there is a ready awareness that their jobs have been made far more interesting and their copy given far greater prominence by McEnroe's presence on the tennis scene, not just as a result of his antics on court, but also through the long and thought-provoking press conferences he gives after his matches. No one can attend one of those without realizing that there is a very lively and belligerently honest intellect at work.

There is no doubt that it is the mind rather than the body — the long-abused and only recently cared-for body — that has kept McEnroe in tennis and extended his career into a decade few thought he would see as a top player. His intelligence, working in tandem with his innate love of the sport he plays, has kept McEnroe committed to a career that has, on occasion, appeared to be coming apart at the seams.

Patrick Collins, writing in *The Mail on Sunday* in November 1982, recognized the commitment but, like so many others, misread McEnroe's extraordinary resilience: the champion's bloody-minded ability to push through pain barriers, both mental and physical, with an intensity few can comprehend. After interviewing McEnroe while he was being attended to by one of his favourite physiotherapists, Cynthia Tucker, during the Benson & Hedges Championships at Wembley – a tournament he was to win that year for the third time – Collins wrote:

'He goes through his act, of course, scowling, barking, bawling out the odd linesman, milking the slow handclap from a few numbskulls in the crowd.

'But what you see is a man, rich beyond reason, who has flown 3,396 miles, simply because he had promised to turn up. A man who is starting to look old beyond his 23 years. A man on a treadmill, blessed with a talent he had no time to savour, endowed with a fortune he has no time to enjoy.

'And always he is scrutinized by his savage self-criticism. "Jeez, that was sick . . . Path-etic! . . . For Chrissakes, John, can ya play this goddam game?" He inflicts upon himself the kind of pressure which would cause less durable characters to be led away by the gentlemen in white coats.

'[And yet] . . . you wondered how much more he could take. And you reflected, not for the first time, that one of the most exciting careers in modern sport may yet prove to be one of the shortest.'

Collins, perceptive as ever, recognized McEnroe's durability, yet could not believe that someone who looked as worn and vulnerable as did this semi-demented perfectionist could survive in such a brutally demanding and imperfect world. He was not alone. As the pressure grew to have McEnroe thrown out of the Davis Cup team following the fiasco in Gothenburg in 1984, the smart talk on the cocktail party circuit in New York was of 'McEnroe's problems'. He was cracking up; he was on dope; he was seeing a shrink; his physical problems were chronic and would never allow him to play his best tennis again. It was the usual concoction of lies, half-truths, hearsay and fantasy with which the lives of mega-celebrities are stitched together.

By the time he was twenty-five, McEnroe was not only a self-made millionaire several times over but as famous and easily recognizable across the globe as all but a handful of people in any walk of life. He was envied as well as vilified for a life-style that encompassed all one could achieve of the American Dream – buying a Malibu beach house from talk show host Johnny Carson, amongst the best-known men in America but unrecognized in countries where McEnroe could not walk down the street without being mobbed; asking Jack Nicholson to wait for him in the locker room while he changed before going off to watch a Lakers basketball game together in Los Angeles; and marrying a film star and chartering planes to fly his family around Europe between tournaments.

But did this bring happiness? Of a kind, yes, because McEnroe playing with his kids or watching a basketball game with his buddies is as normal as one could be – a doting father and a boisterous, amusing, totally unpretentious sports fan. But if we are talking about happiness as total fulfilment, then, no, McEnroe was a long way from that during the mid-eighties as he struggled to get to grips with the two obsessions of his life – his family and his tennis.

To say that they were incompatible would be an over-simplification because, equally, neither could have survived without the other. Throughout his adult life McEnroe has needed just one woman as a lover, friend and partner and, after two lengthy relationships, one with Stacy Margolin, a tennis player, and the other with Stella Hall, a model, McEnroe met Tatum O'Neal and that was it. Their relationship was always going to be intense and volatile – anything less would not have held his interest – but even he was surprised by the amount of energy that was required to make it work. It was energy that, previously, he had reserved for his tennis.

'God, Richard, you have no idea how much we take out of each other,' he would tell me in between bouts of despair as his tennis started to deteriorate after his triumphant year in 1984. 'It's hard, man, I tell you. I couldn't do without her but it takes so much time and effort.'

But it wasn't just the energy that he was putting into his marriage that caused the loss of form on the tennis court. Although this was a factor, I think the steady realization that he was unable to control himself while competing was the prime reason for his decision to walk away from the game for seven months in 1986, coupled, to a lesser extent, with the need to heal an ailing body.

And while the energy-sapping relationship with Tatum had undoubtedly contributed to his frustration level on court, the fact that he had her to run to was, in the long term, what saved his career. Without the opportunity to retreat into a stimulating relationship with someone he loved, he would never have had the courage to turn his back on his life's work at the age of twenty-seven.

He knew, however, that his talent was being destroyed through more and more arguments, more fines and suspensions and ever-more acrimonious battles with officialdom. Aware that his genius as a player was being submerged by the welter of appalling publicity over his behaviour, he knew he was in danger of becoming a laughing stock. For a man of his intelligence who had just taken on the responsibility of fatherhood, that was an intolerable prospect.

People who have never met him have a great deal of difficulty understanding just how mature and intelligent McEnroe is in certain departments of his life, because there can be no doubting the level of petulant, childish immaturity that exists in others. But this is not unusual in people of rare ability. Many of the greatest figures in history have had character defects as large as McEnroe's. One need look no further than Sir Winston Churchill.

Churchill wasn't mad in the clinical sense of the word – although many of his critics tried to paint him as such before he became the nation's saviour – but was Mozart mad? Is McEnroe? The actor Tom Hulce studied some of the tennis player's behavioural patterns while preparing for his role as Mozart in *Amadeus*, as did the great Shakespearean actor Ian McKellan for *Coriolanus*. If one reads Peter Levi's *The Life and Times of William Shakespeare* it is easy to see what led McKellan to study McEnroe as a guide to his interpretation of the role. Quoting the classical source on which the play is based, Levi describes Coriolanus thus:

> 'The origin of all lay in his unsociable, supercilious and self-willed disposition, which in all cases is offensive to most people; and when combined with a passion for distinction passes into absolute savageness and mercilessness . . . Such are the faulty parts of his character, which in all other respects is a noble one.'

It would be difficult to pluck a more accurate description of a living figure from the texts of ancient literature. I have never doubted for an instant that McEnroe has a noble character. He is totally loyal and far too honest for his own good; highly principled in the manner in which he conducts his private life, he is a living, breathing antidote to hypocrisy. And that's quite apart from being a perfectionist. It is hard to ask more of a friend.

Yet the blind spot is very real and very damaging. It took him an inordinate length of time truly to understand the extent to which his 'unsociable disposition' was 'offensive to most people'.

If the penny was starting to drop after the Davis Cup sponsors and many leading members of the US Tennis Association (USTA) had used their influence to get McEnroe banned from the team because of his supposedly bad behaviour against Sweden in Gothenburg in 1984, it did not really start to sink in properly until he retired to Malibu and found that the tennis world went on happily without him — so happily, in fact, than some British writers actually rejoiced in his absence from Wimbledon that year.

'No one's missing me too much over there, huh?' he laughed, covering the hurt, when I phoned him in California during the 1986 Championships. 'Not too many people have called to say "Hi!"'

Those months at the beach with a wife and baby son gave McEnroe his first real opportunity to step back and put his life in some sort of perspective. Like Björn Borg who had walked away from thirteen years of tennis, week in, week out, McEnroe too had just been through a decade of high-pressure competition that had left both the mind and the body in a state of frazzled nervous exhaustion.

But, unlike Borg – a man he admired and liked as a fellow player, but could barely comprehend off the court – McEnroe could not simply switch off, retire to an island and stare into space. Even the great, low-key Swede decided that was a bit too low-key after a while and found himself a voluptuous Italian rock star for company. Having put tennis to one side, McEnroe needed the constant stimulation of a fully engaged, wholly entwined relationship and, in Tatum, he had just that.

Although he enjoyed the experience of normal living – if having a bunch of film stars as neighbours can be described as such – it was the necessity of matching wits with his wife that did him the most good.

'I finally discovered what a regular sort of life is all about,' he laughed when I spoke to him one day after he had spent a couple of months off the tour. 'You get up in the morning and worry about what needs fixing in the house.'

More to the point, I suspect he worried about what aspect of his general behaviour Tatum would pick on next. For if McEnroe set high standards for his tennis – standards that were not carried over into matters of social etiquette – so Tatum set standards of social behaviour that John found himself having to adhere to on pain of a tongue-lashing. He had not married a sock-darning wallflower. He had consciously chosen someone who could give as well as she got. In a sense, he had married another perfectionist.

The fact that McEnroe was a conscientious child who did his homework and never gave his mother any more trouble than the average energetic boy of prep school age may have lulled Kay McEnroe into a sense of false wellbeing. Both Kay and John Senior admit that their upbringing of John Junior was less than perfect. The biggest gap in 'Junior's' education lay in his contact, or lack of, with grown-ups. Innately shy, young John would be only too happy to go up to his room in the family house in Douglaston, New York and munch on a hamburger if his parents had adult company for dinner. This not only led to an almost total absence of poise and social grace when, suddenly at the age of seventeen, he was pitchforked into the limelight of the adult world, but horrendous table manners as well. Hardly surprising, really, if he almost never sat at table.

'We were rookies at the parent job,' Mr McEnroe will offer in defence of their efforts. 'But we got better at it.'

That much is undisputable. The second son, Mark, had his wilder moments, but has now settled down to follow his father into the New York Bar, and Patrick, now a world-class doubles player in his own right, is as pleasant and well-mannered a young man as you could wish to meet.

So although John improved in the years before he met Tatum, especially while he was escorting the gracious and outgoing Stella Hall who was constantly filling the courtesy gaps with all the 'hellos' and 'thank yous' that seemed to pass McEnroe by, there was still a great deal of refining to be done when he came to spend an appreciable length of time at home rather than paying only the typical tennis player's flying five-day visit. To a larger extent than even some of his friends realize, McEnroe's improvement in the public arena is due to the uncompromising attitude of his wife.

The rise in his popularity in Europe, especially in France and Italy where he is turning into a cult figure, has naturally given his self-confidence a tremendous boost and he has been both surprised and delighted by it. The arm-raised salute he now offers to the crowds in Paris, Rome, Milan and even London is an obvious reflection of that confidence. He has come to terms with the fact that he is a gilt-edged celebrity who attracts interest among people with only a peripheral connection with the game he plays. In the early days he was genuinely embarrassed, annoyed even, when journalists who were not genuine sports writers attempted to lift him off the back page to feature in other parts of a newspaper. When *Newsweek* afforded him the supposed accolade of a cover story, the stunned reporter assigned to the task of interviewing the subject was confronted by a less-than-impressed McEnroe demanding to know if the magazine did not have to get his permission first. He simply found it absurd that a tennis player should be considered newsworthy enough to merit a picture on the cover of a serious news magazine.

'I am honoured to be put on the cover of *Sports Illustrated* because I am an athlete,' I remember him telling me at the time. 'But *Newsweek*? That's ridiculous. I'm not a president or something.'

Moving in Tatum's world gave McEnroe a better understanding of how to handle the intrusive pressures of stardom, although that did not make him any more comfortable with the phoneyness of smiling just because a cameraman wanted a 'smile picture'.

'But Tatum has taught me a lot in that respect. She's been at it since the age of two or whenever,' he told me recently. 'She taught me that it really is easier, quicker and more pleasant for everyone to give the photographers what they want, rather than create a scene about it.'

However, it is hard for anyone who has never been close to the publicity process that envelops celebrities to understand just what kind of imposition it inflicts. During the Paris Open of 1989, John and Tatum wanted to take the kids for a stroll in the lovely gardens of the Parc Monceau near their hotel. A quick picture as they headed off down the Boulevard Courcelles, perhaps? Oh, yes, just one – and then a hundred more. There were four photographers waiting for them and it was a full half-hour before they finally agreed to stop trailing after the family around the park, sticking lenses into the kids' faces. Don't imagine it is easy.

But if McEnroe gets ratty under those circumstances, he can be a different person away from the probing eye of the newshound. On his way to play in the big exhibition event in Ede, a pleasant Dutch town not far from Arnhem, in May 1989, McEnroe had stopped off for a one-night exhibition against Amos Mansdorf in Nancy near the Franco-German border. Feeling in need of exercise, McEnroe set off with Sergio Palmieri for a run in the local park. Shortly they came across a couple of little ten-year-olds kicking a football around. The ball rolled over to McEnroe as they passed and McEnroe kicked it back. That's how you start a game of football, really. One guy just kicks it to another guy. No matter that the one is a small boy from a provincial town in France and the other a multi-millionaire American tennis star. The football is the thing, a common orb that rolls as easily to one as to the other. So the kick-about started on a patch of concrete by the park and the two youngsters discovered they had come across some talented opposition. Palmieri, like all sports-minded Italians, was brought up with a football at his feet, and McEnroe played on the left wing for Trinity School in Manhattan.

Soon some older boys arrived and very quickly a fifteen-year-old found himself being dug in the ribs by a friend. '*Eh, ce n'est pas McEnroe? C'est pas possible!*'

But it was possible because McEnroe, surrounded by kids with a football, is the least pretentious superstar in the world. Competitive, of course, because games are to be won – which is why he played so hard in a pair of old sneakers that he arrived in Ede with blisters all over his feet. But he played totally without fear or favour. Just mucking in. The kids, of course, were in heaven and, after an hour or more, eventually rushed off home with a story some parents might have found hard to believe. It is not difficult to visualize the scene. Little Jean-Claude bolts into the kitchen, late as usual, and offers the excuse that he has just been playing football with John McEnroe.

'Oh, sure,' replies Maman, giving the little tyke a cuff over the ear. 'And I suppose President Mitterrand was in goal? Now, enough of these stories. Eat your dinner!'

A mother in Nancy would not be the only one to have trouble believing such a story, which is a pity because the incident only highlights one of the great truisms concerning John McEnroe: all the bad is displayed in front of the world's television cameras; that which is hidden from the public eye is virtually all good.

'We all had such a great time,' Palmieri enthused. 'You know how good John is with kids. They loved him.'

They always do. Children who meet him by chance and adults who know him really well all like McEnroe.

'Anybody who knows you understands,' said Jakob Hlasek, the Swiss No. 1 who frequently plays doubles with him now, as the three of us discussed some minor problem McEnroe was having during the Silk Cut Championships at Wembley last year. 'It's only the people who don't know you who get the bad impression.'

Hlasek was right but, despite the improvement in McEnroe's behaviour, many parents don't want their kids even supporting him, let alone getting close to him. You hear this all the time from coaches and other people involved in the game who have to deal with the up-and-coming generation.

Trevor King, the young Englishman who is the tennis director at the Hotel Sotogrande near Gibraltar, offered the perfect example of the problem McEnroe has created for himself when we recently discussed the way the top stars are perceived.

'McEnroe's always been my hero just because he plays such fantastic tennis,' said King. 'But only yesterday I was ticked off right royally by some mother of a kid I was teaching when I expounded those views. Didn't want her child hearing anything good about McEnroe. Sets such a bad example, she said.' Then, grinning, King added, 'Mind you, I didn't notice all that concern about behaviour put any restriction on her own use of four-letter words when she got on court. Maybe she'd been watching him too much herself!'

This parent, and presumably thousands of others, would no doubt find it difficult to reconcile their views about McEnroe being such an unsuitable role model for kids with the scenes in Nancy or, indeed, in Stuttgart later in the year when the New Yorker was playing in Ion Tiriac's million-dollar special event. Tatum had decided not to join him until later on during an extensive and unusually long European tour. So was this an opportunity for the young millionaire to hit the playgrounds of Europe and seek out, nudge, nudge, a little on the side? People who think that really have no clue as to what John McEnroe is all about.

Hating the thought of being away from all his family for so long, McEnroe had brought his youngest son, Sean, and the boy's nanny for the two weeks in Stuttgart and, later, Toulouse. In between the normal demands on a tennis player's time of practising, eating and match playing, there were hours set aside every day for time with Sean. Time to reveal a gentleness and a patience with the two-year-old that would have melted the heart of his severest critic. Even Sergio, who is on the road constantly with McEnroe when he is in Europe, had to learn when to step back and allow time for John to play with Sean.

And yet this was the same man who, in a fit of rage in the locker room in Düsseldorf two years before, had stomped on a toy belonging to his elder boy Kevin, smashing it to smithereens. Kevin got a new toy but, for as long as he allows himself to descend into such acts of childishness, it will be difficult for McEnroe to gain a new reputation.

But he is trying hard and, as I also wrote eight years ago, as he changes with time, so time will ultimately change the way he is perceived. That is already happening, but keeping it up is not easy. With John McEnroe nothing, except allowing a drop volley to fall from his racket like petals from a rose, is easy.

But before we delve too deeply into the recent life and times of this endlessly fascinating performer, let us go back and take a look at the formative years and seek some answers to the puzzle that is McEnroe . . .

3

A Swamp Party in Douglaston

By the early hours of New Year's Day 1982, the Swamp Party was facing a crisis. It was running out of beer. That was not altogether surprising as over seventy young people were packed into the squat and far from beautiful house that stands at the bottom of Bayshore Drive, right on the very edge of Douglaston and Little Neck. Cars were backed up for several hundred yards along the steep curving road that leads past the large pond – soon to be iced over as the Big Freeze hit – and into the heart of the pretty and opulent dormitory community of Douglaston, New York.

The Swamp Party – so called because it was . . . well, kind of swampy as far as the well-heeled middle-class kids who attended it were concerned: hence its attraction – was definitely the place to be on this particular New Year's Eve. The house, made of overlapping slate and shingle which gives the less expensive buildings a scaly, reptilian appearance, was not really ready for the kind of invasion it received that night. It had been rented a few nights before by Tom Sobeck and John Dickey, a couple of local lads who were both carpenters by trade and were in the process of knocking the place into shape.

It was not, by consensus, the fault of the guest singer that part of the roof fell in. The three-piece band had been making quite enough noise on its own long before he had arrived and the swaying press of bodies was sufficient to test the foundations of the whole building. But, in the absence of biblical trumpets to bring the walls crashing down, the place stood and the curly-haired young man at the microphone finally worked up enough confidence to get into a Stones song, 'You Can't Always Get What You Want'.

Maybe it was the irony of the title that caught someone's

attention, for until then nobody had taken any particular note of exactly what was going on. Eventually somebody said, 'Hey, do you realize who that is singing up there? That's John McEnroe and we're all behaving as if it's routine. It's weird, man.' If I know John McEnroc at all, the man himself would have been very happy that everyone was taking it as just routine. Much as he loves to sing and to envisage himself up there performing alongside Mick Jagger, he knew full well just how far he needed to go with his musical ambitions before he could do anything more than make a token guest appearance at a charity concert.

So it was precisely because he knew nobody would give a damn that he was up there, wailing away into the mike at the Swamp Party on New Year's morning as his friends, most of whom had known him since they were all just out of nappies, searched around in desperation for the last cans of beer.

It was at parties in and around Douglaston and at local hang-outs like Patrick's Pub, which is as Irish as its name, and the Weeping Beech that McEnroe could shed the protective shell he carries with him around the world, and simply be himself.

It is a shame his public cannot see Himself as Himself, to use an Irishism. Because Himself is not at all the kind of fellow you see projected through a television screen. So often his behaviour invites his critics to see him as a loner, a man against the world, an aloof and cantankerous superstar with no more than a couple of close friends. Even on tour where McEnroe does, indeed, have a few enemies, that loner image is something of a joke amongst the other players who find him an agreeable and amusing locker room companion.

Peter Fleming, who was his closest friend on or off the tour in the early days, played the joke for all it was worth during the Australian Indoors in Sydney one year. Fleming had agreed to do an interview for Australian television and the cameras were set up in a small office right next to the locker room at the Hordern Pavilion. Although it was being taped, the set in the locker room was picking up the sound on closed circuit inside the stadium. Doug Mason of Channel 10 television opened up by asking Peter how he and McEnroe had come to play doubles together in the first place.

'Because neither of us had any other friends,' Fleming replied with a wonderfully straight face. He might have been able to carry it through had not hoots of laughter erupted from Tom Gullikson, Peter Rennert and a few of the other players listening next door. At that Peter broke up, too, and the whole interview had to be started again.

The full absurdity of such a suggestion became readily apparent whenever McEnroe was playing in the New York area. Apart from really close friends like Doug Saputo and Jimmy Malhame, various contemporaries were always dropping by the locker room. They could be childhood friends from Douglaston, old school chums or kids he used to play against on the junior circuit. I have often been impressed by the totally natural way he greets them. Neither he nor they ever seem embarrassed or even particularly conscious of the somewhat dramatic change in status that had taken place in a remarkably short space of time. This, of course, can be partially explained by the fact that many of John's friends come from well-to-do families and were in the process of making successful starts to their own careers.

But even with fellow tennis players there is still the same kind of easy 'How've you been?' informality that completely precludes the awkward possibility of the conversation taking a stilted or one-sided tone. No struggling twenty-one-year-old player is going to walk up to a superstar, no matter how well he has known him in the past, if he thinks there is the remotest chance of being hit with a line like 'I've just been making a couple of million bucks. What have you been doing?'

It says a lot for the way in which his contemporaries regard him that someone like Billy Porter could feel perfectly at ease going up to McEnroe at the Cove Racket Club on Long Island as he did one day to catch up with his news. Only four years before, McEnroe and Porter had been promising juniors around the Eastern circuit. Now Porter was back home from a long European tour, having battled his way around the Satellite circuit in France and Belgium in the hope of picking up a few precious ATP computer ranking points without which he would not even be able to qualify for the big Volvo Grand Prix events. Even though his results were improving a great deal toward the end, he would have been lucky to break even financially after four months away from home. McEnroe was at Cove that day to film a TV commercial for Dunlop – a company that had been paying him in excess of half a million dollars a year over five years to use their rackets.

This discrepancy in their fortunes was not mentioned as the two of them chatted easily about their tennis and old times. There was no evidence of the shyness and suspicion with which McEnroe greets strangers and even acquaintances from the world at large. With friends of his own age, whom he got to know before fame and fortune swept him far from the comfortingly familiar boundaries of Douglaston, he is a totally different person. And for years, even, with his duplex apartment in Manhattan and his condominium at Turnberry Isle in Florida, it was to Douglaston that he returned whenever he had some real time off from the circuit to recuperate and relax.

He spent the better part of three weeks there during the 1981 Christmas break. Apart from a couple of appearances for charity, he never touched a racket, which was good for him, and he practically never exercised, which wasn't.

Most evenings would find him ensconced at a large round table at the Weeping Beech, a pub-like restaurant owned by an English-woman Marta Brown and her American husband Russell. It is named after a tree which drapes itself with a forlorn kind of beauty over a little square situated just across the railroad tracks from the restaurant. Some typically callous developers wanted to chop it down a few years ago, but the good people of Douglaston raised a petition and forced the property men to leave their tree alone.

It was after that little triumph that the Weeping Beech was christened and the place quickly became a favourite hang-out for the neighbourhood's younger set. Although quite spacious, the pub exudes a cosy conviviality which is enhanced by the brick walls behind the bar and the dark green decor around the dining area, where one can enjoy such exotic variations of traditional fare as a Weeping Bacon Cheeseburger. Arrayed along the walls are mounted heads of stags and animals that fared less well than the tree. At one end of the bar there is a bison which bears a vague resemblance to the establishment's most famous client when he is passably content, and at the other hangs a bull moose wearing an expression many umpires would recognize as a fair imitation of McEnroe just after he has yelled at them.

McEnroe doesn't do much yelling at the Weeping Beech. Whatever his on-court behaviour might suggest, he is not a hell-raiser in a bar. Certainly he is a babe in arms compared with the likes of Peter O'Toole and Richard Harris, who used to shake the branches of another pub with arborous connections – the Queen's Elm in London's Fulham Road – until the leaves fell off. But then all these esteemed members of the acting profession, most of whom are now under doctor's orders to give up the booze on pain of death, are hearty extroverts by nature. McEnroe, just as Irish as O'Toole and Harris in many other ways, is the precise opposite – a shy introvert who lets his music do his yelling for him when he is trying to relax.

Amongst friends he had grown up with, McEnroe was perfectly content to while away the evenings before Christmas at that large table by the door, getting quietly bombed on half a dozen beers as he bought round after round for people who joined the group for a while and then moved on.

This was his haven away from screaming crowds and probing press and fawning hangers-on; a quiet corner where he was known, respected and liked simply as a kid from down the road who made it big. Strangers would have no chance of penetrating that group because, like most good locals, everyone knows everyone at the Weeping Beech. And they all tend to get quite protective about their most famous son.

But generally he was treated just the way he likes to be treated at home – as one of the crowd. But, of course, the status he had achieved in the outside world offers his friends all the ammunition they need for a little gentle humour. Earlier in December, McEnroe had been named one of the twenty-five most intriguing personalities of 1981 by *People* magazine. The day after the Swamp Party McEnroe was stretched out in the corner of another friend's house, looking mildly incoherent after the exertions of the previous night, when a friend called Robbie Jackson gave him a playful nudge with his foot and demanded, 'Hey Mac – say something intriguing!'

He didn't get a reply.

4

Beginnings

Life did not begin for John Patrick McEnroe Junior in Douglaston, but in the US Air Base Hospital at Wiesbaden, West Germany, at 10.30 p.m. on 16 February 1959 when Kay McEnroe was delivered – by an Austrian midwife – of an eight-pound son. The fact that this future Wimbledon Champion was born in Germany was purely coincidental. He was born there because his father was serving in the US Air Force and he was taken home to America when he was nine months old. Needless to say, he remembers none of it – in fact, he remembers very little at all from his childhood – and Wiesbaden only became a reality for him when he went back there with his parents in 1980.

There was a nostalgic meeting with Frau Hanni Schultheis, in her eighties by then, who had been the landlady of the house in which John and Kay McEnroe had lived before moving into accommodation on the Base. The McEnroes had been especially fond of Frau Schultheis and they were delighted to see her looking so fit as she emerged from her house on Lahnstrasse to greet them. They were amused, too, to see her eyes open wide as she recognized the young man getting out of the car. 'So this *is* your boy!' she exclaimed in amazement. 'I have read about him, of course, and seen his pictures in the papers but I never connected the two. I thought there would be many McEnroes!'

But that is the closest attachment John has felt to Germany. 'I suppose I had the choice of West German citizenship when I was 21, but of course it never entered my head,' he told me. 'I haven't exactly been inundated with offers to play for Germany in the Davis Cup, either!'

So if it is unlikely that the Wiesbaden City Council will ever see fit to rename one of their streets McEnroestrasse, that is as it should be, for the youngster's roots were soon firmly planted in New York. Not, initially, in Douglaston, but prophetically enough in Flushing, where the young couple and their infant son took an apartment in one of those tall blocks that stand no more than five minutes' drive from Louis Armstrong Stadium, then a dilapidated open-air arena. Eighteen years later it was to be transformed into the National Tennis Centre, just in time for a volcanic teenager to test the acoustics with a different pair of lungs, but as much flair and talent with his racket as old Satchmo ever blew down his horn.

By then, John Senior had left the Air Force and was attending law school while Kay was busy giving birth to another son, Mark.* Although they made life-long friends amongst some of their neighbours in Flushing, the McEnroes started looking for accommodation in a neighbourhood more conducive to raising a family. An advertisement in the *New York Times* drew them to Douglaston and although the apartment listed turned out to be no good, Kay was recommended another nearby. So, in 1963, the McEnroes made a move that was destined to put the conservative little community on the map. There are, needless to say, some especially retiring residents of Douglaston who wish that had never happened.

By the time John was eight, the McEnroes had moved into a family-sized house in the exclusive Douglas Manor district. It is a particularly pleasant neighbourhood, with the usual architectural variety that is common in expensive residential areas in America. No American with a little cash to spare wants his home to look like the one next door. Fronted by well-manicured lawns, many of the houses are wood-framed, while some are brick and others a combination that includes slate tiling.

Although far from rich, the McEnroes were beginning to feel financially comfortable by the end of the sixties. Despite the turmoil that was gripping so much of the nation, with race riots in Watts, Newark and Detroit fanning the flames of political unrest and a

---

* The birth of their third son, Patrick, in 1966, provided John with one of his earliest memories – possibly because a friend beat him in the race back to the house to greet the arrival of baby brother from the hospital. At the age of seven, John's competitive instincts were already at work.

whole teenage generation seemingly at war with its parents, Douglaston remained something of a backwater, especially for families with children too young to be concerned with hippies in San Francisco or the draft call for Vietnam. The first time John's father ever set eyes on Douglaston he could not believe it was actually part of New York City. It is something of a municipal quirk that it is for, geographically, it should really be part of the borough of Queen's. But such technical details were of little importance to this young couple who were well on their way to fulfilling the American Dream.

It is, I think, important to remember as we examine the McEnroe phenomenon that while John Junior was a self-made multi-millionaire by the age of twenty-one, his father in a less spectacular but equally remarkable way had proved that hard work and intellect can in a very short space of time break down the class barriers that exist in American society. John Junior's paternal grandparents were both born in Ireland. His grandfather, who finished his working life as a security guard at the Chase Manhattan Bank in New York, was born in Cavan and brought up in Dublin. His grandmother, a switchboard operator and clerk at a New York brokerage house, was born in County Westmeath. By the time their eldest grandson was nine, both had passed away.

Kay McEnroe, whose ancestry is half Irish and half English, feels that it is especially sad that Grandfather McEnroe did not live to see John soar to the top of the tennis world: 'He was immensely proud of John and would have had such fun boasting about his exploits to his cronies over a drink in one of his favourite pubs.'

No doubt the old man would have been equally proud one day in 1974 when the McEnroe household waited breathlessly to hear whether John Senior had been accepted as a partner in the prestigious New York law firm of Paul, Weiss, Rifkind, Wharton and Garrison. 'I went shopping that afternoon, just so as to have something to do,' Kay recalls. 'I had dropped young John off for his tennis at Port Washington and I will never forget returning there to collect him and seeing him rush out to tell me, "It's OK. Dad's just called. He's made it. He's in." John was fifteen at the time and the only one of the boys really to comprehend what it meant to us.'

It meant, of course, that a first-generation son of a working-class Irish immigrant had secured an extremely comfortable middle-class existence for himself and his growing family in one concerted leap. The American Dream eludes the majority, but John McEnroe had turned it into reality several years before his own son began making the kind of money that transcends dreams.

For Kay, whose grandfather was born in Northumberland and came from a family of hatters, the upward journey through the echelons of American society had been only marginally less swift. Her own father had run a trucking company and there were no immediate prospects of sumptuous middle-class living when she married an extrovert young New Yorker with a quick mind, a hot Irish temper and a sweet, almost cherubic smile. But she never had any doubts as to where they were heading. Kay McEnroe is a determined woman; very charming, very feminine but also very strong.

'I always believed that, as a family, we would be successful,' she told me. 'I have never been one to accept second-best. Mostly I was delighted with young Johnnie's work at school, but even if he got ninety-five per cent in some test or other I wanted to know what happened to the missing five per cent. I think I probably pushed him harder than his father did.'

As I discovered while working with Allen Fox, a doctor of psychology and a former Top Ten tennis player in the United States, scientific tests have proved that the classical formula for a successful son is a hard-driving mother and a father who is content to praise and encourage but not to dominate. In the book that Fox and I wrote, *If I'm the Better Player, Why Can't I Win?* we point out that in a study carried out by the psychologists Rosen and D'Andrade in 1959 there is a drastic difference, with boys in particular, between high achievers and low achievers, depending on which parent does the pushing. There is nothing more intimidating for a young boy than to be driven by a father who keeps demanding, 'Be like me!' A youngster of eight or nine, or even fifteen, can't be like his father — he is not as big, not as strong, not as experienced. If he is forced to compete on that unequal level, his ego is in grave danger of being crushed. The same is not true as far as the mother is concerned. The boy is not trying to emulate his mother. He is merely trying to please her.

Although John Senior was a good basketball player, it was perhaps lucky that neither he nor Kay had played tennis before they joined the Douglaston Club – a social and sporting establishment that is housed in an imposing, white-painted, three-storey building situated just a few blocks from the McEnroes' present house – the third they occupied in Douglaston.

The Douglaston Club has five tennis courts and it was not until their eldest son was ready to play that the McEnroes took up the game themselves. John's father was in his thirties by then, so there was little danger of him turning into the kind of player who could continue to defeat a superbly gifted and highly co-ordinated young athlete. 'I like to say that I beat John McEnroe for two straight years,' says his father with an impish grin. 'From the age of eight to ten!'

So, by virtue of his own extraordinary talent, John Junior eliminated the possibility of his father becoming a threat in a sphere of endeavour that had immediately caught his interest. Instead of being a dominating, overwhelming figure, Dad was removed from the competitive arena in young John's life to that place where fathers are most effective – on the side-lines, cheering. The prodding and the pushing – when they were needed – came from mother who, one assumes, from the way she laughingly refers to herself as the Wicked Witch of the West, was the one who kept an iron hand on the household.

'Oh, John was disciplined; don't misunderstand me,' his father emphasizes. 'Just like all other children, he was sent to his room and he got beaten on the behind; sometimes with my hand, sometimes with a paddle. But not very hard. And I must admit that five minutes later I was often hit with remorse. I was depressed at the thought of having to hit my son.'

Before all the armchair disciplinarians start nodding sagely and saying, 'There you are! Told you that was the problem. Wasn't beaten hard enough or often enough,' let me pose this question. Why should he have been? Because he deserved it? All the evidence points to the fact that he didn't. To a very large degree John

McEnroe Junior could be described as a model child who was far too preoccupied with the considerable demands of being a success in the classroom, as well as on the sports field, to give his parents any real trouble.

That is not to say he wasn't high-spirited. It would have been difficult for a child with that amount of excess energy to be anything else. But apart from one run-in with the Port Washington Tennis Academy, of which more later, young John was never in serious trouble either at home or at school. 'Even at the age of fifteen he wasn't allowed out during the week,' says Kay, 'but apart from one occasion, right at the end of his high school days when he turned up at three in the morning and got it in the ear, he was never late home when he went out at weekends. And I never, ever, had to tell him to go and do his homework in the evenings. He took responsibilities like that very seriously.'

If this picture of a conscientious, self-disciplined child seems a little too good to be true considering the 'spoiled brat' image he earned — and, to some degree, deserved — by his behaviour on court in later years, it must be emphasized that it is not purely the assessment of doting parents. Friends of his own age will confirm that, apart from sloppy dress and appalling table manners, John was certainly no worse than any of the other well brought up, middle-class kids of the neighbourhood. More importantly, the Headmaster of Trinity School would have said exactly the same.

Again, it may grate against the image many people have of this apparently loudmouthed, antisocial young man that the education John McEnroe received in America would translate in English terms to the equivalent of Westminster and Cambridge. Come to think of it, some very respectable upper middle-class British parents may not be that surprised because, if I may use an example close to home, my niece Fiona had a punk boyfriend with strangely cut and coloured hair and drainpipe trousers who was known to all and sundry as 'Bog Rat' and who went to Eton. Very nice fellow, too. But not quite what one would expect from the nation's premier public school.

The contradiction between McEnroe's public image and his private education — very private and very exclusive by American standards – is another intriguing and not altogether explicable facet of the story. If his behaviour on court would lead one to think in terms of a teenager emerging from the vicious, undisciplined world of the blackboard jungle, it should be erased from the mind.

After attending Buckley Country Day School in Roslyn, not far from his home, John was sent at the age of thirteen to Trinity School on Manhattan's Upper West Side. Trinity is not only an old educational establishment by American standards but by English standards, too. It was founded in 1709 by royal charter of Queen Anne and is linked to a Dutch Reform school dating back to 1638. In 1894, Trinity moved to 139 West 91st Street from the parish church that had housed and sponsored it up till then. With the completion of the Hawley Wing in 1970, the school buildings, which include a modern twenty-storey apartment tower, now occupy an entire city block. It is the oldest continuously operated school in New York City.

From the personality and appearance of the Headmaster with his tweed jacket, bow tie and pipe, to the atmosphere that pervades the imposing entrance hall and classrooms, Trinity exudes an air that is instantly recognizable to anyone with a British public school education. It is a coeducational day school with over eight hundred pupils – its size being partially dictated by the fact that it serves as both preparatory and high school, taking some children from kindergarten age right the way through to the time they leave for university at eighteen. The academic standard is high – a fact borne out by the number of leading universities that accepted Trinity students from the class of '81 alone – ten went to Yale; nine to Cornell; seven to Vassar and four each to Harvard and Princeton, amongst numerous others.

Trinity, in other words, is accustomed to handling the cream of the crop as far as Manhattan families are concerned and, on his arrival in 1973, there was nothing to suggest that a certain Master McEnroe, one of the relatively few children who had to travel in from the suburbs, would end up being one of the school's most famous sons or, indeed, one of its biggest benefactors.

'If you had lined up all 300 boys in his approximate age group when he arrived here and asked us to place them in the order of who was most likely to succeed as an international athlete, John would have come in 299,' Dr Robin Lester told me. 'He had a cherubic, full-moon Irish face, an unimpressive torso and was outright pudgy, with dimples on his knees. However, it didn't take us long to realize he had amazing hand-eye coordination.'

Dr Lester was the history master in McEnroe's time at Trinity, becoming Headmaster in 1975. He remembers John as a slightly above-average student in an average year; a shy boy with scrawly handwriting who always sat at the back of the class.

'But being shy didn't mean he was silent,' Dr Lester laughed. 'He had a healthy scepticism about certain historical figures and was not afraid of voicing his opinions. He was what I would call a master of the back-of-the-room witty aside. One could say the back row found him pretty entertaining. But with me he never crossed that line which would have made him a smart ass or a trouble maker.'

Although maths was his best subject, John McEnroe was a good Latinist in a school that prides itself on what is described as 'the current healthy state of classics at Trinity'. That alone would make Trinity a happy rarity among American high schools, but much of the credit for this must go to the English-born classics master, Frank Smith. Now retired, Smith was apparently the master who under-stood McEnroe best and who struck up the easiest rapport with a youngster who always had a problem opening up to adults. Again McEnroe's contradictory nature rears its complicated head. A middle-aged Englishman, and one teaching classics, would hardly seem to be the most likely candidate to secure McEnroe's trust.

By the time he was fifteen, John was considered mature enough to travel to school each day by himself. The journey was a daunting one, and the fact that his parents were comparatively at ease with the idea of allowing him to make it five times a week illustrates as well as anything the confidence they placed in their son's common sense and instinct for survival. Undoubtedly those daily journeys gave McEnroe a new and not very savoury look at the world and taught him how to stand up for himself. New York City is not a place where manners count for very much. It is a jungle at the best of times – a concrete jungle inhabited by every species of humanity, including some who make wild animals seem positively benign.

Quite a few of the less desirable ones lurk in the vicinity of Penn Station, and it was there that young John McEnroe, still quite small for his age, had to change trains every day. The journey from Douglaston to Penn Station takes thirty minutes and from there John had a four-minute walk to the subway in order to catch the 7th Avenue IRT line up to 91st Street – another twenty minutes away. Geographically there is no equivalent in London, but a child having to travel from his home in Sutton or Beckenham to Victoria and then catch a tube to High Street Kensington would face a similar kind of journey. In other words, it was a long haul.

'I wouldn't say I liked the idea very much,' Kay admits. 'But there wasn't really an alternative solution so I just tried not to dwell on the possibilities. And John was very good about getting back home on time.'

As it was, young John was only mugged once. The guy hit him a glancing blow in the face and the victim reacted in the best way possible for someone with a very fast pair of legs. He ran. Another incident McEnroe remembers from all those subway rides, rubbing shoulders with the smart office workers and the drunks and riffraff of that bewildering city, is absolutely typical because it spotlights so accurately the kind of things that attract his attention: the things that he finds important in life. 'A man with a sign around his neck saying "Deaf & Dumb" was shuffling past us on the train and someone called his bluff and goes, "You're not deaf, you asshole" or something really bad like that and, just for a split second, I saw the guy react. He had his back to us as the man said it so, of course, I knew he had heard. That taught me a lot about New York City and what kind of phoneyness there is around.'

Already McEnroe was deciding one of the things he liked least in the world was a phoney. Nor did he have much tolerance for cheats. Dr Lester, who as a tennis fan was accustomed to attending Wimbledon each year long before a kid called McEnroe walked into his history class, used to watch John play many of his school matches and he remembers one when the other boy was obviously cheating on line calls.

'Of course, there were no umpires or linesmen, so everyone was on their honour as far as line calling was concerned,' Dr Lester pointed out. 'But things were getting so bad in this particular match that eventually John walked up to the net and asked the boy if he was really sure of that last call. He was giving him a final opportunity but the fellow missed his cue. So John simply went back and proceeded to cut him to ribbons. He just humiliated him with his tennis.'

This is interesting, not just because of McEnroe's reaction to a cheat, but because throughout his junior years it seems that he was often playing within himself. The full force of the intensity that we see from him now virtually every time he walks on court was missing in those days, except when he was playing against opponents of near equal ability in national junior tournaments. The primary reason for this would seem to be that tennis was by no means the sole recipient of his interest and energy. Apart from his academic work, he played numerous sports, including basketball, baseball, soccer and American football and excelled at them all. But another reason seems to stem from a reluctance to make his opponents look complete fools — unless they gave him good reason to.

Soccer was a game that matched his fast-moving temperament and made satisfying demands on his abundance of skill. It was also, after tennis, the sport he played with the greatest success at Trinity. He played left wing and was the school's leading goal scorer in his senior year when Trinity led the Ivy Preparatory Leagues. Utilizing what soccer writers might describe as a cultured left foot, he perfected the curving cross and was even known to score directly from corner kicks.

But despite McEnroe's love of games and the amount of time it took him to pursue them, Dr Lester insists that it never affected his work. Nor did he ever ask for any time away from school to play tennis. 'Neither John nor his parents asked for any special favours on that score,' says the Headmaster. 'Even in his final year when he was rushing off on a Friday afternoon to catch a plane to play in some pro tournament or other — I remember one weekend he had to play Nastase and Lutz — he was always back in class on Monday morning well prepared; obviously having found time to do his homework. And it wasn't easy work, either. He was doing advanced placement calculus, which is basically a very difficult programme.'

The only event in his school career which John did miss was an important one – his graduation ceremony. 'He was very upset about it, but that was one occasion when tennis did come first – with our blessing,' explains Dr Lester. 'We made playing in the French Open and Wimbledon his Senior Year Project. So he was absent when all his classmates – a very bright and well adjusted group of young people like Alex Seaver and Tony Kiam, who are now both at Harvard, and Laura Hughes who is already a successful young actress on Broadway – graduated at the traditional ceremony which is held at Trinity Church near Wall Street. I know John would have loved to have been there.'

But quite apart from the fact that both brothers followed him to Trinity, John did not turn his back on his old school. On 5 May 1981, the Tuesday evening of the WCT Tournament of Champions at Forest Hills, Trinity hosted a dinner in the club grounds to raise money for the McEnroe Scholarship Fund. 'The aim of this fund', John explained to his guests, 'is to help provide a first-rate education to some New York City children who might otherwise be unable to afford it.'

The only thing that went wrong that night was that McEnroe lost, somewhat unexpectedly, to Brazil's Carlos Kirmayr in the first round. That, however, did not stop him appearing to sign autographs and answer questions posed by Trinity students and their families. According to the Trinity newsletter, McEnroe deserved thanks, not simply for raising $14,000, but for providing a fine example for everyone through his generosity and grace under pressure.

'He certainly does set us a wonderful example in that respect,' said Dr Lester. 'He is especially good with the parents, somewhat surprisingly advising them to keep things in perspective and allow their children to enjoy all the sports and facilities available to them and to resist the temptation to specialize too early.

'But, of course, one can't ignore the criticism he has quite rightly received for some of his behaviour on court. That is very disappointing to us but I don't have any answers. An Irish temper obviously runs through the family. Mark had a few problems with that in basketball games, but John was never out of control when he played sport here at Trinity. Noisy, certainly, but he was always complaining about himself, not others. I just hope he will learn to live more comfortably with the mantle of the No. 1 player in the world around his shoulders.'

5

Junior Tennis

If John McEnroe, the unruly superstar, was an exemplary student and loving son, who gave teachers and parents a great deal less cause for concern than many youngsters of his generation, the surprises and contradictions that litter his early teenage years do not end there. For, as a junior tennis player, this wonderfully gifted athlete who was to burst into the public consciousness as a Wimbledon semi-finalist at the age of eighteen was never ranked No. 1 in the United States prior to 1977, let alone No. 1 in the junior rankings of the great big world he was to dominate so soon.

Considering the natural ability that was evident from the moment he first kicked, hit or threw a ball as a tiny child and the hunger for victory which was lurking in his make-up throughout his childhood years, I find this to be one of the greatest anomalies in a life story that is filled with a bewildering array of unlikely and often illogical data.

However, Tony Palafox, the patient, good-natured former Mexican Davis Cup player who, along with the great Australian coach Harry Hopman, has been responsible for McEnroe's technical development, had coincidentally borne witness to an equally sudden flowering of talent early in his own career. Ironically, it concerned another left-handed Hopman protégé: a shy, freckle-faced Australian who was to become McEnroe's idol – Rod Laver.

'I used to practise all the time with Rod in 1958,' Palafox recalled. 'There was plenty of opportunity to do so that year because Rod was losing in the first or second round almost every week. I remember we finished the tour in Budapest and I said, "See you next year." But there was a lot less time to practise the next year because Rod was in all three Wimbledon finals – singles, doubles and mixed!

'I saw a similar sort of change come over John. There comes a moment when the head connects with the body. Everything clicks into place and the improvement is very fast. I must admit I never thought John would become so good so quickly. When he was sixteen he was only one of five guys I was looking after – Rennert, Fromm, Friedman and Kohlberg were the others – and although John had the greatest natural ability there really wasn't much to choose between them.'

Palafox was working as a coach at the Port Washington Tennis Academy on Long Island in 1970 when Kay McEnroe arrived one afternoon with her eleven-year-old son. Tony didn't need more than a few minutes on court with the child to recognize the easy, fluent talent he possessed with a racket, and he had virtually made up his mind to accept him into the Academy by the time he received a phone call the following day from Chuck McKinley, the 1963 Wimbledon Champion. Apparently McKinley, who died at a tragically young age in 1985, was calling at the request of someone he knew who worked in the same law office as John McEnroe Snr.

'What do you think of that kid McEnroe who came to see you yesterday, Tony?' Chuck asked.

'He's OK,' Palafox replied. 'He's got a good feel and can hit shots from all parts of the court. I reckon he's worth a try.'

Within twenty-four hours, application forms for enrolment in the Port Washington Academy arrived, signed by Father, and young John was all set for several hours of serious tennis tuition each week.

In September that year, at about the same time that Ken Rosewall, one of his earliest protégés, was winning the US Open a few miles away at Forest Hills, Harry Hopman saw McEnroe for the first time. 'It was a Friday evening when some of the more talented kids were there and John made an immediate impression on me,' Hop told me from the camp he ran in Largo, Florida, having left the Academy in 1975. 'Although his serve was nothing like the one he has now, he reminded me a bit of Neale Fraser [another of Hop's

Wimbledon Champions] because, apart from also being a leftie, he was always trying to do different things with the delivery.'

Later Frank Sedgman, Lew Hoad and Rod Laver were names Hopman mentioned in the same breath as the young man he helped to guide to that place in the tennis stratosphere that, at various moments over the past four decades, has seemed to be reserved exclusively for pupils of the Hopman school – No. 1 in the world.

Quite apart from the fact that he is not Australian, there are, however, some other rather obvious differences between McEnroe and other stars from Hop's stable. During his days as the most successful Davis Cup captain in history, the tough little Aussie built his reputation on discipline, and consequently a great deal of tennis talent belonging to the likes of Bob Hewitt, Ken Fletcher and Marty Mulligan fled Australia in the sixties because it could not tolerate the Hopman régime. So how, in turn, could Hopman tolerate McEnroe? Did Hopman, who was still an active and sprightly director of his camp when he died suddenly of a heart attack at the age of seventy-nine, mellow in his later years?

Hop had just come off court after a few more hours coaching in the burning Florida sun when I phoned one day, and the suggestion was met with a laugh as dry as tinder from the Australian bush. 'I like John's temperament,' he replied flatly. 'He is always striving so hard for the perfect shot. I like players who get angry when they fail to meet the standards they set themselves. John Bromwich was like that. I remember him throwing up his hands at the White City in Sydney as if he was praying for help.'

'Despite his generally quiet demeanour wasn't Rosewall that way?' I suggested. 'So often I've seen him throw down his racket in disgust after missing a backhand.'

'Kenny just didn't like to lose a point,' Hop replied with a quick, revealing insight inferring, surprisingly perhaps, that McEnroe is more interested in perfection for its own sake than the victory which perfection inevitably will bring.

As far as tennis is concerned there may be some truth to that, for the dream of playing the perfect tennis match is never far from his mind. But there is no denying the strength of the competitive drive; the need, when the mood takes him, to win just for the sake of it, for the thrill of a challenge. Kay McEnroe remembers being at the Douglaston Club one afternoon when John was still a youngster and there was a medal on offer for the child who could swim one hundred laps of the club pool. This was more an endurance test than anything and Kay didn't expect the idea to interest her son very much, because swimming had never been a sport at which he had excelled to the same degree as he had at tennis or football. However, when she was about to return to the house, John hung back and mumbled, 'I'll see you later. I think I'll give the swimming competition a try.' Later on in the afternoon, Kay returned and John was standing there with the medal. 'Yes, I won it,' he shrugged. 'No big deal.'

What drove him then? The idea of doing something, just about anything, better than a bunch of his peers obviously was sufficient to overcome the laziness that is also a distinct yet, once again, contradictory part of his make-up. Here we have a child who is always quite voluntarily on the go, bursting with energy and drive: a child who rushes into the house at lunch-time during the school holidays and grabs whatever his mother has cooking and rushes out again; a child who never has the patience to read a book other than for school work because he's always involved in a game of soccer or soft ball or ice-hockey on the frozen pond down the road. And this child is lazy?

'When Hop came to the Academy, John used to try and hide,' says Palafox. 'Hop believed in drills and lots of hard work and John didn't like hard work. He never wanted to practise as much as the other guys.'

A truant from tennis practice but a self-disciplined stickler for homework? However unusual that might be, there can be no faulting McEnroe on his priorities. School was serious, tennis was fun. School was difficult while tennis, for McEnroe, was easy. So why turn fun into drudgery? According to the logic that was forming in this boy's astute young mind, one should only be serious about the things one needs to be serious about. Work fell into that category because his parents were constantly reminding him of the need for a good education. But tennis practice certainly didn't. Tennis was time off; time in which to relax. If one wants to know why McEnroe takes his matches in such deadly earnest, the clue is here. Matches have replaced work while practice, in his mind, is still time off. In this respect he is the complete opposite of Laver, who spent more hours on the practice court than any player I've ever known, save perhaps for Brian Gottfried.

Here, I think, we get another inkling of another wholly unlikely aspect of the McEnroe character. Then and now John McEnroe is at heart the true amateur sportsman. I realize how preposterous that may sound to anyone who has only observed the millionaire athlete screaming his head off at some underpaid linesman. But that is McEnroe all wound up in the competitive arena. In a sense, he becomes a different human being the moment he walks on court to play a match. But there is an equally real side of him that, in an earlier, calmer age, would have fitted perfectly into the world of amateur sport as it was played – and still is played for that matter – at Oxford and Cambridge and the Queen's Club on a Saturday afternoon. One can just see him wandering around Queen's with his socks round his ankles, clad in the same pair of wrinkled shorts that he had worn to whip some bemused opponent the week before, his school scarf trailing from his neck. Once on court the same intensity would have been evident. But generally, both on court and off, I suspect that McEnroe would have been much happier amidst the camaraderie of the amateur sporting world with its code of honour than the code of conduct he faces on today's cut-throat professional circuit.

The code of honour that existed in American junior tennis as far as players calling their own lines was concerned suited young McEnroe just fine – even if a fear of cheating his opponent out of points occasionally worked against him. The rule in the junior ranks was that a linesman could be called for if either player felt there was a problem. According to his father, John never called for a linesman while competing in junior tournaments and in fact Mr McEnroe was rather startled one day at Port Washington when Herman Newfield, who was helping to run junior programmes at the Academy, came up to him and said, 'You know, you should never let John go on court without a linesman.'

'For a moment I was taken aback,' John Senior recalls. I thought

"What is he saying?" But then Herman went on to explain that he had never seen a youngster call so many close balls against himself as John. He said he was just cheating himself out of points by trying to be too fair and that it would be better for him to have a linesman.'

Knowing John as I do, I have no difficulty believing that story despite its rich irony. Even if the paranoia and virtual persecution complex that he suffers from today sometimes affects his judgement — and there is no doubt that he often complains needlessly about perfectly good calls — McEnroe's outbursts on court are almost always triggered by one of two things: his own imperfect play or what he considers to be an injustice. The inability — or the blind, stubborn refusal — to accept that life is a journey through a minefield of injustices lies at the source of many of McEnroe's problems, and his hatred of anything less than direct or honest would make it perfectly plausible for him to steer well clear of giving an opponent even the slightest opportunity of calling him a cheat. In his naive and unsullied youth, I am sure John would have happily given away a few points rather than leave himself open to charges like that.

So the 'amateur' code would have suited McEnroe very well in many ways and his affinity to that old-fashioned amateur world — an affinity that is well camouflaged, obviously, by all that intensity and less than gentlemanly behaviour — struck me most forcibly when I saw that marvellous film, *Chariots of Fire*. I realized then that Harold Abrahams, back in the twenties when professionalism was considered a nasty and probably contagious disease, was far more professional at heart than McEnroe is today in this age of multi-million dollar pay cheques. Just as Borg had his Bergelin and Vilas his Tiriac, so Abrahams, contrary to all Olympic ethics, became a pioneer of the whole coaching concept by having his Sam Mussabeni, the small Italian, played so movingly in the film by Ian Holm, who dared not watch his pupil race, not even from the back of the crowd. McEnroe has no Mussabeni. In the early days, only when a friend such as George Martin, a New York restaurant owner, acted as a kind of part-time assistant at tournaments to provide a buffer between John and all the people who want bits of his time, did he even have someone with him. But it certainly wasn't a coach. On the very rare occasions that Palafox watched one of his matches, the advice was kept to a minimum. For a top professional, McEnroe's pre-match preparation is just a trifle cavalier. As we have noted already, serious practice is a sort of last resort, used only if he hasn't been playing enough matches. Stroke production problems tend to get worked out in the doubles which McEnroe, quite apart from enjoying them, uses in lieu of practice.

So there were no real problems with opponents or officials in the junior ranks although, as his father readily admits, John quickly gained a reputation for being a very intense competitor – and a very noisy one, too. But all the 'hootin' and hollerin'', as Mr McEnroe describes it, was self-directed anger at his own poor play.

Apart from Hopman and Palafox, there were a few other people, some speaking from experience and some from instinct, who realized that this sloppy, pudgy kid was destined to become something special. One of them was Gene Scott, publisher of *Tennis Week* and a Forest Hills semi-finalist in 1967. Having guided Vitas Gerulaitis through his formative years, Scott is always quick to spot exceptional young players on the Eastern seaboard, and he played doubles with McEnroe in a local tournament when John was only fifteen. 'I knew immediately he was going to be a class player,' says Scott. 'He produced angles I had never even thought of. Anyone who has an instinctive grasp of how to play doubles at that age should have no trouble in reaching the top.'

But no one, perhaps, has an earlier memory of McEnroe on a tennis court than Mary Carillo, whose family still live just a few blocks away, towards the wide expanse of water called Little Neck Bay. A year older than John and a fine athlete herself, Mary used to join in all the boys' games that were played on the nearby sports field. Given Mary's happy, outgoing disposition – all that sunny Italian charm melting the Irish mist – I have no doubt that she helped him overcome any initial shyness he might have had with older children, as well as helping him develop his natural athletic talents.

'We played everything – basketball, football, ice-hockey,' Mary recalls. 'John was by far the best athlete around. His was the team you definitely felt like being on! But we also used to play a lot of tennis against each other when he was eleven and twelve. There was no problem getting courts at the club and we used to play five sets regularly during the summer months.'

Eventually John suggested to Mary that she too take lessons at Port Washington, and even there the two occasionally played. 'But that was as a result of disciplinary action taken by Harry Hopman,' Mary pointed out. 'Hop used to get mad because John would start dinking around and using all that loose-wristed stuff to produce outrageous spins in the middle of some straightforward drill. So Hop told him that if he wanted to play like a girl he could come over to our court and play with real girls! John didn't think much of that and it was a pretty long face that used to join us. But he got over it pretty quick.'

It was back at the Douglaston Club, however, that Miss Carillo turned prophet and caught sight of a very accurate reflection in her crystal ball. 'It must have been when he was about thirteen,' Mary said. 'He was beating up on me pretty bad by then. But at home I was still one of the best players around so he was quite happy to play with me.

'One day after we had just finished another heated battle I sort of collapsed by the court-side and just as a kind of reaction from having to deal with all that talent, I suppose, I said, "Oh, God, John, you're going to be the best player in the world."'

Typically, McEnroe wasn't impressed.

'Oh, shut up,' he replied, using a little mild aggression to hide a combination of embarrassment at the compliment and of realization, even then, of the enormity of what Mary had just suggested. 'You haven't seen anyone play. You can't judge.'

There is no doubt that McEnroe already realized that he had talent but, like any schoolboy, he was in awe of the great champions of the time. When Mary mentioned the best player in the world, John had only one frame of reference in his own mind — Rod Laver, his idol. Mary didn't know as much about Laver as John did, but she knew something exceptional was developing in Douglaston and it seemed to her that anyone of that age who could play so many different strokes so easily simply had to end up being the best player in the world. She was right.

There was early evidence that she would be proved correct in Paris in 1977 when she and John were both competing at the French Open for the first time. 'We looked at the sign-up board for the mixed doubles and said, "Why not?"' It is not hard to imagine the thrill they both felt when they went on to win the title. 'Mixed doubles champions at the French Open! Wow, we could hardly believe it. Four of our friends from Douglaston just happened to be in Europe and we all sat around the table and popped the champagne and made jokes about how half the town had come to Paris to see us win the mixed. It was a great evening!'

But this is jumping ahead of the story. Paris and champagne were still a little way off when the one blemish on McEnroe's career in junior tennis occurred. Sadly enough, it involved the Port Washington Tennis Academy, an institution that had been so good for him at the very start of his young career. The Academy, which thrived for many years under the directorship of Alex Aitchison, an Australian friend of Hopman's, is the brainchild of its owner, Hy Zausner, a rich American with a genuine philanthropic bent. The facilities of the Academy are such that the place runs at a loss, despite being filled to capacity with about a thousand students attending classes at junior and senior level at various times each week and a thousand more playing in one of the 150 tournaments held there each year. It survives only through tax exemption as a non-profit organization and generous financial contributions from Zausner himself.

Unfortunately, Zausner appears to have been a little high-handed in the way he dealt with an incident that occurred, not at the Academy itself but during a junior tournament held at the Concord Hotel in upstate New York in 1976.

'It was a schoolboy prank that got out of hand,' admits McEnroe. 'One night Peter Rennert and I decided we could create a little havoc in the girls' dorm. So Peter got a fire bucket and positioned himself outside the door while I lit a small towel we had rolled up and threw it into the room.'

Apparently Rennert then leapt into the room as McEnroe yelled 'Fire!' and sprayed the place with water, being careful to hit the burning towel and not being too careful about what else he hit – beds, clothes, girls in nightdresses, girls half undressed. Pandemonium, hysteria, great fun.

'Except, of course, that it was damned dangerous and therefore an irresponsible thing to do,' says McEnroe looking back with the wisdom of the passing years.

The story got back to Zausner because one of three boys – and McEnroe is still not sure which – ratted on Peter and himself. The result was a letter that turned up at the McEnroes' house in Douglaston a few days later, addressed to John Jnr, informing him that he had been suspended from the Academy, along with Rennert, for the rest of the summer.

'I thought it was a shocking way to handle the situation for two reasons,' John's father told me. Firstly, Hy Zausner knew me quite well enough to pick up the phone and, at the very least, warn me that the letter was coming. That would have been basic courtesy especially as John was one of his best students and we, as a family, were pretty enthusiastic supporters of the place, having sent Mark and Patrick there as well.

'Secondly, I didn't quite understand what it had to do with the Academy. The incident hadn't occurred at Port Washington and John and Peter were not playing at the Concord as representatives of the Academy. Without condoning in any way what had occurred I was frankly shocked and disappointed at Zausner's action.'

Although it was made clear to John that he would be welcome back for the winter semester, the feeling in the McEnroe household, always a proud and tight-knit family group in times of crisis, was that it would be better for the star pupil to continue his tennis education elsewhere.

'We put no pressure at all on the other boys but Mark immediately said that he had no wish to go back to a place where his brother was not welcome,' said Mr McEnroe. 'I felt like hugging him for that kind of loyalty.'

The decision was certainly made easier owing to both Hopman and Palafox having left Port Washington by that time and Tony working at Cove Racket Club, which is situated almost as near Douglaston as the Academy. So, fortuitously as it turned out, McEnroe and Palafox were reunited.

'I hadn't seen him for seven or eight months when he came to work with me at Cove and he had obviously improved,' Palafox recalls. 'But he needed some work on the backhand and to start with we spent at least fifty per cent of the time working on a top-spin backhand. Until the age of sixteen he could only hit the shot flat or with under-slice.'

Thus, in the quieter and more personally concentrated atmosphere of a small club, working with a man he trusted implicitly. McEnroe was able to add the finishing touches to a game that was to blossom so suddenly a year later.

Rennert, meanwhile, had moved with his family to California so he, too, never returned to Port Washington, although it was thought at the time that both he and his parents accepted the disciplinary action as just. In a *Tennis Week* interview with Linda Pentz in December 1981, Alex Aitchison was quoted as saying that Rennert admitted the Academy had been right. That remark prompted Rennert to write the following letter to *Tennis Week*, which was published in the 30 January issue of 1982:

'Just to set the record straight, I would like to correct a quotation attributed to me by Alex Aitchison . . . In their suspension of John McEnroe and myself in 1976, not only did I not think they were right, but I thought they acted hastily and insensitively without even attempting to hear our side of the story . . . I talked with Hy Zausner afterwards in an attempt to understand their point of view and apparently Alex chose to interpret my comments then as an acknowledgement that "they were right" . . . I didn't think so then and now that I have graduated from the junior ranks and have, I hope, attained a more mature point of view, I still don't think so.'

Even before he left Port Washington, McEnroe had decided that all the other sports he enjoyed and excelled at would have to take second place to tennis or be eliminated altogether. American football, the gridiron game, was one of the first to go. Being the best athlete on the team and the one with the quickest brain, McEnroe had inevitably ended up as quarterback – a position even more pivotal and demanding in American football than that of scrumhalf in rugby. But at fourteen McEnroe was still small for his age and therefore in ever-increasing danger of being seriously mauled by some opposing giant. His parents had been trying to persuade him to give up the game for fear that he would suffer an injury that would wreck his chances of realizing his full potential in tennis. But it was Horace Reid, a big black kid at the Academy who played on the pro circuit for a few years later on, who finally got John to listen to reason. 'You're crazy playing football, man,' Reid told him. 'Especially as a quarterback where you're throwing with your left arm. That's your tennis arm you are putting at risk. Don't do it.' Thanks to Horace that was the end of John McEnroe, quarterback.

By the time he was fifteen, McEnroe was becoming a veteran of the junior tournament circuit. His parents had taken it in turns to escort him to events in the East and mid-West during the early years, but increasingly John, despite his shyness with adults, was happy to travel on his own, finding no difficulty in enjoying his time at tournaments with kids his own age.

Eliot Teltscher, the wiry little Californian who was to dog McEnroe's footsteps all the way into the world's top ten, remembers playing him for the first time in Dallas when they were both fourteen. 'I know we had an umpire for that match, which was kind of unusual, because it was Anne Smith's father [Anne became a top player on the women's tour] but mostly we were calling our own lines,' Teltscher recalls. 'It was all very intense and competitive at the top junior level but basically Mac had fewer problems calling his own lines than he does with linesmen on the court today. He beat me 6–3, 6–4 that time with both of us playing from the back court. Mac was just kicking in his serve in those days. None of us had any serves to speak of.'

By the time he was selected for the US Junior Davis Cup team at the age of sixteen, McEnroe was developing a serve and a lot more besides. Nonetheless big national junior titles always eluded him.

Determination is written all over his face.

Above: McEnroe's idol, Rod Laver, is still out there on the Over 45 Tour.

Right: Jimmy Connors, as vocal as ever, with his new Slazenger Ceramic racket.

Right: Ilie Nastase at the Adidas booth in Atlanta during the Tennis Fair.

Below: McEnroe has played tennis giant Björn Borg fourteen times.

*McEnroe's current apponents
include Mats Wilander (above
opposite).
Michael Chang (right).
Brad Gilbert (below).
Boris Becker (below opposite).*

PHOTO: CHERYL TRAENDLY/PHOTOGENICS

Since Peter Fleming retired, McEnroe has chosen his doubles partners carefully. Here in San Francisco there is an encouraging word for Australian left-hander Mark Woodforde. They won the TransAmerica title and, a year later, lifted the 1989 US Open doubles crown at Flushing Meadow. It was McEnroe's eighth Grand Slam men's doubles title and his first without Fleming.

PHOTO: PROFESSIONAL SPORT

McEnroe with Peter Fleming. Together they won fifty-seven doubles titles – a Grand Prix record.

A doubles team that doesn't work – Patrick and John McEnroe. 'It might one day,' says John, 'But if you think he gets nervous, what about me? Too much pressure, man.'

PHOTO: RUSS ADAMS PRODUCTIONS

McEnroe winning his first Wimbledon in 1981.

Although he won his fair share of doubles, the name of McEnroe is not to be found on the list of National USTA Champions, indoors or outdoors: not at the age of twelve, fourteen or even sixteen. Yet by eighteen, of course, he had made that quantum jump to the senior level and the dizzy heights of the Wimbledon semi-final.

Larry Gottfried, Brian's younger brother, was the boy who most frequently denied McEnroe those junior titles and, ironically, Larry was one of the few top juniors of the era who never followed through to make it in the pro ranks. Apart from Teltscher, Van Winitsky, a good-looking, cocksure prankster who was always getting ragged by his team mates on the Junior Davis Cup squad for his boundless self-confidence, was another of McEnroe's great rivals and at that age one of his better friends. There were times when a long-suffering coach called Bill McGowan took this high-spirited group of Junior Davis Cuppers – apart from McEnroe, Teltscher and Van Winitsky, Tony Giammalva, Robert Van t'Hof and Jay di Louie were also on board – on a nationwide tour, sometimes by plane and sometimes in a long limousine with seven or eight packed in the back. Heaven knows how they survived.

'We were a pretty wild bunch,' admits Winitsky. 'Once in a coffee shop in San Francisco the waitress eventually tore off her apron and stormed out after we had kept sending her back for one more glass of water. She just went bananas. I used to get the most shit from coach McGowan. Then, I suppose, it was McEnroe who got in the most trouble. We seemed to have a lot in common in those days, especially in music. He and I were into Deep Purple while Rennert liked Traffic.'

McEnroe had already got a close-up look at the big world of professional tennis when he started ball-boying during the US Open at Forest Hills.

'I ball-boyed for Ilana Kloss and Regina Marsikova when they were playing in the juniors – can you believe that?' McEnroe grinned. 'And I ball-boyed when Pilic played Borg one year and Nikki gave me a lot of shit. But it gave me a good chance to see how those guys played.'

Although McEnroe quickly graduated to higher things, some of the kids who used to ball-boy with him are still at it. 'They just enjoy being involved for a couple of weeks in the summer,' McEnroe explains. 'They work some of my matches now and I'll suddenly remember their names as I turn round and say, "Let's have that ball, Bruce." It's sort of strange.'

McEnroe first played at the US Open when he was sixteen, partnering Tony Palafox in the doubles.

Ironically they were drawn against Vitas Gerulaitis and Peter Fleming who had stepped in as a last-minute replacement for Sandy Mayer who was injured. So Palafox found himself on court with three players he had coached! It was not until a couple of years later that McEnroe and Fleming came together on the same side of the net. They played together in Los Angeles and San Francisco and did well enough – reaching the semi-final both times – to want to try again when McEnroe left Stanford. By 1978 they were in the Wimbledon final and in 1979 they were champions. They ended up winning fifty-seven Grand Prix titles together – more than anyone in history apart from Bob Hewitt and Frew McMillan.

After reaching the Wimbledon semi-final in 1977, there was much speculation in the press as to whether McEnroe would continue with his plan of going to Stanford University in northern California, or whether he would be seduced at the age of eighteen by the allure of the professional circuit and its amazing riches.

'But there was never any real doubt that he was going to go,' says his father. 'It was something he had been working for all his life and even if he didn't stay for more than a year, we all felt it was important for him to go and get a taste of college life.'

McEnroe agrees. 'The good thing was that I had passed my entrance exams before doing well at Wimbledon so I had the added incentive of not wanting to throw away all that work. I'm really glad I went. I had a really good time.'

McEnroe started studying mathematics and calculus and initially signed up for a whole variety of subjects. But eventually, as it became apparent that professional tennis really was going to be his career, he searched around for something that did not require a great deal of written work. The emphasis had suddenly switched. Tennis had taken priority; tennis was work, and work, in the accepted sense, had been relegated to the role of an interesting pastime.

'Eventually I found this exposition class where the lady said, "No papers, no tests required, we're just going to talk." So we just had to sit around and rap about things that bothered us and it was good because some really weird things came out which taught us a lot about people.

'There was this guy who admitted for the first time in his life that he was a homosexual. Imagine doing that in front of twenty-five people! And then there was someone else who talked about a friend of his who had been mugged by a black man and somehow implied that mugging was a racial thing. There were two black girls in the class and one of them got really upset and stood up and said, "My mother was raped by a white man and I'm the result." Then she rushed out in tears. We all thought. "Oh, my God, what do we do now?" It was real heavy duty stuff, man, I tell you. So we told the guy to go and apologize.'

Under the tutelage of the well-respected Stanford coach Dick Gould, McEnroe was also continuing his education on the tennis court. Although John didn't put in as many hours on the practice court as team-mates like Bill Maze, Matt Mitchell and his old pal Peter Rennert, Gould has nothing but praise for the way his No. 1 player conducted himself as a member of the team.

'A coach couldn't have asked for more,' Gould told me. 'Apart from being the finest all-round athlete I have ever had here he was also the greatest team player I have ever known. He always had a deep concern for the other guys. He would always take the time to console those who had lost and help them work on their games if they needed it.

'And his dedication was never in question. One occasion I remember especially occurred when we were in Austin, Texas, and had to drive down to San Antonio to play Trinity, where Larry Gottfried was No. 1. John wasn't feeling well and, in fact, he was running a fever of 104° by the time we left. But he insisted on playing and went out there in front of a really hostile crowd and played his guts out and never lost his composure. And then he came back and played doubles, too. It was a really impressive effort.'

But the pinnacle of achievement at Stanford as far as McEnroe was concerned came when he followed in the footsteps of Jimmy Connors (1971) and Billy Martin (1975) by winning the National Collegiate Amateur Athletic Championships in his freshman year. Held at the University of Georgia's Henry Field Stadium, the NCAA finals are a high point in any American tennis player's career, and veteran observers amongst the three thousand crowd on a blazingly hot June day in 1978 have rated McEnroe's 7–6, 7–6, 5–7, 7–6 victory over John Sadri, then a senior at North Carolina State, as the greatest college match they have ever seen. It lasted four hours and in the end only one point divided them on aggregate – McEnroe having won 144 to Sadri's 143.

It required all McEnroe's speed of eye and exquisite timing to blunt the ferocious power of Sadri's serve, which was already being talked of as one of the fastest in the game at any level. But he triumphed, ending his days in the younger echelons of tennis at the top of the heap. The length of time it had taken him to get there can, I think, be partially explained by that realization at Stanford that it was as a tennis player that he was going to be judged and that nothing else really mattered. As soon as he had made up his mind about that, all the fierce endeavour and compulsive competitive urge which had been evident in his varied activities as a child came to be focused on just one thing – his tennis.

There were beginning to be times, of course, when the fierceness of that effort boiled over, but some keen observers had never doubted his ability to channel that effort and that talent into an unwavering pursuit of excellence.

Tommy Tucker, one of the game's great enthusiasts who is now director of tennis at the Mission Hills Country Club at Rancho Mirage California, first noticed something extraordinary about McEnroe when he was fifteen. 'I had never seen anyone reaching for perfection with such intensity,' Tucker told me. 'It was all in his face; the contortion, the pain, the effort. In a way I found it beautiful.'

At about this time McEnroe was beginning to think about beauty of a different kind. Stacy Margolin was his contemporary on the junior circuit and became the first girl to catch and to hold his eye. 'It was easy then,' John recalled a little wistfully one day. 'We were both just a couple of young players of about the same standard enjoying the same things. It got a little bit more complicated when we started playing different circuits.'

But even then John went to extraordinary lengths to keep the relationship going and, despite a few inevitable problems created by the pressures of fame, Stacy remained his only girlfriend for three years. It was in many ways an unlikely partnership and one which was typical of the cosmopolitan tennis circuit. Through tennis a New York Irish Catholic boy and a Beverly Hills Jewish girl, divided perhaps by more than a continent, met and discovered things in common.

6

An Autumn Tour – and the Talent Blossoms

After his first-round loss to Erik Van Dillen at Wimbledon and a summer devoted to college tennis, McEnroe still had much to prove as he set out on a long tour of the Grand Prix circuit in the autumn of 1978. He had done well enough at the US Open, dropping only one set on his way to the semi-final, where Jimmy Connors once again proved too experienced for him, winning with disdainful ease 6–2, 6–2, 7–5.

Yet Connors' victory seemed to confirm that the game's established hierarchy was not yet ready to let any nineteen-year-old upstart with a huge talent and hot temper muscle in on its jealously guarded perch at the top of the tennis world. Björn Borg and Jimmy Connors were the undisputed leaders of a familiar group of top ten players which inclued Guillermo Vilas, Eddie Dibbs, Vitas Gerulaitis, Brian Gottfried, Raul Ramirez, Roscoe Tanner and Harold Solomon. Few experts had any doubt that John McEnroe would soon be in amongst them, but nobody was really prepared for the speed and the brilliance of the assault he was about to launch – an assault he would carry right around the world to bloody the game's acknowledged king at his own Swedish court.

Immediately after the US Open at Flushing Meadow, McEnroe won his first Grand Prix singles title at a small event in Hartford, Connecticut. The news of that victory reached those of us attending the Arco Open in Los Angeles like a warning shot from the East. It seemed logical to assume that this would be the first of many. Within a week McEnroe was out West for the $175,000 Trans-America Open in San Francisco, proving all his supporters right.

It was there, at the famous Cow Palace, scene of so many great political and sporting occasions, that I came to a personal decision about John Patrick McEnroe Jnr. Looking back, I suppose it was a far-sighted attempt to preserve my sanity and, in a perverse sort of way, I have Jimmy Connors to thank for it. During the previous ten years I had been driven to the brink of despair on numerous occasions by Connors' behaviour on court and his attitude off it. I was often unable to decide which appalled me more, having to watch his matches with his strutting, arrogant and often obscene acts of bravado, or his truly embarrassing performances in press conferences as he struggled to recognize the meaning of 'defeat' — a word he had never been taught as a child.

I tried to concentrate on the brilliance of his tennis but always found it very difficult to ignore the rest. It is all much easier now, of course, because Jimmy has grown up, matured, got married to a wondrously beautiful girl and generally come to terms with the fact that being the second- or third-best tennis player in the world is really not all that bad. He has become at times an articulate spokesman for his sport and, as an entertainer who always gives his all, is worth his weight in gold.

But when I saw McEnroe appear on the horizon I thought, 'Oh, God, here we go again!' I recognized the short-tempered, highly-strung, intensely competitive signs that had been so apparent in Connors at the same age, and I didn't like what I saw. But, equally, I had no intention of spending the next ten years sitting in press conferences around the world watching a player whose behaviour I didn't like and didn't understand. So, in San Francisco I decided to do something about it. I decided to try to get to know this strange-looking and obviously intensely shy young man. I had never got to know Connors on a personal basis, which was hardly surprising because I had been highly critical of him in print and he, quite understandably, did not go out of his way to treat me as a friend.

In getting to know McEnroe, Peter Fleming was obviously my best bet. Peter had already been on the circuit a couple of years and we had become more than casual acquaintances during the previous two weeks because he had been kind enough to loan me his car. This proved to be a Datsun 240Z, which had been sitting in the bowels of a garage near the UCLA campus ever since he had left the University, and which was badly in need of some exercise. Actually it required quite a bit of exercise to drive the car – a powerful, snorting, wonderfully eccentric little monster that punished the driver noisily for any errors of timing with the clutch. In many ways it provided the best possible practice for getting to know John McEnroe.

But, in fact, I quickly found him much more agreeable off court than I had supposed. With Peter there to break the ice, he treated me with a great deal less suspicion than he would other adults trying to get too close. And, to my surprise, I soon discovered Fleming was right when he described John as 'very mature for his age'. I know that the on-court image is one of childishness and immaturity, but that is the performer wearing his performer's clothes. It is not a voluntary guise but a schizoid state common amongst many hyper-tense entertainers.

Away from the competitive arena there was no doubt that McEnroe came across as a quiet, thoughtful and sensible young man who was very quick on the uptake. Not exactly what I had been led to expect. But Fleming had insisted this was so and he was right. The pair had first met at Port Washington when Peter was sixteen and John twelve. Before long they had become friends and the age difference, usually considerable for boys in their teens, never seemed to matter very much. Peter calling McEnroe 'Junior' was the only obvious outward sign that the pair were not exact contemporaries.

'It didn't take me long to find out how good he was,' Peter told me when we talked about their first meeting some time later:

'I looked at this twelve-year-old kid in the coffee shop at Port Washington and told him I'd give him five games a set. My game was OK, nothing amazing, you understand, but hell, I was four years older and I thought I'd be able to handle it. The best I did was 6–2. After that we began practising together a lot. I mean, we must have played each other hundreds and hundreds of times. As you know John is not big on practice, but we always used to play for a couple of beers or dinner or something and we played our guts out. He deliberately used to call me names and get me annoyed so as to get my competitive juices flowing. I think it was the only way he could make a practice match hold his interest. Intentionally or not, it sure helped me. I learned from him just by watching the way he competed. And then later, I think I probably helped him a bit by being around as a friend when he first came onto the tour. Not that he was slow to make friends with other players. He's always been pretty relaxed in the locker room. But we were especially close and still are.'

With Borg and Gerulaitis as top seeds and Gottfried, Dibbs and Tanner as back-up cast, promoter Barry McKay, the former US Davis Cup player and Kramer touring pro, would have been more than satisfied with his field in San Francisco. But even before the talented South African Andrew Pattison upset Borg in the third round, McEnroe was attracting an inordinate amount of attention for a No. 8 seed. David Schneider, another South African, with a lopsided grin and a restless curiosity about the world, came nearest to causing McEnroe real stress in the early rounds by forcing him into a third-set tie-break. But after that the group of Stanford University friends who came up each night from nearby Palo Alto to cheer their hero was given few worries as McEnroe's lethal serving disposed of three tour veterans, Marty Riessen, Kim Warwick and Adriano Panatta, without the loss of a set. Little Eddie Dibbs, one of the game's great unsung humorists, didn't find much to laugh about as McEnroe's incredible variety of skills edged him out of a tense battle 6–4, 7–6.

'I mean, what can I say?' shrugged Dibbs afterwards, looking as if the dog he'd backed at his favourite Miami race track had just fallen on its nose. 'The kid's amazing. He's got all this stuff coming at you from everywhere and he's quick, I'll tell you that, he's quick.'

In the final, McEnroe appeared to be in deep trouble as another experienced campaigner Dick Stockton, a Wimbledon semi-finalist in 1974, produced a near-perfect illustration of serve and volley tennis during the first two sets. For the first hour Stockton was finding the mark with eighty-two per cent of his first serves and it was only the fighting qualities he displayed in winning the second-set tie-break by seven points to five that saved McEnroe from defeat.

After that, Stockton went off the boil and McEnroe claimed his first important Grand Prix title by 2–6, 7–6, 6–2.

In press conference McEnroe showed that he could analyse a match with as much precision as he could play it. 'Tennis is all about momentum,' observed McEnroe accurately. 'There is no doubt that Dick should have won in straight sets. Until the tie-break I was having trouble getting his first serve back over the net. Then suddenly I started moving better. I felt I could hit the ball again. And as soon as I was able to put some pressure on him he started to make mistakes. It's hard to serve like he was for three sets.'

Unlike a lot of cities in America, San Francisco does actually have some sports writers who know one end of a tennis racket from the other. But even for those who still insisted on calling a rally a volley – oh, you'd be surprised how many still do – that little critical summation by the new TransAmerica Champion should have told them all they needed to know.

While I headed back to Santa Monica to wrestle with Allen Fox's book and Peter Fleming's Datsun Z, McEnroe sharpened his skills in two smaller Grand Prix events: first, on the Hawaiian island of Maui, where he lost to the eventual winner, Bill Scanlon, in the semi-final; and then all the way over to Switzerland, where Guillermo Vilas beat him in the final at Basle. It was time for the next Super Series event on his schedule, the Stockholm Open – a tournament that had during its comparatively brief nine-year history earned the reputation of being one of the best run in the world.

Even before Nikki Pilic won the first Stockholm Open in 1969, the famous Kunglihallen on the outskirts of that charming city had been a breeding ground for some of Europe's great indoor champions. Players like Lennart Bergelin, later Borg's coach, Sven Davidson, Jan-Erik Lundquist and Ulf Schmidt had all played much of their formative tennis there as, indeed, had Borg himself. But if the special tiled courts – a surface unique, in my experience, to the Kunglihallen – had always been fast, they were certainly getting no slower with age. This was partially the reason why Borg, already a three-time winner at Wimbledon, had never been able to win his local event.

As soon as I saw the way the tiles reacted to McEnroe's serve, I knew it would take something special to stop him joining the long list of American success stories in Stockholm. Serve and volley experts like Arthur Ashe, Stan Smith, Tom Gorman and Sandy Mayer had all carried off little replicas of the Skandia Cup to place on their trophy-laden mantelpieces. Sure enough, McEnroe did not take long to join them. Tom Okker, still a sprightly and dangerous opponent, gave him pause in a closely fought second-set tie-break but no one else came as near to taking a set off him — certainly not poor Tim Gullikson who got crushed 6–2, 6–2 in the final.

But, of course, it was McEnroe's semi-final defeat of Björn Borg by the entirely deserving margin of 6–3, 6–4 that left Sweden dumbstruck. The match made front-page news the entire length of the country and one could almost hear television sets in Lapland freeze over and reindeer drop icy tears as the severity of the defeat became known. It was not just the fact that their national hero had lost which shocked the Swedes. The tennis experts among them had been aware of the possibility because the speed of the court so obviously favoured McEnroe's game. But for Borg to lose in one hour and fourteen minutes without ever seeming capable of offering any real resistance was almost humiliating.

But neither the Swedish press nor, indeed, Borg himself attempted to offer any excuses. There really weren't any to make. 'McEnroe was, to be honest, never in any trouble at all,' wrote Björn Hellberg in the *Slazenger Year Book*. 'So strong was the American's serve that Borg – regarded as the best returner in the game – only got seven points against it in the entire match!'

A disappointed Borg was philosophical. 'There was little I could do,' he said. 'John just played too well for me.'

Interestingly it was the first time that Borg, himself a teenage wonder, had lost to a player younger than himself. Their future matches would rarely be as one-sided, but the decisiveness of that first victory was important for McEnroe as it gave him a little psychological armour for the battles that lay ahead.

And so to London. The Benson & Hedges Championships, which became so much a part of the winter sporting scene, were a mere two years old when McEnroe made his first appearance at Wembley. The tournament might have been young but, like the

Kunglihallen, the old arena was rich in tennis history, as well as being the home of so many other sports. I first saw Pancho Segura there, illuminating the old London Professional Championships with his bow-legged, double-fisted brilliance. I saw Lew Hoad take a set off the other Pancho — Gonzalez — 6–0 in thirteen minutes on the fast boards that they used in those days. But Hoad secured only the first set, Gonzalez won the other two. And it was at one of those bars behind the restaurant that a young Mike Davies, full of Welsh fire and visionary enthusiasm, bought me a beer back in 1961 as he outlined his dreams for professional tennis. Later, as Executive Director of World Championship Tennis, he made some of them come true.

There had been doubts about bringing top-class tennis back to Wembley, which is not the most central location in the London area. But Benson & Hedges are five-star sponsors and when Jimmy Connors won the first tournament and Björn Borg the second, a new tradition had been born. In 1978, with neither Connors nor Borg present, the event badly needed a draw card to maintain the level of interest. John McEnroe arrived just in time.

David Lloyd, Tom Okker, Corrado Barazzutti and Dick Stockton were swept aside without the loss of a set but in the final, facing the determined Tim Gullikson for the second straight week, McEnroe found himself seriously challenged for the first time since losing to Vilas in Basle.

Tim, the right-handed of the Gullikson twins, utilized to full effect the great strength of his game, the return of serve, and won the first set on the tie-break, but not before McEnroe, exploding with rage and indignation, had threatened to walk off court after a bad umpiring mistake. On the first set-point to Gullikson in the tie-break, Tim went for a backhand down the line and the ball actually hit the net-cord judge before falling between the tramlines. Apparently the umpire wasn't looking because he gave the set to Gullikson. Even though the mistake was blatantly obvious, it took two or three minutes of shouting on McEnroe's part before the umpire, after consulting his linespeople, got the message and reversed his decision.

The fit McEnroe threw was not a pretty sight, but would justice have been better served if he had politely said, 'Excuse me, but I think there has been an error' and been ignored? Was yelling and screaming the only way to get things put right? One would like to think not, but I must confess that I am far from sure.

As it turned out it became immaterial because Gullikson won the tie-break fair and square four points later and a large audience was treated to a ruggedly contested feast of serve and volley tennis, with McEnroe's greater range of skills gradually gaining the upper hand to win the last three sets 6–4, 7–6, 6–2.

'If I win, I'll treat you to dinner,' McEnroe had promised me before the match. Although his tastes are a mite more sophisticated now, his idea of a good meal at the age of nineteen was a double helping of the best hamburger at Wolfe's in Park Lane. That was fair enough because, as he and Peter had won the doubles, it was a double celebration. Although his fame was spreading, he still wasn't as well known as he is today, but he was certainly known at Wolfe's. He had been cleaning out the kitchen there most of the week, judging by the reception he received from the tall, shapely waitresses. In that respect he was behaving like the typical tennis pro. If they find a place they like, they turn it into a substitute home for the week – quite a natural reaction for people who are constantly on the move.

In the five weeks since San Francisco McEnroe had been on the move in more senses than one. He had been moving up the Association of Tennis Professionals (ATP) computer so fast that even Borg and Connors were beginning to feel the draught. It would be a while before he would actually overtake either of them but, based on what I had witnessed on the tour that autumn, I had no hesitation in writing in the 9 December issue of *Tennis Week*, 'In my opinion John McEnroe is currently the best tennis player in the world.' It was an evaluation based, of course, on who was playing the best tennis at that particular stage of the year. There was no question of suggesting that he deserved the No. 1 ranking, because that can only be earned by a player winning at least one of the Grand Slam Titles. But from September to December 1978, I had not seen anyone come near to emulating McEnroe's record of consistency or rivalling the sheer brilliance of his play.

I did not base my judgement just upon his annihilation of Borg in Stockholm, although that proved beyond doubt that he was not afraid of reputations. I was more convinced by the fact that I had never seen any player come straight out of the college ranks and begin *routinely* beating hardened, high-ranking tour veterans in straight sets week after week: Stockton, Okker, Panatta, Dibbs, Riessen, Tim Gullikson — these were no push-over opponents. But this young man was pushing them to one side as if he was in a hurry to get up to the very top of the mountain in one great leap.

Actually, McEnroe was remarkably realistic and patient about the amount of time it would take him to do that, and it is another major plus for his character that he was never a bragger or a boaster. He was never one to lay claim to something he did not genuinely feel was his. So he knew it would take time. But the start he made in the autumn of 1978 left me in no doubt at all that, probably sooner than later, he would indeed be recognized as the best tennis player in the world.

7

1979 – a Year of Consolidation

The following twelve months removed the final doubts, if any remained, concerning John McEnroe's pedigree. By the time he had won the Masters in January 1979, the WCT Dallas Finals in May, and the US Open in September, no one needed any more convincing that he was the twenty-four-carat genuine article – a true world-class champion not merely by virtue of his amazing virtuosity with a racket but also because of that other vital ingredient, the ability to win under pressure.

Wimbledon, of course, remained a special problem after his surprising fourth-round loss to none other than Tim Gullikson. But that apart, he had become the third force in the Borg-Connors-McEnroe triumvirate that won everything that really mattered during the course of the year and a lot else besides.

His rise had been swift and spectacular in his utter domination of the rank and file. It is an old adage in tennis that every player needs a killer shot to become a champion. But it would be simplifying the issue to pick out one shot from McEnroe's vast and varied armoury. Rather, it is the actual variety that is so stunning. A player who possesses such an array of available options automatically puts fearful pressure on his opponent. What is he going to do next? The question eats away at the back of the mind, eroding the most carefully drawn-up tactical plan, and withering the will. It is not by shouting and complaining that McEnroe wins the all-important and so often overlooked psychological battles that are always raging unseen out there on court in a top-class professional match, but simply by tactically preventing his opponent from playing the way he wants. Although his own pavonine skills, often so arrogantly and effortlessly brilliant, tend to capture all the attention, they frequently act as a smokescreen for the tactical ploys that are slowly but surely dismantling the other man's game.

It is because McEnroe is so intensely involved in this all-encompasing physical and psychological warfare that he has no time for the niceties of acknowledging a good shot from the other side of the net. Instantly McEnroe is blaming himself for having *allowed* his opponent to get into a position from where he was able to unleash the winning forehand or backhand lob. The fact that the man he is playing can hit shots of equal power and brilliance is not the issue as far as McEnroe is concerned. He knows that, and is more than ready to acknowledge it before or after the match. As soon as battle commences, McEnroe becomes totally engrossed in the task of preventing those shots from hurting him. And when they do, the pain can be seen in his face. And yet he is not really thinking about the ball that just flew past him for a spectacular winner. His mind has already locked onto the ball *he* hit. Obviously it was too fast or too slow or not accurate enough — hence the self-recrimination.

That kind of reaction will not be seen, however, if Borg latches on to his best serve wide to the ad court and smacks it back down the line for a winner. That was McEnroe's best effort and Borg's best effort. Too tough. McEnroe has no problem with that. So, in a sense, he is a spoiler. Players, especially players he has met often and really studied, come off court knowing that he has not allowed them to play. Only a man with a wide variety of skills can do that. But, of course, he needs the big weapons too, and in McEnroe's case I would have to pick on the serve and the ability to do almost anything he wants with a volley that make him, at times, virtually unplayable. The feel and timing he possesses are quite remarkable. I have never seen anyone quite so adept at being able to turn the most blistering return into a featherweight drop volley.

Nevertheless it is interesting that coach Palafox picks on the volley as one of the few areas for criticism in John's game. 'He is in to the net so fast that sometimes, with the forehand grip, he has no time to adjust,' Palafox points out. 'So he hits up because he is lacking that fraction of a second to set himself right.'

It was Palafox, incidentally, who taught McEnroe to ease up on crucial points and resist the temptation to hit the ball too hard. 'As a junior he had a tendency to go for the big shot at 15–40. I stopped that. He still likes to hit the ball harder in doubles and that is correct because there is more chance of someone intercepting in a limited space. But in singles he likes to move people around and do more things with the ball.' It was chance, however, and not Palafox, that taught McEnroe his unique serve. 'I suppose I was already a little bit sideways on because that seemed sort of natural for a left-hander.' John explained:

'But the action I have today really evolved when I was eighteen. I had a back problem and was wearing a brace when I played Erik Van Dillen at the US Open. I wasn't comfortable with it so I took it off and started bending forward really low just before I served so as to loosen the back muscles.

'Quite by accident I found that the movement pulled me round to an even more sideways stance. Then, as I continued the muscle loosening exercises every time I served in other matches, I started to notice that I could hit better angles and that people were having a tougher time reading each delivery. So, even though the back is fine, and I don't bend low any more, I decided to keep the service action just as it was.'

Ironically, it was not his lethal serve that carried McEnroe to the first major title of his fledgling career at Madison Square Garden in January 1979. The serve, in fact, was the least impressive part of his game as he hung on to beat Arthur Ashe after Arthur, whose career was to be so cruelly cut short just a few months later, had missed two match points in the Masters final. Incredibly, McEnroe had allowed the first set to slip from his grasp when he served three consecutive double faults with the score standing at 5–4: 40–love. Ashe peered querulously through his contact lenses at his young opponent and quickly accepted the gift, winning the set on the tie-break. Having lost the second 6–3, Ashe actually led 4–1 in the decider before McEnroe's fighting qualities were put to their first real test in a crunch stituation, and they did not fail him as the native New Yorker showed the pro-Ashe crowd of seventeen thousand just what he could do by reeling off six straight games for victory.

It was not a vintage Masters — with Borg, Vilas and Gerulaitis all boycotting the event in another of the game's petty feuds, there was never much chance of that — and even McEnroe's first every victory over Connors was robbed of much of its significance by the fact that Jimmy was forced to retire with a badly blistered foot at 0–3 down in the second set. But even allowing for Connors' handicap, one detected the first signs that McEnroe was learning how to handle an opponent who had completely dominated him in the past. He was discovering how to put the handcuffs on his tormentor. A few months later he would have Jimmy well and truly under lock and key.

But a Masters title was proof of that pedigree; certainly proof enough for John Barrett, who wrote in the *Slazenger Year Book*, '. . . he has proved beyond doubt that his technique, his skill with a racket, his speed of thought and movement and, above all, his courage and will to win are of the highest order. The $500,000 he has won in his seven months as a professional has been earned on merit alone. Forget about luck, forget about the absence of certain players. Concentrate instead on his ability and recognize him for what he is: a worthy successor to Laver, Ashe, Connors and Borg.'

But, having skipped the Masters, Borg was waiting for his new rival on the WCT tour just a few weeks later. In the semi-final at Richmond, Virginia, Björn survived a hair-raising second-set tie-break, eventually winning it by ten points to eight after McEnroe had reached match point four times. By all accounts Borg's 4–6, 7–6, 6–3 victory remains one of their most dramatic and brilliantly fought battles, but it was rivalled a month later when McEnroe turned the tables in New Orleans at another WCT event promoted by the former British player, Peter Curtis. It was a memorable week in many ways, not least for the fact that Ilie Nastase actually got thrown off court in the third set of his first-round match with Bob Lutz. After that uproar died down, we were treated to some superb tennis. The Czech, Tomas Smid, sharpened McEnroe's game for him in the quarters before going down in three hard-fought sets, and that set the stage for another semi-final showdown with Borg. After being completely outplayed in the second set, Borg tested the younger man's nerve and skill to the nth degree in the third as he forced the match into the deciding tie-break. But once again McEnroe proved he could stand the pressure as he came up with some lethal serves and acrobatic volleys to clinch a 5–7, 6–1, 7–6 victory. After that Roscoe Tanner was swept aside in straight sets in the final 6–4, 6–2 – a sudden reversal of fortunes for Roscoe who had beaten McEnroe with comparative ease in the quarters of the US Pro Indoors in Philadelphia just a few weeks before. But McEnroe was growing in stature week by week now and, although he and Peter Fleming had already won the WCT Braniff World Doubles title in London at the beginning of the year, New Orleans provided him with his first WCT singles crown and it proved to be a good omen for Dallas.

But there was some travelling to be done before his rendezvous at High Noon in the Big D. Twenty-four hours after beating Tanner in New Orleans John McEnroe was in Milan, a city that, after London, became as familiar to him as any in the world outside the United States. McEnroe's Italian connection really came about as a result of his close and somewhat unlikely friendship with that feisty little ex-player called Sergio Palmieri. Tough and resourceful, Palmieri is not afraid to make himself unpopular in pursuit of something he believes to be right – and in that, of course, he shares common ground with McEnroe.

Although he was a somewhat controversial director of the Italian Open for a couple of years, it was as right-hand man to two of the most successful personalities in Italian tennis, Sergio Tacchini and Carlo della Vida, that Palmieri's hard-driving talents have been best employed. A contemporary of Palmieri's as a player, Tacchini quickly built his clothing company into a top line name in tennis fashion and, like his rivals Fila and, later, Ellesse, recognized the need to have his shirts on the backs of the best players in the world. So, as a Tacchini rep at the French Open in 1977, Palmieri was naturally interested in all the promising newcomers competing at Stade Roland Garros that year.

'The problem was, the first time we met I didn't recognize him,' laughed Sergio. 'I don't think he was too pleased. He was wearing

Fila clothes then and Marty Mulligan, who was working for both Fila and Diadora shoes at the time, dropped a pair of shoes round at my booth for John to pick up. When I returned to the booth later in the day I saw this guy standing there asking for shoes and I said, "Who are you?" Eh, bellissimo, such a good start. But we got on better after that.'

So much better, in fact, that after Palmieri had shown McEnroe the confidence he had in him by inviting him to play in 1978, in an exhibition in Milan with Borg, Gerulaitis and Panatta – starry-eyed company for a youngster still at college – Sergio became one of McEnroe's closest European friends. Naturally a Tacchini contract was waiting for him as soon as he left Stanford and McEnroe, while still shying away from the rigours of the red clay at the Foro Italico in Rome, nevertheless became a regular visitor to the two major indoor events that Palmieri ran in Milan each year for della Vida, one of Europe's best promoters of sporting events.

At the Palazzo dello Sport, McEnroe quickly felt at home and his tennis reflected his happy frame of mind right from the start. Crushing Gerulaitis 6–0, 6–3 in the semis, and encountering only marginally more resistance from Australian veteran John Alexander in the final, McEnroe won the Ramazzotti Cup, which was then a combined WCT/Grand Prix event, in style. Although he was to have his ups and downs in the exhibitions that followed much later each year, he was to retain the Cup in 1980, beating Vijay Amritraj in the final, and again in 1981 with one of his most decisive victories over Borg.

In 1979, however, Borg got the better of McEnroe on the next stop of the WCT tour in Rotterdam by beating him 6–4, 6–2 in a rather disappointing final. But the young New Yorker had, of course done more than enough to qualify for the eight-man field in Dallas. Although Borg had won three WCT titles to his two, McEnroe actually finished top of the points table by virtue of having played in Philadelphia where greater prize money earned double points. Could McEnroe justify being top man in a field that included Borg, Connors, Gerulaitis and Tanner? Results at the Alan King Classic at Caesar's Palace Hotel in Las Vegas the previous week raised doubts about that. Playing under lights on a balmy desert

night, McEnroe had once again failed to handle Connors' aggress-
ive stroke-play in a semi-final full of spectacular shotmaking and
had gone down 7–5, 6–4. Borg, extending a winning streak to
seventeen matches, then crowned himself the new Caesar by beating
Connors in the final.

But a whole different wheel of fortune was awaiting them in
Dallas, McEnroe opened with a 6–4, 6–0, 6–2 drubbing of John
Alexander who promptly announced in press conference that
McEnroe was as good as anyone he had ever played. 'And I in-
clude Laver, Newcombe, Borg and Connors in that assessment,'
Alexander added.

The words had a prophetic ring because in the semis Connors
suddenly discovered that he no longer held the whip hand over this
shrewd and tenacious competitor who had finally got the 'How to
beat Connors' tactics fixed firmly in his head. Keeping Jimmy under
constant pressure with the brilliance of his serving, the New Yorker
mixed patience and steadiness from the back court with darting
sorties to the net. And he always deprived Connors of the pace he
craves. 6–1, 6–4, 6–4 was the score and it was as decisive as it
sounds. With that psychological barrier lifted, McEnroe was mentally ready for yet another battle with Borg. In the end it was
probably mental freshness that decided the issue, coupled with the
unrelenting accuracy of McEnroe's wide, swinging serve into the ad
court. Borg had played a little more tennis than he would have liked
going into Dallas – he had won Monte Carlo before flying straight
to Las Vegas – and the steely determination that he carries with him
on court was just a fraction flimsier than usual. So the hungrier man
got his deserts after an absorbing duel by 7–5, 4–6, 6–2, 7–6, and
afterwards Borg said of the new champion. 'To play John, you must
always play at the very top of your game.' Coming from Björn, that
was the ultimate compliment.

So, within the space of five months, McEnroe had won the two
big play-off finals of the world's circuit, and if his success at the
Masters had proved primarily that he could seize his luck and win
when he was playing below his best, the well-heeled, tennis-wise
crowd of Texans who packed Moody Coliseum was left in no doubt
as to McEnroe's ability to raise his game to just whatever level was

required against the very best players in the world. Not since Ashe's memorable triumph at Wimbledon in 1975 had anyone beaten both Borg and Connors in the same tournament. That in itself was a significant achievement, but McEnroe was not getting carried away.

'No, I don't think I'm the No. 1 player in the world,' he told the usual large assortment of international press that WCT invite to Dallas every year. 'It's great to beat Connors and Borg but I've got a lot to do before I can regard myself as No. 1. I mean, I haven't even won a Grand Slam title yet.'

But it wouldn't be long. By September I was writing this report in *Tennis Week*:

'After the racket had been flung in the air; the speeches made and the interviews given; after the hugs and handshakes and the very private conversation with father in a corner of the locker room, John McEnroe paused as he struggled into a crumpled pair of white jeans and said, "Jesus, I can't believe I just won the US Open . . . I mean, the *US Open*, man, can you believe that?"

Sure. McEnroe's 7–5, 6–3, 6–3 win over Vitas Gerulaitis; his clinical straight set destruction of defending champion Jimmy Connors in the semi-final and his victory in the doubles with Peter Fleming – all this was merely a confirmation of what some of us had realized some time ago. Winning a major title – and winning it soon – was in this young man's stars. Nothing was going to stop him. The talent was too huge; the will too strong.'

By winning the US Open at the age of twenty, McEnroe had become the youngest player to wear that coveted crown since Pancho Gonzalez in 1948. Now another young firebrand had seized control of American tennis, but if there were similarities in temperament between the two champions, the thirty-one years separating their individual triumphs had seen the US Championships undergo an incredible metamorphosis: from all-amateur to Open; from the West Side Tennis Club at Forest Hills to the National Tennis Centre at Flushing Meadow; from patrician crowds drawn from country clubs and other exclusive bastions of the game to the howling, drunken mob of New York sports fans who descended on Flushing

Meadow the night – that infamous Thursday night – when McEnroe played Nastase. These were changes that had made the game unrecognizable and unpalatable to many. But reality was no longer clothed in long white flannels. Gene Scott got it right when he wrote in *Tennis Week*:

'We have entered a new era of spectator tennis. And those who insist we return to the fans of yesteryear with jackets and ties and "excuse me's" after an audible cough are out of touch. Professional football, baseball and [ice-] hockey have had raucous scenes in the stands for years. Fighting and violence on and off the field are commonplace – however distasteful we find it.

'In the wild growth we have encouraged for our sport in the past decade, there is a sort of rage inherent in the process. We have created a fire-breathing dragon and can't now retreat from harnessing her destructive force and presiding over her ultimate taming.'

Certainly some taming was required after the scenes that erupted on that Thursday night when the idea of the game's two great bad boys meeting in the second round attracted a drunken, boorish crowd that gave tennis an unwelcome taste of just how some New York sports fans like to spend their evenings. In the end, after the spectators and officials had managed to turn the whole thing into a pantomime of the absurd, the two players were virtually turned into innocent bystanders.

True, Nastase and, to a lesser extent, McEnroe had knocked out a rough draft, whipped up a bit of enthusiasm and set the stage. But after that people who were supposed to be nothing more than the supporting cast stole the show.

Frank Hammond, a Falstaffian figure in the chair, forgot all his best lines in the scene entitled 'Big Match Crowd Control' and not only overreacted to Nastase but then completely blew his cool with the spectators. Mike Blanchard, a gentle and elderly referee, got into the act when matters started to deteriorate rather rapidly at 2–1 in the fourth set, with McEnroe leading by two sets to one. Hammond had accused Nastase of stalling and had started docking him penalty points and then an entire game when he refused to face McEnroe's serve. By this time the crowd, which had caused Nastase to stall in the first place, upped its noise level to ear-splitting proportions. Blanchard, still believing in sweet reason and common decency and all those other phrases that so many New Yorkers were never taught in English class, first tried to address them through a malfunctioning microphone and then, fumbling about with a ladder in an attempt to reach up to Hammond's mike, was lucky he didn't complete the farce by falling off.

By that time Billy Talbert, the tournament director, had enlarged the growing cast by walking on court, ignoring Hammond's clearly announced default of Nastase which had occurred moments earlier, and ordering Blanchard to take over from Frank in the chair. With ten thousand people making as long and as shrill a demonstration of sustained anger and abuse as I have ever heard in a sports arena, it was quite impossible to play tennis. So, despite all the commands and counter-commands from officials who were running around like chickens with their heads off, the two players just stood there looking more than a mite bewildered at the way their little play was panning out.

By their own standards, which aren't too terrific, I admit, neither Nastase nor McEnroe had done anything very bad, and the real tragedy was that during the first two sets they had produced tennis that was often breathtaking in its beauty. But all that had evaporated as the spectators seized on every little grimace and glance, every gesture of annoyance or line call query to force a confrontation and create what they had come for — a full-scale horror show. That they got it was their fault and the officials' fault. But, of course, there was no denying that a couple of tennis players called Nastase and McEnroe also played their part.

The spectators were never that bad again but neither were they sweetness and light, especially as far as their two local heroes — McEnroe and Gerulaitis — were concerned. So it was poetic justice that, having spent most of the fortnight cheering the opponents of those players, they should end up with a final that would force them to cheer for one or the other. I have always found it the ultimate hypocrisy for New York crowds to boo John McEnroe for his behaviour. McEnroe's behaviour is New York behaviour. Putting aside his Irish temper, the rough edges to his personality are pure New York; the result of too many rides on the subway with the elbow-jabbers and seat-snatchers and the strangers who walk up to you and say, 'Got a light, kid?' and then let the door slam in your face – or worse. A nice, harmonious home in the suburbs doesn't eliminate the inevitable assimilation of that kind of behaviour; that very real need to stand up and fight back before you get trampled to death. So New Yorkers who object to McEnroe – and, for slightly more complicated reasons, to Gerulaitis – should go home and take a long, hard look at themselves in the mirror. For New Yorkers to boo their home-grown stars is tantamount to booing themselves. But then some of them are into self-flagellation, too.

So the US Open crowd at Flushing Meadow in 1979 got the final it deserved and, perversely, it was more than some of them deserved. Beginning as the dying embers of a glorious September day threw an orange glow over the Manhattan skyline and finishing in the floodlit glare that had worried Björn Borg, the match was never close enough to be a classic. But Gerulaitis should derive some comfort from the fact that he participated in a duel rich in the game's finest skills.

Responding at last, the crowd was often left gasping at the sheer speed and athletic ability of the two men as they chased and parried; lunged and recovered both balance and composure in time to play yet another shot of perfect length and direction. But, hard though he tried, Vitas could never find a chink in McEnroe's armour. Was there one? Not apparently with McEnroe playing to his full potential on the medium-paced composite surface called Decoturf. The firm footing gave him an even better springboard than usual from which to launch himself into the attack behind his serve and, for most of the match, he was hitting his first volley closer to the net than anyone I have ever seen, save, perhaps, for John Newcombe at his best. He was returning serve brilliantly, too, forcing Vitas to dig heavily top-spun returns out from around his ankles. Despite the older man's great speed and dexterity it was all too much for him, and long before the end it had become apparent that the boy from

Douglaston would make the short drive home that night as the new Champion of the United States.

But the triumphs did not stop there. Before he helped his country retain the Davis Cup with a crushing victory over Italy in San Francisco in December, McEnroe had already passed that way, stamping his name on the TransAmerican trophy he had won the year before. Then, as if confirmation was needed that his was as rare and as special a talent as tennis had seen at any stage of its history, he flew off to Stockholm and London and retained those Super Series titles as well. All in all it had been a very good year.

8

Summers in the South of France

'Say hello to the guys in Vichy,' he said as I left him, shirtless in the burning Provence sun, squatting on the steps of a grand old hotel in Aix. John McEnroe was the best Under 21 player in the world in the summer of '79 and I was heading north to Vichy where the Galea Cup, the world's premier Under 21 team competition, was already in progress. McEnroe, tapping out a beat to an Eddie Money cassette, was waiting for the other members of the group, Jimmy Connors, Ilie Nastase, Guillermo Vilas and their various aides, mothers and agents to finish lunch. Then they would travel on to Cap d'Agde and Pierre Barthes' mammoth sixty-court tennis camp for the third and final leg of an exhibition tour that would net this high-priced quartet more money in a week than any of the Galea Cup competitors had seen in their lives.

Nevertheless, just for a fleeting second, I thought I detected a hint of regret in McEnroe's voice – that instinctive reaction to the challenge of real competition: the compulsive desire to prove oneself. Looking back now, I am sure I was not mistaken. For a start the players at Vichy that year, players like Ivan Lendl, Yannick Noah and Pascale Portes, were far closer to his age group than his colleagues on the 'Carré d'As' exhibition tour, although ironically, as it happened, Vilas turned out to be a far better friend in later years than Lendl.

But there was also the attraction of representing one's country in a meaningful competition – the thought of which certainly stirred McEnroe's interest almost as much as just making money. But as far as the Galea Cup was concerned that was never a possibility, because, at the time, the USTA had never entered a team. The Galea Cup is an event which, alongside the Orange Bowl in Miami, ranks as the best junior tournament in the world. With the final rounds played over the best of five sets with no tie-breakers on slow red clay, it provides the best possible testing ground for a young player's stamina and ability to withstand pressure.

Had McEnroe – and a great many other Americans for that matter – spent a couple of summers in Vichy, he might have taken a great deal less time to adapt to the technical and psychological demands of those courts at Stade Roland Garros where, at least prior to 1982, his hopes of winning the French Open lay buried.

As it was, McEnroe had started to spend a brief part of each summer in France, but in the South of France: Nice, Fréjus, Aix-en-Provence and Cap d'Agde, a mixture of the old and the new as far as tennis tradition was concerned. For the big money exhibition tour, matches were played in places that were either new for tennis but old for other things – like the Roman amphitheatre at Fréjus – or just plain new, like the vast Exhibition Hall in Nice, and the whole area is as resonant as any in the world with memories for virtually every leading player that the game has known since the Great War.

In summers long gone the courts of the Côte d'Azur had been filled with figures like Suzanne Lenglen and Elizabeth Ryan, with a youthful Teddy Tinling in attendance as both player and umpire. King Gustav of Sweden was an active enthusiast and, apart from the five-year hiatus during World War II, the world's top players kept on coming, as they still do every spring for Grand Prix events in Nice and Monte Carlo.

It remains, despite Le Fast Food and Les Traffic Jams, a very special part of the world and in the years to come I imagine it will retain a special place in John McEnroe's memory because, for one week each August, it provided him with the opportunity to pause and reflect while playing tennis and earning money at the same time. Not a bad combination.

Each year, of course, he returned a little wiser – although not necessarily any closer to solving his problems – and his visit in 1981 was particularly pleasant because he invited his mother ('I thought it was about time I gave her a holiday'), and it gave the pair of them more time to spend together over quiet and delicious dinners than at any previous period of his young adulthood.

But it was two years before, on his first trip in 1979, that I saw him in Aix. In less than a month he would win the US Open for the first time and establish beyond further argument his credentials as one of the great players of his era. But that year, in particular, his week in the South of France offered him a chance for experimentation and introspection.

The matches on that leg of the tour were being played at the famous tennis club just outside Aix under the direction of Max Guérin, whose Raquet d'Or tournament had been thrown out of the Grand Prix the previous year in a fruitless and quite unfair attempt to make an example of someone suspected of committing the widespread crime of paying to players under-the-counter guarantees. Max's response was to give the tennis establishment a great big sad Gallic shrug and promptly to join forces with the show business promoters who were sponsoring the Carré d'As, which was much frowned upon by the powers in Paris.

The night that I was there McEnroe was scheduled for a last match against Connors, and by the time he had lost the first set it was getting quite chilly for that time of year. It was also getting late. A good crowd of two or three thousand were starting to think of home and, under the circumstances, many players would have gone through the motions of another set and called it a day. But there is a flame that flickers away inside McEnroe that refuses to be snuffed out – not by a chill, damp night, or by the lateness of the hour, or by the unimportance of the occasion. For McEnroe it is important to be earnest – at the very least about the things which matter most to him.

So he kept us there another ninety minutes while he ran and fought and finally beat Connors, who doesn't like losing either. It was after 2.00 a.m. by the time we got back to the Novotel, one of many in those roadside chains that are scattered around France in a good plastic imitation of the American motel concept, and John was too wound up to sleep. He was also thirsty. Miraculously, a young lady appeared to offer something resembling service and proceeded to squeeze fresh orange juice behind the bar while we talked.

'Thanks for keeping us up all night,' I said.

He laughed and shook his head. 'I don't know what it is churning away inside me, I really don't. I know exhibition matches like this offer a great opportunity to practise relaxing on court; maybe even to have a bit of fun. But I just can't let go. I still get uptight when I get a bad call. I tell myself it's no big deal but it doesn't do any good.'

McEnroe pushed his glass across the bar and produced one of the very few words in his French vocabulary. 'Encore.'

The girl looked at this bedraggled young man, standing there in his track suit in a deserted bar at 2.45 in the morning, and replied incredulously, 'You want more?'

She had already squashed him enough oranges for three glasses, but she obviously wasn't familiar with an athlete's capacity for liquids after a match.

We talked some more until his thirst was quenched and the energy seeped away to be replaced by a natural state of sleepiness and he wandered off to bed. He was still pondering the problem when he drove into the centre of the city to join the other players the following day. Waiting on the steps of the hotel he said, 'It's as if something inside me is going to burst if I don't do something to release it. It's something I haven't yet learned to control. But I suppose I'll have to find a way because I really want to take the pressure off myself and *enjoy* playing these guys.'

The solution wasn't readily at hand, and a year later different problems were starting to crowd in on a young man who was beginning to find fame an increasing burden. By August 1980 he had, of course, not only won the US Open but fought Borg to the death in that fantastic Wimbledon final which included the unforgettable tie-breaker John simply refused to lose. Compared with the year before, he had been transformed from a promising young star into an international celebrity as far as the general public was concerned.

Two girls, who had been at Stanford with John, and who happened to be touring Europe that summer were with us at a table in the corner of the bar, where a pianist was tinkling everyone's favourite tunes. The atmosphere was mellow and relaxed. There were a couple of lovers at a nearby table and just by the grand piano a slightly more boisterous group of middle-aged men with a couple of attractive girls were making a night of it. Later it transpired that they were the director, cast and crew of a big-budget British television commercial being made on the Côte d'Azur.

Eventually the director, a tall, dark-haired man with a faintly menacing expression, came over to our table and with no formal preamble butted in on our conversation. Suddenly we – and, I noticed, McEnroe in particular – were being bombarded with questions about the music, which songs we liked, etc. We all remained distantly polite and finally he meandered off.

About half an hour later, a black American who worked at a club in Cannes dropped by to say hello to the pianist and began to improvise a few songs in a deep, rich voice. The sounds were so good that we moved over to the stools around the piano.

Suddenly the director plonked himself down beside us, and asked John if he knew the title of the old Cole Porter melody that we were listening to. John admitted that he didn't.

'Aren't you ashamed of yourself?' demanded the drunk, leaning across the bar belligerently. 'Aren't you ashamed not to know the name of that song?'

I looked across at the girls and we all held our breath. The reaction, when it came, was a great deal more controlled than we might have feared.

'No, I can't say I am,' McEnroe replied evenly, staring down into his beer. 'I don't care about your song; or you or what you think.'

'Hell, now you're getting rude,' the director retorted, sniffing the scent of the brawl that he was looking for. 'I reckon you've got problems, young man. What do you do anyway? I make films – so what are you good at?'

'I surf,' said McEnroe. 'I'm the 123rd best surfer in America.'

Somehow we all managed to keep a straight face and quickly drew John back into our own conversation. The director, disappointed, returned to his party, which included a Scot in a far worse state than he was.

A little while later, having made friends with the pianist and the American singer, one of the Stanford girls agreed to sing a James Taylor number while McEnroe accompanied her, somewhat stiffly, on the piano. The director returned, tried to get one of us to admit what our friend did and then, exasperated, blurted out, 'Well, I hope he plays tennis better than he plays the piano,' and staggered out of the room.

But we were not done yet. It was now the Scot's turn to infiltrate the party with all the pathetic belligerence that goes hand in hand with too much whisky.

'You calling me an American – don't you dare call me an American!' he yelled at McEnroe, who hadn't called him anything. The man had already fallen off his bar stool twice and broken three glasses during the course of the evening and now proceeded to collapse again. Against my better judgement I leant down to pick him up and restored him to his uncertain pedestal, whereupon McEnroe, still incredibly unfussed by the constant baiting he had received, engaged the man in a little good-natured banter. But it was obviously going to be one of those nights when we couldn't win.

Tolerance and good humour, apparently, were not to be appreciated. A third member of the group, a striking, dark-haired girl who was presumably one of the actresses, walked up to the bar and started telling McEnroe to leave the Scottish drunk alone because he was really a very sweet, talented guy who had been working very hard and was now just a little bit tipsy. When John protested that he hadn't done anything to initiate the exchange and would be very happy to leave the guy alone if only he would let him, the girl gave him a haughty stare and said, 'Oh, really, you're so conceited.'

A pleasant evening had been turned into a no-win situation and John agreed that it was time to move out. He was beginning to realize just what worldwide fame was all about. Although, thank heavens, it is highly unlikely that every bar he enters will be filled with quite such a boozy crowd as we ran into at the Hyatt, it is obvious that his reputation even then – and it hasn't got any better – set him up as a target for any loudmouthed show-off who felt the need to prove something.

That, indeed, may be the price of fame but it is a higher price than many people might imagine. The liberties some members of the public take are barely believable. There is another instance of this kind that sticks in the memory because it was so unexpected.

Just after McEnroe and Peter Fleming had won the Benson & Hedges doubles title a couple of years ago I was in their dressing room at Wembley. By chance John had a towel around him and Peter was dressed – they might well both have been naked – when the door was flung open by a woman in her forties with a grand but faintly Australian accent, flourishing a programme.

'Here you, sign this,' she said, thrusting the programme at McEnroe. 'I have a young fan of yours who wants your autograph.' The woman then turned to a shy girl of about twenty who was cringing in the corridor with embarrassment. When I suggested that the women had no right to be in the players' dressing room she gave me one of those hate-filled, unsteady stares that people can summon up when alcohol starts to take a grip of their senses.

'I've got a perfect right to ask this young man for his autograph,' she replied and then, turning back to McEnroe who was sitting, stunned and silent, in the corner, added, 'Although frankly I think you are . . . Puh! That's what I think of you . . . Puh.'

By that time an official had arrived and she was escorted out, still protesting her divine right to intrude on people's privacy.

Obviously McEnroe's behaviour on court and his less than charming attitude to strangers – even those who are simply trying to be nice – provokes this kind of incident. But again, contrary to what one might expect, he does not shout and scream at the interlopers and drunks. More often than not he is incredibly restrained.

After our tactical withdrawal from the Hyatt bar in Nice we all felt in need of some fresh air. So we walked across the Promenade des Anglais onto the deserted pebbled beach. The evening had still been fun, despite the interruptions, and John had put the bad parts behind him as quickly as he forgets a bad defeat. Soon he was challenging us to a contest to see how many times we could make a stone skip over the calm, warm waters of the Mediterranean. With the moon offering no more than a dull orange glow as it hung over Cap d'Antibes, it was difficult to follow the stones as they flipped out into the darkness, and after a while John lost interest in the challenge and bid us all good night. Happily, there was no one to molest him as he shuffled back across the road into the hotel lobby, head down, hands in pockets, thinking, no doubt, that the world was a difficult and confusing sort of place.

9

Life at the Top is not so Easy

Even for those with the gifts of the gods and a bulging bank balance to offer proof of material rewards, life can be difficult and complicated and a little confusing, especially when you are still very young and are being swept along on the heady wave of success; trying too hard; travelling too much and saying 'yes' to too many people. All that McEnroe discovered the hard way in the first months of 1980 as injury bit, form slipped and criticism mounted.

The first disappointment was the loss of his Masters crown. Ironically it was friend and neighbour Vitas Gerulaitis who paved the way for his downfall at Madison Square Garden. Along with Borg, Vilas and all the other top points winners of the year-long Grand Prix tour of 1979, Gerulaitis had elected to play in the New York showpiece this time and, after successfully negotiating the early round robin matches, the pair met on the Friday night to decide who would finish top of his Group. The $10,000 bonus for finishing up a Group winner was the lesser of two incentives – the greater being the fact that the winner would meet Connors in the knockout semi-final while the loser would have to face Borg.

Maybe after his loss in the final of the US Open four months earlier, Gerulaitis had more to prove. Maybe he had a fraction more incentive to drive himself on, not so much towards victory, but away from the haunting spectre of another defeat at the hands of his New York rival. Not that McEnroe was exactly giving anything away, but one sensed that the greater motivation was surging from Gerulaitis' side of the net. But motivation itself is never enough. On this particular night Vitas had the tools to finish the job – a much steadier and more penetrating serve, an instinctive knowledge of his opponent's game that only heightened his already electric speed about court, and increasing confidence on the return of serve which blunted one of McEnroe's most potent weapons. It was enough, although the 3–6, 7–6, 7–6 score revealed just how close it was.

So McEnroe's opponent in the semi-final was to be Borg. And again he was up against a man with a special sense of motivation – as if playing the American left-hander wasn't motivation enough for this proud Swede. But this time there was something else because Björn was well aware of what everybody had been saying, and it irked him. They were saying, after his defeats at the US Open, that he couldn't win in New York. And New York – and especially Madison Square Garden – was the place where the greatest champions in sport were expected to put their talent and their courage on the line and, if they were truly champions, emerge triumphant. In addition, Borg had never won the Masters, even when it was a nomadic event moving from city to city around the world. So he wanted this one badly.

For a time it didn't look as if McEnroe would let him have it. Using his incredible touch to jerk the Swede around court, John fought back from 2–4 down in the first set to win it on the tie-break. Borg was still having trouble with his timing midway through the second until, at 4–3, a typical backhand pass left the New Yorker groping in its wake and the all-important breach was made. Winning the set 6–3, Borg still couldn't break free until he raised his game to a new plateau of excellence in the deciding tie-break and took advantage of a surprisingly wild, slashing forehand volley from his rival on the fifth point to wrap it up by the unexpectedly lopsided margin of seven points to one.

Borg hushed the New York crowd into awe-struck silence by beating Gerulaitis for the fifteenth consecutive time in the final. The score was 6–2, 6–2 and the game took just seventy-six minutes. So Björn Borg, to his obvious delight, was the new Master and still the No. 1 player in the world. McEnroe had work to do.

For a player who had been winning virtually at will in the latter months of 1979, the work load suddenly seemed to get heavier. Inexperience lay at the root of the problem. Thinking match play alone would keep him fit, McEnroe filled his schedule with too many tournaments and never gave his body a chance to recover from minor aches and strains. And, of course, he was never very good at doing the preventive exercises that even a body about to enter its twenty-first year requires to keep it properly tuned.

So the defeats began to pile up. A wounding five-set loss to Connors in the final of the US Pro Indoors in Philadelphia, after he had been on court at the Spectrum most of the previous day in singles and doubles, was the next setback. The effort left him emotionally as well as physically drained for, as Laurie Pignon observed in the *Daily Mail*, the crowd behaved like a mob. 'The match had all the atmosphere of a street fight,' wrote Pignon. 'The crowd clapped McEnroe's ten double faults and they clapped when he fell over three times.' The pressure of always being the villain of the piece was beginning to tell.

He gained some measure of revenge by beating Connors 7–6, 7–6 in the final of the US National Indoors at Memphis and there were title-winning triumphs, too, in WCT tournaments in Richmond, Virginia and Milan during the first three months of the year. But he went down to Gerulaitis again in the Pepsi Grand Slam in Florida; was forced to pull out of WCT Frankfurt through injury; lost his way on the red clay of the Monte Carlo Country Club against Vilas; and was beaten 6–4, 6–1 by Harold Solomon in the quarter-final of the Alan King Classic in Las Vegas. But most demoralizing of all, perhaps, was the thumping defeat that the United States suffered at the hands of Argentina and the raucously partisan Buenos Aires crowd in the Davis Cup. McEnroe was beaten by both Vilas and Clerc after not having conceded so much as a set in eleven previous Davis Cup singles.

So it was a slightly chastened young man who arrived in Dallas to defend his WCT crown, but a realistic one. 'In the long run the Buenos Aires experience probably did me good. I've had a few problems, sure, but to give yourself excuses is the wrong approach.'

Again one marvelled at the inner strength and outward maturity of this youngster who was already labouring under the nickname of 'Super Brat'. He continued to take his beatings like a man, even though there was no immediate improvement in his form. The irrepressible Connors snatched away his WCT title in a four-set Dallas final and a week later, having battled his way through to the final of the WCT Tournament of Champions on clay at Forest Hills, Gerulaitis got him again – 6–0 in the third.

After that the prospect of the French Open and the even slower clay at Stade Roland Garros was daunting in the extreme, and McEnroe never looked remotely capable of living up to the No. 2 seeding he had earned solely on the basis of his ATP computer ranking. 'One year I am going to prepare properly for the French,' he told me, neither for the first nor the last time. Even though he managed to win love sets against a veteran clay-courter, Patrice Dominguez, in the first round and a younger one, Per Hjertquist, in the second, he was never quite sure enough of his own ability to stem the brilliantly sustained attack he met from the bobbing, weaving, bouncing Australian Paul McNamee, and lost a wildly exciting and spectacular dogfight 7–6, 6–7, 7–6, 7–6.

So it was hardly surprising that McEnroe was relieved to see the sight of grass at the Queen's Club when he arrived in England in June for what he had promised himself would be a carefully planned assault on Wimbledon. After making a mess of it for two years in a row, he knew that he could not afford any more bad losses in the world's premier tournament if he was to be recognized as a valid contender for the crown Borg had been wearing with such style for the previous four years.

Even though the first of the really vicious press criticism had hit him during the Stella Artois Championships at Queen's the year before, he had come to enjoy the tournament. The reasons were very simple. Both tournament director Clive Bernstein and advertising wizard Frank Lowe, whose company has been responsible for all those wonderful caricatures of Nastase, Connors and McEnroe that are plastered on billboards all over London prior to the event each year, had gone out of their way to be nice to him and make him feel at home. Quite naturally he responded and, by the time he made his third consecutive appearance in the Championships, Bernstein was publicly calling him 'a true professional who never lets the public down'.

That made a welcome change from some of the things that had been written about him the previous year after a series of minor incidents blew up into a raging inferno of a row during a quarter-final match against Sandy Mayer. Sandy, who has not always been the most civil of players himself, fanned the flames by suggesting McEnroe should be banned, and the press took it from there. 'Go Home, Super Brat!' screamed the tabloids, picking up on a phrase penned by Ian Barnes of the *Daily Express* in a slightly different context a few months earlier.

But soon it wasn't just the headlines which made McEnroe shake his head in wonderment and disbelief. In the *Daily Express* ace feature writer Jean Rook was sharpening her quill – and when she jabs that weapon, it hurts. While admitting that John was quite nice to her when they met, she announced, nonetheless, that he was '. . . loud, rude, vain, childish, sulky and bloody-minded. John McEnroe, at twenty, is a spoilt child only his mother could love.' That little homily was spread across nine columns of the paper. And there were others like it. Apart from being hurt, McEnroe was genuinely perplexed.

'I mean, I know I lost my cool and shouted at a couple of people when I shouldn't have, but I didn't expect everyone to react like they did. I thought they might understand or give me a second chance or forgive or whatever. I couldn't believe it was blown up into such a big deal.'

But now he was back in a calmer frame of mind. As is often the case, a little adversity had done him good. The third-round loss to McNamee in Paris had given him a few days off and the chance to settle into the flat that he and Stacy were renting for the month he expected to be in London. That, hopefully, would eliminate the popping flashbulbs that had greeted him every time he stepped out of the Kensington Hilton during the previous year's Wimbledon.

'I'm so relaxed I can hardly believe in myself,' he told John Oakley of the *Evening News*. 'I'm not saying I'll never blow my top again or start screaming at umpires, but I honestly don't want it. I want the British public to see there is another side of John McEnroe; that I am not just the big bully-boy they all believe I am.'

He certainly got off to a good start. No sooner had Queen's started in typical monsoon conditions that Laurie Pignon was suggesting he deserved a medal for agreeing to play the big-serving Californian Tom Leonard 'with a suspect ankle, on an outside court made dangerous by rain'. But he did it because Bernstein asked him to and he was leading 6–3, 3–4 when the referee decided conditions were simply too bad to continue. He won soon enough when play resumed and went on to beat Australia's Kim Warwick in the final, after eliminating in the semis the man he had beaten in the 1979 final: Paraguay's languid, talented giant Victor Pecci.

So, despite the risks he had taken playing on wet grass, the ankle, heavily strapped, had come through unscathed and was growing stronger day by day. Despite the rain and the frustrations of trying to find a practice court, his own weather chart seemed to be set fair. The omens were correct. Three weeks later the tennis world was in a state of euphoria after what many described as the greatest Wimbledon final of all time. Borg had done it again, but this time McEnroe was also the hero after a match that was nothing less than a celebration of the modern game. More than the excitement, I recall it now as a joyous occasion for all of us who love tennis. I tried to capture that mood in the report I wrote for *Tennis Week*:

'After two of the wettest and most frustrating weeks in the history of the Championships, it came as such sweet thunder – this final of finals, this clash of Titans, gracing the world's most famous sporting stage as it had never been graced before.

'Twice, as Björn Borg climbed still higher on his endless ladder to the stars, the sun peeped out and, then, as if in shame, disappeared again behind the familiar blanket of cloud. Begone, fickle friend! We did not need you to illuminate this glorious scene.

'Two men of skill and steel, locking their talents and courage in a battle so closely fought that only the genius of the game's scoring system could divide them, needed no assistance nor, heaven forbid, any further disturbance from the elements. They had ploughed through rain and hail: skidded on slippery grass and dug deep into muddy baselines on their way to this great finale and, once there, it was they who produced the thunder and the lightning, sending shock waves of electricity through the enraptured Centre Court.

'All they needed was a stage to play their game. And what a game they played! Was there ever a better final than this? Has one match ever produced dramas, tenacity, power and sportsmanship in greater abundance? Can anyone now deny that Björn Borg is one of the greatest players of all time or that John McEnroe stands on the very threshold of greatness?

'While we ponder these questions, let us savour the memory of this remarkable contest for we shall be fortunate indeed to see its like again. Borg and McEnroe will doubtless play many more great matches — already they have produced three other classic encounters at Richmond, New Orleans and in the Masters last January — but it will take a great many factors and no little luck for them to arrive in the Wimbledon final a second time and play as well again.

'We are getting spoiled with our finals at Wimbledon. Unlike the previous two decades when a Trabert, a Hoad, or a Laver would frequently crush some hapless opponent, the seventies provided a plethora of excitement on finals day. Smith–Nastase; Ashe–Connors; the first Borg–Connors; and last year's Borg–Tanner were all great matches and now this, which may be the greatest of all.

'For once the statistics alone reveal something of the drama. Björn Borg became Wimbledon Champion for the fifth successive year by defeating John McEnroe 1–6, 7–5, 6–3, 6–7, 8–6 with the fourth-set tie-break stretching to eighteen points to sixteen. McEnroe eventually won that set on his seventh set point and Borg finally won the match on his eighth match point. And if further evidence is needed of just how close this three-hour 53 minute marathon really was, the total number of points and games won and lost will do it. Borg won 190 points to McEnroe's 186 and 28 games to his opponent's 27.

'At the beginning Borg was surprisingly bad. The mistakes that spun off his racket were partially due to the wicked accuracy of McEnroe's shots and partially as a result of his failure to anticipate just how much faster the worn, brown Centre Court had become after a couple of days' respite from the rain. The racket he began with was, by his own very special standards, too loose and when McEnroe held serve to love for a 3–0 lead, Borg changed it for a tighter one.

'But it was not until the eleventh game of the second set, when he held serve to love, having settled on the tactics of coming in behind his first serve and staying back on his second, that he could finally look McEnroe in the eye with any degree of confidence. By that time he had escaped from four break points; three of them in the crucial ninth game. The Swede had opened that game with his fourth double fault but on each of the three occasions that McEnroe stood within a point of a 5–4 lead with his serve to follow, Borg greeted the crisis with a vicious first serve. As the drama unfolded, the value and importance of those three magnificent deliveries grew. A two-set to love deficit might well have been too big a gap to bridge against McEnroe in this mood – even for Borg.

'So, at 5–6, McEnroe served to save the set and suddenly gave Borg a foot in the door by dumping one intended stop volley into the net and then foolishly attempting another off the very next point. McEnroe's exquisite touch is sometimes good enough to outwit Borg, but the timing has to be perfect and this time it was not. Björn raced on to it and tapped away a winner, 15–30. Then came the killer blow. Lunging to his left, Borg hammered a superb double-fisted backhand down the line off precisely the kind of first serve that was supposed to be McEnroe's most potent weapon.

'It gave Borg two set points and he clinched it on the second when McEnroe netted a backhand volley off another fine service return.

'More fine service returns helped Borg to an early lead in the third, but he had to fight his way out of a 0–40 situation in the seventh game before serving out for 6–3. By this stage, it was becoming a duel of the highest class. Both men had honed their game to near perfection, sprinkling the wrinkled court with power and guile and so much skill that even the bad bounces were handled with a deft turn of the wrist or adjustment of the racket head.

'At 4–4 in the magnificent fourth set, Borg forced another breach in the New Yorker's armour. Again it was his ability to meet McEnroe's sizzling first serve, which flew at him off the apex of the service box, with a crushing cross-court return that earned him the break, and when he reached double match-point at 40–15 in the next game, we prepared for the end.

It was then that the twenty-one-year-old American wrote himself into the folklore of the game, proving, for those who still doubted it, that his strength of character matched his skill. He hit Björn with a firm back-hand pass down the line on the first match-point and a forehand pass on the second, and the crowd realized the Swede was not the only player out there with nerves of steel.

A great back-hand service return sealed the break back and soon we were into the historic tie-break. It stretched over twenty-two minutes and thirty-four points – more than would be needed to win an entire set 6–1 – and was so finely balanced that match-points and set-points seemed to ricochet back and forth across the court with the blur of syncopated rhythm. The sequence built crisis by crisis with Borg reaching two match-points (his third and fourth of the match) at 6–5 and 7–6; then McEnroe with two set-points; then Borg back on the threshold again with three more match-points and then a run of four set-points for the American before he clinched it on the fifth with a heavily top-spun service return that was dipping too quickly for Borg to control as he tried for an ambitious stop volley.

The Centre Court erupted. John McEnroe Senior was out of his seat and Junior was clenching his fists and staring at the heavens. Two sets all; the greatest title in tennis was still up for grabs. Could the implacable Swede – the Centre Court's immovable object for the past four years – hold onto his treasured crown? Once again the answer was yes.

Eighty per cent of his first serves found their mark. Incredibly McEnroe could win only three points against serve in the entire set and it was a tribute to his own resilience and skill that the young New Yorker stayed with the Champion for as long as he did. Twice he served confidently to save the match, but in the fourteenth game Borg unleashed two superb returns and reached his eighth match point when John netted a low volley. This time it really was the end. One more deadly backhand cross-court pass and that was it.

'"I am as constant as the northern star," Caesar said before Brutus and his conspirators proved him wrong. But McEnroe was alone out there and, well as he wielded it, one dagger was not enough to fell this Caesar.

'This Nordic Emperor is as constant a factor as the game has ever known and he is not done yet. In fact his powers are growing still. Thank God for McEnroe for otherwise Borg would indeed "bestride this narrow world and hold the palm alone".'

McEnroe's path to the final had been uneven. He had been dreading a return to the notorious No. 2 Court, that graveyard of dreams where he, like many aspiring champions before him, had lost so unexpectedly to Tim Gullikson twelve months before. But in fact this time it was on the adjoining No. 3 Court that he had been given his biggest scare. Playing with the carefree abandon of a man on the verge of giving up the game, Terry Rocavert, a lowly ranked Australian, led McEnroe by two sets to one before going down 6–3 in the fifth. Tom Okker, Kevin Curren (a powerful young South African who pushed him to 7–5, 7–6, 7–6) and none other than Peter Fleming were the next hurdles he cleared successfully, not merely from the point of view of the result but also because the volatile temper was kept largely in check.

But the semi-final was a different matter. The semi-final meant Jimmy Connors. It also presented the psychological barrier of being the stage of the Championships he had never managed to pass before. As far as the state of his nerves was concerned, it was a tougher match for him than facing Borg in the final. He couldn't afford to lose to Jimmy again so soon after Dallas – not if he wanted to retain the No. 2 ranking his US Open victory had secured for him.

So, although the match, once it got under way, was rarely in doubt despite a courageous fight back by Connors which earned him the second set, McEnroe was too tense to control his temper when a few decisions went against him. Once, the umpire refused to award him an ace after a fault had been wrongly signalled. The umpire wanted to play two. 'If in your opinion, my opponent could not have reached the ball it should be my point,' said McEnroe angrily. But despite the fact that he was right and despite the fact that he didn't swear and actually remembered to say 'please' at the start of the conversation, the crowd immediately started whistling and slow hand clapping. Tanner had also made a similar complaint during his match with Connors in the previous round. But Tanner comes across at the clean-cut all-American boy and no one whistles him. They whistle McEnroe not because he is wrong, not because he swears, but just because of his reputation and the way he looks. His behaviour had been virtually impeccable for the previous ten days, but one angry outburst was enough. It is small wonder that, as time has passed, he has occasionally felt the effort of trying to behave well just simply isn't worth it. 'So many times the crowd never understand what I am trying to say and just never give me a chance,' he complains. 'I have a perfect right to point out to an umpire politely that he has made an error.'

But, of course, as the umpire gives him the stony stare and the crowd give him the whistle, the resentment and frustration build to a point where a rational complaint turns into a raging torrent of abuse. It never got to that level of intensity against Connors, thank goodness, and with another masterly performance McEnroe was through to a final that would do more for his reputation and self-esteem than any other he has played so far.

However, his year of highs and lows continued. He lost to Jose-Luis Clerc, the rapidly improving young Argentinian, for the second time in six months in the final of the Grand Prix event at South Orange, New Jersey; was forced to scratch through injury during his second-round match against Erik Van Dillen in the Canadian Open; and then, one of the few times he has ever gone out in the first round, crashed 7–6, 6–4 to Tracy Austin's brother, John, in Atlanta. Hardly the best preparation for the defence of his US Open crown the following week.

But once again McEnroe rose to the big occasion and proved that, like his arch-rival Borg, he too is a proud and brilliant guardian of a hard-earned crown. Ivan Lendl, who was starting to look very threatening indeed, pushed him to 7–5 in the fourth set of a rugged quarter-final clash and then he found Connors – who else? – waiting for him in the semis. The most interesting aspect of this encounter was the fact that the defending champion was able to blow his cool over a series of dubious line calls, totally to lose his rhythm and concentration, to allow Connors to run off a string of eleven consecutive games and still come back to win 6–4, 5–7, 0–6, 6–3, 7–6. McEnroe won the deciding tie-break comfortably enough by seven points to three, but Connors had played to the very limit of his considerable ability and, quite apart from McEnroe's tantrums, the match exuded a cut-throat quality between these two less than friendly rivals that only heightened the sense of drama. It was a match made for New York and its pitch of excitement almost eclipsed the roar of the 727 engines as the jets climbed off the end of the La Guardia Airport runway.

But, as at Wimbledon, a match with Connors seemed to drain McEnroe of all the worst excesses of his combustible temperament and leave him primed and coolly determined for the task of playing Borg.

After that great triumph at Wimbledon, this seemed to be Borg's best ever opportunity of nailing down the one major title that still eluded him. But after coming back from the dead three times in as many rounds: two sets to one down against Tanner in the quarters; two sets to love down against the mercurial little South African, Johan Kriek, in the semis; and two sets to love down against McEnroe in the final, Björn's quest for the Grand Slam died where he least expected it – in the fifth set.

On fourteen occasions since 1976 Borg had been extended to a fifth set by a variety of worthy challengers in various tournaments, but always he had proved himself the calmer, tougher competitor when the chips were down. But not this time; not under lights on a cool September evening at Flushing Meadow; not against John McEnroe. This time, in a mighty test of stamina and skill, it was the New York left-hander who wrenched the prize of victory from the game's most bemedalled warrior. The score by which McEnroe retained his crown was 7–6, 6–1, 6–7, 5–7, 6–4. It contained the same number of games, fifty-five, as their vintage Wimbledon final and, at 4 hours 13 minutes, lasted twenty minutes longer.

It was a strange match: strange for the way in which Borg squandered his chances when he twice served for the first set; strange for the way he slumped into a fit of near-suicidal depression in the second; and strange for the way he fought back only to lose momentum in the home stretch he knows so well. But apparently his astrological chart was a mess that week, so maybe it was all in the stars. But McEnroe, the Aquarian, was only interested in keeping body and mind together in a last Herculean bid to save his crown. He was into a fifth set for the third consecutive day; into his ninth hour of singles play in twenty-four hours.

'In the fourth set I thought my body was falling apart,' McEnroe admitted. 'But then I felt better; better, in fact, in the fifth set than I had done at Wimbledon.'

God alone knows how. If his body didn't actually fall apart on him, it virtually refused to function the day following the final. 'I couldn't get out of bed, man. I tell you, my body just packed up.' No wonder. But when the will to win is as strong as it is in this amazing young man, adrenalin will keep a body pumping past the point of exhaustion and it was that kind of will that Borg had to face in the fifth set. And for once it proved stronger than his own.

Aided by two Borg double faults, McEnroe seized control of that deciding set by snatching a 4–3 lead and then unleashed a series of superb serves, dropping only two points on his remaining two service games. To the amazement of many, McEnroe had proved himself the greater champion on the day, but with Borg still Champion of Wimbledon and France, John knew better than to start proclaiming himself No. 1 in the world. Impatient on court, he remained almost Job-like in his patience off it but he knew now, deep down inside his private self, that it was only a matter of time. It was Wimbledon that mattered most. He needed Wimbledon.

Even though it is easy to look back now and realize that his defeat at Flushing Meadow in 1980 tolled a bell of distant doom in the glorious career of Björn Borg, I said at the time that, by the infinitesimal standards by which we judge great champions, he would never again be quite the same player. I knew he would continue to win big titles occasionally and, as long as his enthusiasm lasted, he would continue to play great tennis. But suddenly he was no longer invulnerable at those moments that separate the quick from the dead. A doubt had been implanted in a previously undoubting mind. And McEnroe would never let him forget it.

10

A Messy Masters – and
Rapid Reappraisal

Whatever seeds of doubt McEnroe had managed to implant in Borg's subconscious, the results were far from instantaneous. When I met McEnroe for a prearranged interview that I had been asked to do for an American magazine, it was *his* face that seemed to be etched with anxiety about the final outcome of their encounter. We were back at Madison Square Garden for the 1981 Volvo Masters. I found him on the trainers' bench being attended to by one of the great characters of the pro tour, the John Denver look-alike, Bill Norris. For a man who spends much of his life cooped up in windowless rooms tending to athletes' limbs, Bill retains a weird and wonderfully inventive sense of humour. He is also exceptionally good at his job.

With McEnroe in the state I found him that afternoon, Bill had a special task on his hands. 'You could say my condition's not too good, that's for sure,' John volunteered. One could tell that just by looking at him. For a start he was overweight, he also had a stomach problem, brought on partially by excess tension, and he had strained his thigh.

'Actually it was a pulled hamstring,' I was informed later by Dave Fechtman, the lanky Texan who was the ATP's other trainer on the tour and, with degrees in science, biology and physical education from North Texas State University, is, like Norris, highly qualified for his specialized profession. 'Between the ages of nineteen and twenty-five there is still a significant degree of bone growth and stabilization going on in the human body,' Fechtman explained. 'And playing tennis at this level on an almost constant basis subjects the body to a tremendous amount of stress. But John handles it pretty well. More than some players he is prepared to play with a minor injury and endure a certain amount of pain as a result. Like Connors, I would say he is exceptional in that respect.'

There was little doubt that McEnroe had been playing in pain at the Garden but, as usual, he wasn't trotting out any excuses in press conference. He didn't really need to after his Thursday night duel with Borg which had turned out to be another little classic, if not for the standard of play, then at least for the drama extracted from a score of 6–4, 6–7, 7–6. Pouncing on errors from an erratic opponent, the Swede won the final tie-break by seven points to two, but he did something else during the course of the match that will be remembered much longer. He argued with the umpire. The crowd of nineteen thousand sat aghast as the Master walked up to British umpire Mike Lugg and complained about a call. But when Lugg told him he was overruling the baseline judge on the call, Björn went on complaining – very quietly. Eventually Lugg was forced to become the first umpire ever to dock Borg first one, and then a second penalty point for refusing to play. Björn was very stubborn, and very angry, too.

'I was in total shock,' McEnroe told the press. 'I mean, I didn't believe what I was seeing. I didn't know whether to tank the next two points, to make up for the points Björn had lost, or what. I certainly didn't want to take the set that way because of course the penalties gave me set points in the tie-break at 6–3. I just didn't feel right about it.'

For different reasons he didn't feel very right about his match with Gene Mayer either and, when he lost to the double-handed player from New Jersey for the first time in his career, he had effectively blown his chances of qualifying for the semi-finals. But there was still the doubles to play and he wasn't about to let Peter Fleming down just because of a gammy leg. (They went on to win the doubles title with a straight set victory over the year's entertaining WCT Braniff Champions, Peter McNamara and Paul McNamee.)

So McEnroe was on the bench being patched up when I started questioning him about a whole range of subjects, beginning with his attitude to keeping himself in shape.

'It's not good, is it?' he smiled. 'I suppose I don't do enough exercises. I'm definitely not the most enthusiastic trainer in the world, I prefer just to play a lot to keep myself fit. But I am beginning to realize that is not enough. Arthur Ashe has recommended a gym here in New York and it's probably about time I did something about it.'

Although the gym never saw very much of him, McEnroe certainly did something about his physical condition because within a matter of weeks he had lost a startling amount of weight, mostly as a result of a proper diet that cut out a lot of the junk food of which he was so fond. What had probably been lingering puppy fat disappeared and he never looked the same again.

He also started talking about the problems of being a star and how difficult he found it being a worldwide celebrity.

'I don't really consider myself a celebrity,' he declared. 'I don't like what goes with it. I want to be myself. I want to be known as a top tennis player, but not all the other bullshit that goes with it. I don't like being a phoney – and that's what happens when you start meeting hundreds of different people all over the place. I prefer to be honest. I think that's more important than being liked by everyone. But I know I have to learn to handle people and you could say there's still some room for improvement there!'

The US boycott of the Moscow Olympics had been the hot topic of the preceding months but McEnroe had no wish to air his views for public record:

'I'd love to talk about that subject for hours but, really, who cares what I think? Politics should be left to politicians. I don't know all the facts. Even Ronald Reagan didn't know everything that was going on in the White House when he was running for President. I'd like to see athletes do well because I'm an athlete. But I've never been to Russia. I don't know what's going on. I think it's totally inappropriate for someone to sound off about something just because he's in the limelight. He's no different from anyone else and certainly no more important when it comes to politics. There are probably a lot of union workers in New Jersey who know a hell of a lot more about politics than I do. But, privately, I like to keep abreast of events. I think it's important to be informed.'

I wondered as he finished that little speech how many other supposedly spoilt twenty-one-year-old superstars had such a rational, modest and intelligent understanding of their place in the world.

We went on to discuss a decision he had come to a few weeks earlier that did have political connotations — an invitation that he and Borg had received to play an exhibition match in the black South African state of Bophuthatswana. Borg had been ready to go despite heavy criticism in the Swedish press but McEnroe, who had been guaranteed a staggering $800,000 for one afternoon's work, had turned it down. I asked him why:

'Well, after discussing it with my father and listening to the opinions of a few people who knew something about the situation down there, we both agreed that there was an element of exploitation in the whole thing.

'I just didn't like the idea of being used to show off a supposedly black state that appears to exist at the convenience of the South African Government. I don't want to get into details because, as I have said, I don't believe in coming out with heavy statements about things that I don't know much about. And as I've never been to South Africa and have no particular desire to go there, I obviously can't comment with any degree of accuracy. It was just a feeling I had; call it instinct if you like.

'And in any case I'm not sure these type of challenge matches are particularly good for the game. It depends on the time and the place. It's possible that Borg and I will do a tour of Australia, although the money will be a lot less than we were offered from South Africa. But that's Australia, which is a bit different.'

(In fact McEnroe and Borg did play a three-match series in Australia the following month before John was properly fit. He lost badly in the first two matches and was humbly apologetic to the Australian press. 'I feel embarrassed,' he told them. 'You don't want people to think badly of all this because of all the money involved. All I can do is play my guts out and try to salvage something in the last match in Melbourne.' He did, and won. The money that the pair were guaranteed – over half a million pounds – was fractionally more than half what they would have received in South Africa. The original date for the South Africa match, 6 December 1980, was left free on McEnroe's calendar, so he flew down to Florida to play an exhibition for Harold Solomon's Hunger Project Charity. Instead of $800,000, he received nothing.)

In the light of all this, his reply to my next question was rather sad, despite being truthful for quite different reasons. I asked him, if he could change one thing about himself, what it would be:

'My image. I know I don't help myself by arguing with umpires and answering back when the spectators start yelling abuse at me. I know that's stupid because you can't win. But I just hope that one day they'll understand what I'm trying to say – that it's wrong in tennis to clap double faults; or scream out when you are about to serve or do any of those dumb things a few spectators do. That's probably too much to hope and I'm not sure how long it will take me to change. I'll probably go right out there now and get into an argument with someone. I just can't help myself. I really can't. If I see something that's wrong I just have to say so. You could say I have a temper. I'm Irish, you know.'

That winsome, impish and somehow shy smile crossed his face and I wished, not for the first time, that he could carry it on court with him. It would prove so much more effective a weapon in righting the wrongs that pain him than that belligerent scowl. But as long as he feels the way he does, replacing the scowl with a smile would require wearing a false mask, and that he simply cannot do. To John McEnroe, so logical, rational and intelligent in so many ways, that would amount to being a phoney. He knows it would probably help him. He knows it would probably achieve more than he is achieving now. But deep, deep down in the very fibre of his proud and stubborn being, there is something that keeps on telling him that there is nothing worse in the world than pretending to be something you are not.

So he heaved his body off the table, changed for his doubles with Peter Fleming and went out to face the music. About half an hour later, as I was typing in the pressroom, I heard the boos and I knew that he was at it again, scowling at the world, creating his own special kind of misery. As usual he had left his smile, folded with his sneakers and jeans, back in the locker room.

Once the weight came off and the hamstring mended, McEnroe's fortunes began to pick up again on the WCT tour in Europe. He won tournaments in Milan and Frankfurt, and then returned to Dallas to scythe his way through a Borg-less field to regain the crown he had lost the year before by beating Johan Kriek in the final.

But even with a flat in Montmartre, five days' peaceful practice and Stacy to keep him company, the French Open still turned out to be another struggle through quicksand. On courts made soggy by a depressingly wet Parisian spring, he beat Vince Van Patten in the first round and then actually managed to get past three South American clay-courters: former ATP President Jaime Fillol; Uruguay's Diego Perez; and an old rival from his junior days, Ricardo Ycaza of Ecuador, to reach the quarter-finals. That, by his own limited standards in Paris – winning the mixed with Mary Carillo in 1977 was still by far his best achievement there – was some kind of progress, but the fact that the unknown Perez, a qualifier, had taken him to four sets did not augur well for his ability to handle sterner opposition. And sterner stuff was indeed just around the corner.

Ivan Lendl had never beaten McEnroe before but the twenty-one-year-old Czech had already stamped his mark on the tennis world by leading his country to victory in the Davis Cup, having achieved, in the semi-finals of the 1980 competition, the remarkable feat of beating both Vilas and Clerc in Buenos Aires. Clay was his surface and he knew that, at last, he had got McEnroe where he wanted him. By the time McEnroe had finally persuaded referee Jacques Dorfmann to halt play for the night after loud complaints about the wet and gloomy conditions, Lendl's pounding ground strokes had caught the American out of position on a sufficient number of occasions to secure a 6–4, 6–4, 0–3 lead. On the resumption, McEnroe managed to cling to his service break to lead 5–3, but then everything came apart at the seams and Lendl bludgeoned his way to victory, 7–5, for a thoroughly convincing straight set win.

I asked McEnroe what he thought about his performance:

'Well, I'd say disgraceful is just about the best way of putting it. Conditions were just a little different today and I adjusted slower than he did. The ball was coming through harder and I just wasn't ready for it. I was making careless mistakes. I'm unhappy because I feel I didn't play the way I know I could have. I'm not hitting the ball the way I should. Everything's wrong. It's my fault, no one else's. There's no reason why I shouldn't be able to play on clay so it must be a question of preparation or mental toughness or something.'

Another honest appraisal.

In Paris in 1981 he achieved little other than to give Ivan Lendl, who eventually lost to Borg in the final, a foot in the door in their increasingly antagonistic personal rivalry. It proved to be a psychological boost that the Czech was to exploit to the full later in the year.

11

Wimbledon 1981

Once again the 1981 Stella Artois Championship at the Queen's Club at the beginning of June offered a little preview of what was to come for John McEnroe. There was a bad-tempered confrontation with the big Californian Hank Pfister and unnecessary baiting of umpire Georgina Clark during his defeat of Brian Gottfried in the final. With Wimbledon looming – a Wimbledon he was now certain he could win – McEnroe was feeling the pressure.

His premonitions were quite correct but his preparation, at least on the emotional level, was all wrong. By the time he stepped on No. 1 Court for his first-round match against Tom Gullikson, the left-handed twin, he was so nervous and so tautly strung that the inevitable happened. As he admitted candidly some time later:

'I lost control of myself. I probably didn't realize it was as bad as it looked. I didn't feel I had done anything that terrible by the time I got the second warning. But there were all sorts of things building up inside that I couldn't control. Everything aggravated me because I had put so much pressure on myself to do well. Even before the match started the umpire came up to me as I was sitting on court and said, "I'm Scottish – so we're not going to have any problems now, are we?" I suppose he was trying to break the ice and make out we would understand each other because I am Irish or something. But when I didn't respond he got visibly annoyed. So that was a bad beginning right there. But I just don't want to have any personal contact with officials. I just find the whole thing too difficult. It's business out there and there is no room for personal relationships.'

Most of the business in that match wasn't very pleasant. Although he won handily enough, 7–6, 7–5, 6–3, he was so uncertain of himself that he was continually mocking his own efforts and, in one outburst that would have been funny if all the other stuff hadn't been going on, he announced to the crowd, 'I'm so disgusting you shouldn't watch. Everybody leave!'

Sadly, of course, it was his attitude towards the officials that most people found disgusting – not his tennis. He was rude to the Scottish umpire Edward James, he yelled at linesmen, insulted the referee when Fred Hoyles appeared to try to restore order, smashed his racket and then refused to shake hands with the umpire at the end. The crowd booed him off court, but even as he went a young girl flung her arms around his neck and said, 'I love you.'

Maybe, just maybe, she was one of the few to see through the scowling, pouting, petulant visage and catch a glimpse of the insecurities that lay beneath. But no one had much time for thoughts like those. Super Brat was back with a vengeance as far as the press was concerned and all the good work of the previous year's final had been torn to shreds. The headlines screamed for his blood and completely dwarfed his remarks afterwards which, as usual, were contrite, self-searching and honest. 'My behaviour is unnecessary,' he said. 'I'm the one who gets hurt. No one is to blame but myself. If other players manage to keep calm, why not me?'

The question was left hanging as McEnroe progressed steadily through the Championships but, for many, a different question was more pertinent. If he had been so bad, why hadn't he been defaulted? The answer lay somewhere in the complicated penalty structure as laid down in the Grand Prix Code of Conduct – since revised – and the reluctance of Fred Hoyles to take such drastic action. As it was, McEnroe got hit with a £1,500 fine for the Gullikson match and was warned that any future misconduct would be interpreted as 'aggravated behaviour' and liable to fines of up to ten thousand dollars and/or suspension.

All that he had expected, but nothing infuriated him more than the totally erroneous reports concerning a driving offence that were put out on an agency wire service and therefore reported not merely in *The Times* and on BBC Television but in newspapers throughout the world. The report stated that he had been fined for speeding. That would have been difficult because he wasn't driving – Peter Fleming was. But, in a careless piece of reporting that gives journalism a bad name, someone had jumped to the completely unfounded conclusion that, as McEnroe was involved – to the extent of being in the car – he must be the culprit. He was beginning to realize just how difficult it was to shake off a bad reputation.

Despite all this and despite deteriorating relations with the newshounds among the massive Wimbledon press corps, McEnroe buckled down to business in the singles, beating Raul Ramirez in the second round, the great doubles team of Bob Lutz and Stan Smith in a coincidental one-two in rounds three and four, and then the Florida-based South African Johan Kriek in the quarters. Ramirez had won a set and Smith had served and volleyed with the kind of form that won him the title in 1972 before going down 7–5, 3–6, 6–1, 6–2, but there were no more problems for McEnroe in the singles until he met Rod Frawley in the semi-final.

Frawley, a twenty-eight-year-old Queenslander who had lived and coached in Frankfurt for several years before returning to the circuit in 1979, was an unlikely Wimbledon semi-finalist. Although he had enjoyed a very successful run on the Grand Prix tour in 1980, his form had been slipping in the months preceding Wimbledon and his ATP ranking had slumped from 39 to 110. But right from the first round Rod had settled into a steady rhythm and had always looked the most likely outsider to benefit from the carnage of seeds in that quarter of the draw – Tanner, Vilas and Pecci all having lost before the third round. In fact, Frawley arrived in the semi-final by way of a highly impressive victory over the promising New Englander, Tim Mayotte, having dropped only two sets en route – the same number as McEnroe.

McEnroe should have taken greater heed of all this, but it would have been difficult, given their relative positions in the world rankings, for him not to have gone on court feeling pretty confident. 'I knew he had been playing well, but I thought he would be a little nervous to start off,' admitted McEnroe. 'But instead he goes and breaks my serve in the first game and plays really well. It came as such a surprise that it unnerved me.'

In the end nothing unnerved McEnroe more than the umpire, Wing Commander George Grime. When McEnroe yelled out, 'You're a disgrace to mankind', Grime instantly assumed that McEnroe was referring to him and gave the player a conduct warning. 'But I was saying it to myself, umpire,' McEnroe called out, his face already contorted with despair and growing anger as another apparent injustice came down on his head. 'I was saying "you're a disgrace to mankind" to *myself*. Aren't I allowed to say that to myself?'

With McEnroe's long record of verbal self-abuse there is absolutely no reason to doubt his word, but Grime obviously did not believe him. On his report card he wrote down: 'McEnroe said umpires are a disgrace to mankind.'

There had been a similar misunderstanding on the part of the umpire in the Gullikson match. When McEnroe screamed out: 'You guys are the absolute pits of the world', Edward James jotted down the word 'piss' on his card. That was why he felt he could not repeat it publicly when McEnroe demanded to know why he was being penalized for obscenity. 'Pits', of course, is not obscene, not even in the American vernacular: it merely means 'the bottom'.

But then misunderstanding of the term had been widespread. Valerie Burnett, the Chairman's wife, thought it meant something far worse and was surprised at the mildness of the term when an American friend explained it to her during the US Open some weeks later. But by that stage of the Wimbledon fortnight McEnroe was so firmly entrenched as the villain of the piece that many people were inclined to think the worst of everything he did and said.

Certainly his behaviour was obnoxious at times – bad enough for the All England Club committee to feel justified in upholding Hoyles' recommendation for that $10,000 fine, which was later reduced to $5,000 by the Pro Council Administrator Marshall Happer, and finally thrown out altogether no less than seven months later when Harry Hopman, McEnroe's choice for the three-man panel drawn up to hear the player's appeal, vetoed it.

So once again the conduct problem overshadowed the tennis in McEnroe's semi-final, which was a pity because Frawley proved himself a worthy opponent and, showing not the slightest sign of being overawed by the occasion, challenged the American through three hard-fought sets with solid serve and volley tennis before going down 7–6, 6–4, 7–5.

The other semi-final had been a classic – 'A Banquet for the Gods' announced *The Times* in a rare moment of euphoria – and, indeed, Borg had to scurry around to find his very best recipes before he could get the better of Connors who, as his Las Vegas friends would say, was really cookin'. Sixteen aces helped Borg pull back from a two-set deficit – the first time that anyone had got him in that much trouble since Mark Edmondson in 1977.

The very act of survival against such an inspired opponent only heightened the aura of Borg's invincibility at Wimbledon and increased the feeling among many pundits that he would extend his incredible run of title-winning years to six. But, despite everything that had gone before, McEnroe also had his supporters, especially amongst those who simply felt that a change would be good for the overall health of the game. I personally was convinced he could win – I had seen him beat Borg often enough on cement and Supreme courts, so why not on grass?

To hope for a repeat of the drama and excellence of the final of the previous year was asking too much, and in that we were proved right. Even compared with the Borg–Connors semi-final, the 1981 final was a less tasty feast, but it was close enough and technically good enough to live alongside some of the best Wimbledon finals of preceding years. In retrospect, Borg was a little lucky still to be in front by the time the second set reached 6 all. The Swede had taken the first on a single service-break, but McEnroe had reached break point on the champion's serve no less than eight times in four separate service games.

The first tie-break rather confirmed what the score had thus far failed to do – namely, that the five-time champion was losing control of the match. With McEnroe coming up with precision volleys and cleverly disguised lobs, Borg managed to win only one tie-break point before the American set course for victory by levelling the match 4–6, 7–6.

Borg led 3–1 in the third set but McEnroe, chipping his service low to Borg's feet, broke back in the seventh game and then survived an onslaught on his own delivery in the tenth that proved to be Borg's last real hope of salvaging his crown. With the Centre Court crowd – as noisy as any I have heard in a final – helping to raise the tension level to new heights, Björn produced an unbelievable backhand pass as he raced onto a good, deep volley from McEnroe and reached the first of four set points. Earning his spurs as a prospective champion, McEnroe survived and took the match into another tie-break. A beautiful floated cross-court pass off the forehand deprived the Swede of one service point and a backhand, chipped deep down the line, took away another. They were strokes of exquisite skill and timing – the strokes of a man worthy to hold the game's premier title. Maybe, deep down inside him, Borg sensed that too, for although he fought bravely in the fourth set, he was playing like a man searching for miracles and McEnroe, controlled and resolute, didn't have any on offer. So by the score of 4–6, 7–6, 7–6, 6–4 a new king was enthroned, ending a long and dignified reign.

It was not viewed as a very happy coronation within the hallowed halls of the All England Club. The ridiculous failure to communicate properly over the invitation to the Champions' Dinner only emphasized the fact that there was little love lost between Wimbledon and its new Champion. And that was the saddest thing of all. It was sad, too, to hear a friend like Dan Maskell, the BBC's veteran commentator, tell me, 'I found McEnroe's behaviour so offensive that it completely ruined my enjoyment of this year's Wimbledon.'

As there is no one who has a greater or more abiding love for the game than Maskell, nor indeed many with a deeper knowledge of it, such opinions must be respected. It is not just a question of the old school being unable to cope with the brave new world. Maskell frequently enjoyed and defended Ilie Nastase. But McEnroe, in his rage for perfection and intolerance of injustice, takes matters to a stage that many reasonable people find unacceptable. John simply didn't realize that to start with, although I know that he does now.

In less than four minutes on a blustery afternoon at Flushing Meadow in September 1981, John McEnroe uncorked four knockout blows that finally and irrevocably stripped the mantle of supremacy from Björn Borg's shoulders. The score in the final of the

US Open stood at one set all and 4—3 to Borg in the third with the Swede's serve to come. For the first time in a fluctuating and far from error-free match, Borg was starting to find an easy rhythm with his baseline drives, and the packed Stadium Court crowd of twenty thousand was giving him every encouragement as he glided towards a two set to one lead.

Then suddenly McEnroe turned everything inside out. Five points later McEnroe was a different player and we were watching a different match. John admitted afterwards that the way he played that game made him feel as if he could hit any shot he wanted. Those who saw it could understand why.

McEnroe won four of those five points with outright winners: the first was a scorching backhand cross-court pass on the return of serve; the second a topspin lob deep into Borg's backhand corner that the Swede, caught very close to the net, never bothered to chase. They were both exquisite shots that would have been difficult to reproduce at any stage. But, after allowing Borg one point, the defending champion reproduced both instantly, in sequence, as if he were providing his own live version of instant replay: backhand pass; topspin lob. Borg looked stunned and no wonder. Even he, who had taken a longer, closer look at McEnroe's talent in the past few years than anyone else in the game, was shocked by the streak of genius that had just flashed before him. The power of one shot and the precision of the other, each repeated in perfect harmony at a crucial, pivotal moment of the match, revealed a rare and instinctive gift shared only by the greatest champions. Borg has that gift and seeing it so clearly and so cruelly reflected in his opponent's play made it that much more psychologically damaging.

Borg never recovered. Two games later a stinging forehand winner clinched the set 6—4 for McEnroe. Any chance Björn had of getting back into a match that he had seemed to be on the point of controlling just a few minutes earlier was destroyed by the deft manner in which the American took the pace off his shots; forcing constant reprogramming of the Borg computer as each stroke came back at different levels and different speeds, doctored with varying amounts of spin.

Rod Laver, one of many former champions present for the

Centennial Celebration of the USTA, was impressed and McEnroe would want no better stamp of approval. Laver noted, in particular, the champion's footwork – that precious ability to meet any shot, no matter how hard it is hit, with perfect balance even after being forced to change direction.

And so McEnroe joined Bill Tilden as the only other man since World War I to have claimed the US singles crown in three successive years. His 4–6, 6–2, 6–4, 6–3 victory was a crushing defeat for Borg who had failed once again to win the one major title that had always eluded him. Untypically, he stalked off court without waiting for the prize-giving ceremony and admitted to me, when we met in Geneva a few weeks later, that it had been a deliberate act. 'I was just very, very disappointed,' Borg said honestly. 'I couldn't face the idea of making a nice speech in front of all those people. I suppose I was a bad boy.'

But for McEnroe, of course, it was a triumph. Apart from his exciting and often tempestuous five-set semi-final with friend and neighbour Vitas Gerulaitis, in which the CBS courtside mike took a hammering from the McEnroe racket and the officials took a hammering from the Gerulaitis mouth, only the silkily skilful Indian Ramesh Krishnan had given McEnroe any real trouble. Krishnan, whose father was a Wimbledon semi-finalist twice in the sixties, served for a two set to love lead before McEnroe realized there was serious work to be done and battled his way out of trouble 6–7, 7–6, 6–4, 6–2.

When Heinz Gunthardt of Switzerland was unable to partner Peter McNamara in the doubles final because of illness, McEnroe and Peter Fleming won the title by default. But they had already played a match worthy of the final one round earlier when a pair of veteran Aussies called John Newcombe and Fred Stolle forced them to battle for five long sets before going down 7–6 in the fifth. The crowd loved every minute of it, mainly because the two old pros milked the situation for every drop of entertainment value it was worth, while the young Americans angrily refused to see the joke. Inevitably they were on a hiding to nothing as far as popularity was concerned, and if this was to be a contest of heroes and villains, the die became cast when McEnroe hit Stolle at close range with a full-blooded drive and then took a long time raising his hand in a gesture of apology.

'But that wasn't where he lost me,' said Stolle who, through his association with Gerulaitis, had come to know McEnroe pretty well, especially after John took an apartment at Turnberry Isle in Florida where Fred directs the tennis activities. 'Being hit was no big deal, despite what everyone said afterwards. I would probably have played the same shot. No, what I couldn't stomach was his sarcastic attitude when I pointed to a mark left by one of Peter's serves that had landed wide. John was at the net like myself and when I touched the spot with my racket just to verify that the linesman's call was correct, he said, "Oh, yea Fred, why not pick any mark? Any old mark will do." That was where he lost me.'

It was a sad and familiar story. Off court McEnroe would never seriously suggest that Fred Stolle would try to con anyone out of a point. But on court, in the heat of the battle, rational thinking becomes obliterated by a paranoid conviction that everyone is trying to do him in. It was to be that way frequently during the remaining months of 1981 and it was only after the Volvo Masters in the following January that he realized that it was not just his reputation but his actual play that was beginning to suffer. In the intervening months, however, more friendships were to be put under needless strain.

12

The Davis Cup

In my book *Open Tennis* I claimed that John McEnroe had single-handedly saved the Davis Cup at the beginning of the eighties and many people laughed. Even Rex Bellamy, writing a kindly review in *The Times*, took me to task and suggested I had gone a little over the top. Well, stubborn soul that I am, I will attempt to restate my case. First of all, this is what I wrote:

'(The trend at the time was for the top stars not to play Davis Cup . . .) and by the time McEnroe appeared on the scene it was threatening to turn into a stampede. Had McEnroe joined in, the efforts of Philippe Chatrier and David Gray, who had joined him from the *Guardian* as secretary of the ITF, to streamline the Davis Cup and pump some much needed sponsorship money into the World Group and zonal ties would have come to nought. Without their top stars bothering to turn out, American audiences, parochial in their sporting tastes at the best of times, would have turned off the Davis Cup so fast no promoter worth his dollars and cents would have touched a Davis Cup tie with the end of the outsize racket. And if America had not continued to be a leading Davis Cup nation, no major international sponsor would have been interested, either. Dwight Davis' marvellous idea, which had produced so many glorious sporting moments since its inception in 1900, would have been reduced to a second-rate competition between second-rate nations. Only one person prevented that happening. John McEnroe.

'. . . until he brought officialdom down on his head after the disastrous loss to Sweden in the 1984 final in Gothenburg,

McEnroe's motto was simple: "I'll go anywhere, any time to play Davis Cup for the United States."

'That was a commitment no other top American star was prepared to make. It was a commitment that rekindled interest in the competition in America and was instrumental in allowing the ITF to find a sponsor of the calibre of the Nippon Electric Company (NEC) to take over worldwide sponsorship to the tune of one million dollars.

'The equation was very straightforward: no McEnroe, no America; no America, no NEC; no NEC, no future for the Davis Cup.'

Despite everything that has happened since, which includes a gradual disenchantment with the whole USTA management of the Davis Cup and frequent refusals to play, I do not see any reason to back down from my original assertion that, without McEnroe's loyal support in those crucial years at the start of his career, the Davis Cup would have struggled to survive. How could it have been otherwise? No other top American tennis player was willing to commit to the Davis Cup at the time, so interest would inevitably have waned. Relegation in the early years of the World Group format, which came into being in 1981, would have been a disaster – a quite likely one at that – and would have killed off any chance of securing a big sponsor. And without some sort of prize money, which even today does not match what a player can earn from a couple of nights' exhibition matches, none of the other big stars of the era like Björn Borg, Guillermo Vilas, José-Luis Clerc and José Higueras would have been inclined to increase their commitment to the Davis Cup which was spotty at the best of times.

When America did eventually get relegated, at least McEnroe was there, incensing some people as usual with his overt display of flag-waving nationalism, but ensuring that everyone knew the Davis Cup was a big deal by engaging himself in a six-hour, twenty-minute marathon with Boris Becker, which still stands as the second-longest Davis Cup tie in history. The fact that he lost 4–6, 15–13, 8–10, 6–2, 6–2, and the United States was indeed forced to spend a year fighting its way out of the American Zone, was no longer of such dire consequence (although the NEC would have been much displeased had McEnroe not helped André Agassi lift them back up within a year by beating Argentina in Buenos Aires) because, by the mid-eighties, the power-house tennis nations of Europe like Sweden and West Germany were creating a level of excitement all of their own. But Mats Wilander, Stefan Edberg and Boris Becker had not been around when McEnroe, steeped in Davis Cup tradition by parents who thought there was no higher honour than to represent your country, put his reputation and his pocket-book on the line and said, 'I don't care what anyone else is doing, I'll play.' Not every nineteen- or twenty-year-old would have had such courage of their convictions.

So let me take you back to the very beginning of this career that would turn out to be one of the most brilliant in Davis Cup history. It began, appropriately enough, on what was very nearly virgin land – the expanding oasis that was still eating its way into the fringes of the Californian desert called the Mission Hills Country Club.

Like the courts at La Quinta Hotel and, later, the Grand Champions' resort at Indian Wells, Mission Hills was to become a centre of international tennis activity as well as a paradise for golfers. Situated a few miles from Palm Springs down Highway 111, Mission Hills was so new when Britain upset all predictions by reaching the Davis Cup final in 1978 that you got sand in your shoes just by walking around the back of the Centre Court. Today, palm trees and greenery stretch as far as the eye can see and the retreating desert shimmers in the distance.

It was here that the nineteen-year-old John McEnroe was chosen to play singles for his country for the first time. The report I wrote for *Tennis Week* bears a second look in the light of subsequent events:

'With John McEnroe as point man and Stan Smith and Bob Lutz the linchpin of their success, Tony Trabert's team brought the Davis Cup back to the United States for the first time since 1972 with a thoroughly convincing 4–1 defeat of Britain.

'Yet in all probability, it will be British tennis that will benefit most from the year's campaign that ended on a strangely unreal note at the Mission Hills Country Club near Palm Springs.

'It is unlikely that the average American sports fan will consider regaining the Davis Cup one of his country's major sporting achievements for 1978. To an outside observer it seems that America only really gets behind its athletes in a team sense once every four years at the Olympics. This may change when the United States finally produces a soccer team capable of challenging Argentina, Brazil or West Germany. Until then American sport will continue to live in its cosy, esoteric little world, pretending that the Los Angeles Dodgers playing the New York Yankees actually qualifies as a "World" Series.

'In Britain, however, the achievements of team manager Paul Hutchins in taking his team to the finals against considerable odds should generate sufficient interest and pride to stimulate much needed growth in the game.

'It would have been stretching credibility a little far to have expected a better result against a team as powerful as that fielded by Trabert in the final. But some British visitors were disappointed by the somewhat contrived and artificial atmosphere in which the tie was played.

'Given the time available to set up the final, I doubt if a better site could be found. It was technically and aesthetically correct for the US to want to play outdoors and that, considering the December date, inevitably restricted one's options.

'I think the problem lies in the image so many of us have of the correct setting for a Davis Cup final. Irrationally we retain the memory of twenty thousand people lubricating parched throats from cans of beer at White City or Kooyong under a burning Australian sun. Somehow, three hundred freezing spectators huddled under blankets while coyotes yowl at the desert moon doesn't quite fit. But perhaps we have Harry Hopman to blame for that. In the post-war heyday of the Davis Cup he helped turn the competition into an Australian festival.

'Provided you were watching from the protective warmth of the Mission Hills Clubhouse, that desert setting with the huge silver moon hanging overhead had a charm all of its own as

Buster Mottram saved the possibility of an embarrassing rout by fighting his way back from the brink of extinction against Brian Gottfried. And, of course, when the sun was up to warm the icy desert air during the afternoon the stands were nearly three-quarters full. But the sizeable band of British fans who had journeyed six thousand miles to cheer their heroes had a right to wonder why more of southern California's vast tennis-playing population could not stir themselves to drive the odd hundred miles to witness the famous and traditionally exciting event.

'From an American point of view the biggest plus was the continued growth of the remarkable John McEnroe. By crushing John Lloyd in the opening singles and Mottram in the decisive fourth rubber on Sunday for the total loss of only eleven games, McEnroe created a new record for singles play in a Davis Cup final. The previous best was twelve, a record shared by such notables as Bill Tilden and Björn Borg.

'It had been evident right from the start that the US needed two singles victories from McEnroe to remove the distant threat of an upset, and that was asking quite a lot from a nineteen-year-old arriving from a gruelling indoor European tour – especially since he had never played singles for his country before.

'But McEnroe, channelling his Irish temperament into two periods of intense and unwavering concentration, rose to the challenge with performances that surprised even those of us who consider him to be the greatest talent currently wielding a racket.

'"Not even Connors or Borg have made me look that much of an idiot," remarked John Lloyd. But at least Lloyd managed to break the McEnroe serve. Mottram, like Borg in Sweden four weeks earlier, never got to deuce.

'Against Mark Cox and John Lloyd's brother David in the doubles Smith and Lutz produced as fine a demonstration of the art as one could have wished for. They first played together when McEnroe was five, and it showed. Their defence was watertight and their offence – especially from Smith at the net – devastating.

'When I caught Smith peeking at a video cassette recording of the match at a party given by Mission Hills assistant pro

Tommy Tucker on the Saturday night, he grinned and said, "Just checking on our mistakes . . ."

'Mottram's feat of fighting back from two sets and match point down in the third against Gottfried was a triumph for a player whose erratic past performances have frequently defied logic. Despite two agonizingly unlucky net calls on vital points and no less then eleven foot fault calls, the big Englishman refused to allow anything to distract him from his single-minded determination to dig himself, and Britain, out of a large hole. The fact that he succeeded established him as a competitor of the highest rank.

'It took John McEnroe to garnish Mottram's brilliant 1978 Davis Cup record but then, as the coming months will prove, McEnroe is something else.'

That was a fairly safe prediction and McEnroe did not fail me, not in the following months, nor the following years. But if there was apathy on the part of the local tennis-orientated population in 1978, it did not last. Eight years later, Charlie Pasarell, a former Davis Cup player himself, was planning a 10,500-seat tennis stadium at the new Grand Champions resort and many people told him he was mad. 'You'll never fill a stadium that size in the desert,' they said. Now that the last three days of the Newsweek Cup are oversubscribed one hundred per cent, Pasarell is planning to build a 16,000-seat stadium back down the road near La Quinta and the cynics are silent. He will fill it for the ATP Tour event and, if McEnroe's playing, he would fill it for a Davis Cup tie. In 1989 when the United States, with McEnroe and Agassi playing singles, met France in nearby San Diego, all the tickets for the 12,000-seat arena were sold weeks in advance. That is how far tennis has come in the intervening years and, although many people closely associated with American tennis will grind their teeth before admitting it, no one has fanned the flames of interest more dramatically or more consistently than McEnroe.

However, my crystal ball was a great deal murkier when I predicted, earlier in the article, that it would be Britain, rather than the United States, that would benefit most from the 1978 Davis Cup campaign. Although Paul Hutchins, captain at the time, felt there were spin-off benefits, they have been hard to detect. Inexcusably, British tennis was allowed to stagnate for another decade.

Stagnation was the last thing on McEnroe's mind. Unruly and unchecked, he was storming the conservative bastions of the game with his fiery talent, revealing an ability to thrill and to shock that quickly gained him a notoriety far beyond the confines of his sport. Because of its hallowed position in the game's history, McEnroe's scornful attitude towards the niceties of behaviour in Davis Cup play – which contrasted sharply with the pride he felt at being selected for the team – earned him special retribution. But with the criticism came the interest – and plenty of it.

Despite the morale-crushing defeat McEnroe and his colleagues suffered on the clay of Buenos Aires against Argentina in 1980, the 1981 semi-final victory over Australia in Portland, Oregon, and the revenge exacted over the Argentinians in the final in Cincinnati were two of the most enthusiastically supported ties I can remember in the United States. And one did not have to search very far for the reason. McEnroe had added Wimbledon to his US Open crown that year and was unquestionably the biggest name in the game. The reaction of the average American sports fan was typically simplistic: 'The Davis Cup's gotta be a big deal if McEnroe's playing.'

And so it was. Although neither the traditionalists nor even his own captain appreciated the way he went about it, two things would have happened if McEnroe had joined Jimmy Connors in removing himself from the latter stages of the 1981 campaign. Argentina would have won and no one would have cared.

But, at that stage of his career, McEnroe never stayed away, no matter how poor the opposition or how inconvenient was a tie for his own schedule. Even the fact that Tony Trabert, who McEnroe still rates as the best Davis Cup captain he has known, had made way for Arthur Ashe, a man he never really understood, did not dilute McEnroe's dedication to the cause.

Facing Ivan Lendl on a suffocatingly hot day at Flushing Meadow in the Davis Cup quarter-final was not the way he would have chosen to celebrate his 1981 Wimbledon triumph. But that was what he had to do just five days after surviving the physical and emotional ordeal of beating Borg at the end of a very long fortnight. Small wonder that it proved to be beyond him, but with Connors making a rare appearance on the team McEnroe recovered in time to deliver the *coup de grâce* against Tomas Smid in a conclusive fourth rubber and so deprive Czechoslovakia of the Cup they had won in Prague only seven months before.

For reasons best known to the man himself, that was the first and last America saw of Connors as a Davis Cup player that year, but with Tanner stepping in to score a vital five-set victory over Peter McNamara in the semi-final against Australia in Portland, Jimmy's absence was shrugged off by a team that had learned to live without him often enough.

Ashe, however, found it more difficult to shrug off the behaviour of his doubles pair when McEnroe and Fleming threw a fit over a complete misunderstanding between the umpire and a linesman. As the Americans were beating McNamara and Phil Dent handsomely at the time, the conduct warnings they received as a result of the rumpus that brought Ashe on court in the not very effective role of peacemaker seemed all the more unfortunate and unnecessary.

It was, however, an absolutely typical example of the kind of trouble that erupts when McEnroe — and equally in this case Fleming — simply will not tolerate a genuine mistake that an umpire stubbornly refuses to rectify. Fleming had stopped playing because the linesman behind him had called the ball out. The call had been quiet so that only Fleming and not the umpire heard it. It had also been wrong. The linesman admitted as much to Fleming but refused to tell the umpire because the rules say that the umpire is supposed to *ask* his line-judges before they can offer information of that kind. One is reminded of Mr Bumble in *Oliver Twist* who would have had the perfect answer to such stupidity. 'If the law supposes that,' said Mr Bumble, 'the law is an ass.'

Quite true, but ranting and raving about it wasn't going to get them anywhere and they should have let the matter drop after an initial protest. But, of course, they couldn't and, with the dignified Ashe out there trying to placate two overwrought players, the whole scene descended into a distasteful farce. McNamara and Dent couldn't understand it. If ever there was an example of the basic difference in Australian and American attitudes towards sport this was it – not that McEnroe and Fleming were the first to illustrate the gulf that separates them. Dennis Ralston and Chuck McKinley had been lambasted in the Australian press back in the early sixties for their behaviour in Davis Cup and, in their reaction to this latest incident, McNamara and Dent voiced opinions that could have echoed those of Neale Fraser (now the Australian captain) and Roy Emerson twenty years before. 'We think it's special playing for Australia,' said Dent, 'and it must be bad when you get two warnings when you are playing for your country. I reckon it was a pretty poor show.'

McNamara was bewildered and obviously disgusted. 'I find it hard to believe that they made such a big deal out of nothing. The game's deteriorated somewhat. You're supposed to have thirty seconds between points and we waited around for five minutes. If we had got another set, there is no way we would have lost the match. They would have been defaulted out of it because under Davis Cup rules the third warning means "exit".'

But to McEnroe and Fleming the issue of whether they were winning or losing or whether the incident reflected well on themselves or their country was obviously secondary in their minds to the fact that an injustice had occurred, and injustices must not be tolerated.

'Anyone who makes a decision like that shouldn't be allowed on a tennis court,' McEnroe told a packed press conference afterwards. 'We're the ones who pay in the long run; we're the ones who are made to look bad as a result of a decision like that. The question is not whether the ball was in or out. That wasn't the point. The point was that play was interrupted by an erroneous call which the linesman freely admitted and the umpire refused to accept.'

'Yes, I'm sure the crowd misunderstood as usual,' added Fleming. 'I'm sure they thought we were complaining about the call but we weren't – because the ball was in. But of course then the din starts up and it just makes everything more tense and difficult.'

But McEnroe knew they had overreacted and tried to explain why. 'It might sound like bullshit to say something like this but you get up-tight because it's not only you playing out there. That is the difference in playing Davis Cup. You definitely feel worse if you lose. Not that everyone in the whole country is wondering what's about to happen in Portland, Oregon, but there are a lot of people who are still patriotic and care about it and you try to do your best for them. And I get up-tight. I think you could see I was more nervous than normal.'

That explanation cut little ice with the Aussies. When Neil Amdur of the *New York Times* relayed McEnroe's explanation of nervousness to Dent, the reply was laced with sarcasm. 'He never acted like that before? God, he gets nervous a lot then.'

Primarily the Australians were annoyed that they had become the victims of the inevitable but unintentional chain reaction that is set in motion in these situations. The officials were the original offenders, initially for making a mistake over a line-call which is perfectly understandable, and secondly for refusing to bend stupid rules in order to defuse an incident with a little common sense. The Americans were then at fault for continuing to argue so long because, in doing so, they then broke the very legitimate and very necessary thirty-second rule. Four or five minutes is a long time to hang around on court, trying to maintain both concentration and body warmth while your opponents argue over a point of law.

Back at the Marriott Hotel that evening, jubilation at having clinched the tie 3–0 was tinged with feelings of regret in the American camp over the row. It had spotlighted the seemingly unbridgeable gap that existed between Ashe and two of his players – a gap that had more to do with upbringing than difference in age. It had been drummed into Arthur by his father and his tennis mentor Dr Johnson that the No. 1 rule in life for a black boy trying to make it in the white man's world was never, ever to give anyone the opportunity to reproach you for misbehaviour. Consequently Ashe, who is as nervous as a kitten inside, has very rarely let his emotions show. McEnroe and Fleming, of course, were never placed in that position. For them the need to fight for what was right was one of the first principles of life. But, like so many people, Ashe just felt they went about it the wrong way.

'I thought their behaviour was disgraceful and I told them

so,' Arthur told me when I ran into him in the corridor outside McEnroe's suite. Inside John and Peter were on their third beer. But even though they were high on victory they had not lost sight of the fact that the needless row had created problems within the team as far as their captain was concerned.

'We blew it,' McEnroe said, suddenly and momentarily morose as he let the facts sink in. 'I know, don't tell me man, we blew it.'

In a sense they blew it again against Argentina in Cincinnati three months later. But it was indicative of the enormity of the triumph they achieved that McEnroe should leap into the arms of his captain Arthur Ashe and trainer Bill Norris after he had brought the Cup back to America by beating Jose-Luis Clerc in the decisive fourth rubber. He had barely spoken to Ashe for the previous forty-eight hours. Once again two hopelessly different temperaments had been trying to work for a common cause and had found the task well nigh impossible. Ashe was simply too low-key for McEnroe – and, it must be said, for other members of the team as well – and McEnroe, in turn, was operating at a pitch of emotional endeavour that Ashe could barely understand. In the end victory was the only possible palliative.

This McEnroe provided, more than ably abetted by Fleming in the doubles, with as brilliant a display of skill and tenacity under pressure as anything he had achieved before. Considering what was at stake, I think the fifth set he produced against Clerc was probably as fine a set of tennis as he has ever played in his life. After beating Tanner on the opening day, Clerc had proved he could compete at the Americans' own level on the medium-fast Supreme court at the Riverside Coliseum – a court that was supposed to give the United States almost as much advantage as the Argentinians had enjoyed on their own clay in Buenos Aires. And he continued to prove it by levelling his match with McEnroe at two sets all.

McEnroe, however, had not been assisted by what occurred in the American locker-room during the ten-minute break between the third and fourth sets. 'It was like Fifth Avenue in there,' declared Tony Palafox, who had popped in to see if John needed a little tactical advice (Ashe was not saying a word to him on court) and then left quickly when he saw the crowd swarming around the player. 'I just told him to keep serving to the forehand and into the body and then got out of there. I always used to insist on a closed locker-room at the break when I was playing for Mexico, and John should have done the same.'

Ironically McEnroe had not done so for fear of causing another rumpus. 'I just didn't want to make any waves,' he told me. 'I didn't want to get accused of being any more difficult. I thought we'd had enough problems but I suppose that was one thing I should have insisted on. Half the USTA seemed to be in there and so many people were trying to say the right things that I completely lost my concentration.'

It was not until the fifth set that McEnroe got himself together again and channelled all that ferocious energy and skill into one final, awesome bid for victory.

Despite the fact that the score would only be 2–2 if he lost, McEnroe knew that Guillermo Vilas was well capable of beating Tanner, and his pride would not let him contemplate putting Roscoe under that kind of pressure. In his mind this was the set; this was the match; this was the whole Davis Cup campaign right here and he was prepared to fight all out for it. There was no more time to yell at linesmen or worry about Ashe. Everything he had learned as a tennis player and competitor was levelled at a strong and worthy opponent and, in the end, one felt a little sorry for Clerc. No one could have survived the tidal wave of talent that engulfed him. It was all there: the viciously accurate serving; the masterful change of pace; the flashing winners that seemed to explode out of nowhere past Clerc's outstretched racket; and those mesmerizing drop volleys that wafted off his racket with such spell-binding delicacy.

But it was not just the skill and the shot-making. John McEnroe was as hyped up as I had ever seen him and yet so obviously in total control. It was intimidating to watch from courtside, so heaven knows what it was like from the other side of the net. 'Yeah!' he yelled, punching air to celebrate the unloading of another ace. The crowd roared. Father, like so many spectators, was waving a little American flag in glee. Even Ashe leapt out of his chair to applaud.

'My, is this man pumped up!' exclaimed former ATP President

Cliff Drysdale in his role as TV commentator. 'This is a truly remarkable performance.'

And, indeed, it was. 6–3 was the eventual score in that fifth set and Clerc did well to get three games.

The celebrations were long and noisy. Back at the hotel rock music blared in McEnroe's suite as well-wishers, some welcome and some not, poured in. 'The walls,' wrote John Edwards graphically in the *Daily Mirror*, 'thumped like an elephant's heart.'

It wasn't all Edwards had to say. To put it mildly, he was more impressed with Bob Jenkins' umpiring than McEnroe's behaviour in between his bouts of brilliance. As a newcomer to the tennis scene, but a veteran and much-lauded observer of everything from Vietnam to the Royal Wedding, Edwards had obviously been shocked by the vitriol that poured out of McEnroe in moments of high stress. Edwards was not alone in this. ITF President Philippe Chatrier, a former French Davis Cup captain, was also shocked by some of the things McEnroe said to USTA officials sitting at court-side.

The worst of it had occurred on the second day in the doubles which, no matter how much one disapproved of the antagonism that broke out on court amongst the players, became compelling entertainment. At one stage Ashe had to order McEnroe back to the base-line as he and Clerc advanced towards each other like gun-fighters in Dodge City. But the best drama lay purely in the tennis. The score of 6–3, 4–6, 6–4, 4–6, 11–9 with Vilas serving for the match at 7–6 in the fifth (there were no tie-breakers in Davis Cup then) was extraordinary enough in itself considering that Clerc and Vilas were two unfriendly singles players trying to weld themselves into a doubles team born of necessity rather than desire. But the level of skill displayed made it as fine a game of doubles as I have ever seen, for all four men played at the top of their form, not least Fleming who was something of a revelation. He was on court with three of the best six singles players in the world yet no one would have detected that he was, in that sense, the odd man out from the way he held steady when the heat was on; serving brilliantly and volleying with savage power.

But throughout that great victory and the first four sets of his match with Clerc, McEnroe apparently felt the need to continually carp and frequently abuse the officials. Once he called a middle-aged black linesman 'boy', which was about as stupid a thing as he has ever said in his life, not merely because it was unpardonable but because, as he has proved over and over again, he has no racial prejudices whatsoever. But there is no doubt that his prejudices against everyone who sits in authority over him on a tennis court are very real and very alarming.

The following year, McEnroe swept through the entire campaign undefeated, culminating in the retention of the Cup against France in Grenoble. But at least one match proved to be a monumental test of his stamina, resilience and concentration. In the second round against Sweden in St Louis, McEnroe battled the new seventeen-year-old French Open champion Mats Wilander through a six-hour, twenty-two-minute marathon that still stands as the longest match in history. The score was 9–7, 6–2, 15–17, 3–6, 8–6 but, despite being two sets to one down, McEnroe never felt that he was going to lose. On the indoor Supreme carpet he was in his element and, at courtside, Ashe shared his confidence.

'It was a great effort,' Ashe told me. 'But I always thought John was going to come through.'

In Grenoble, on the specially laid indoor clay court – a ploy that the Swedes would copy to such good effect in later years – McEnroe had another tough battle on his hands against Yannick Noah. But, once again, he revealed the quality of a true champion by over-coming a two set to one deficit, as well as a surface and a crowd that both favoured his opponent, to win 6–3 in the fifth set.

When he and Peter Fleming beat Noah and Henri Leconte in the doubles, the Cup was assured of staying in American hands because Gene Mayer had given the United States a 2–0 lead on the opening day by beating Leconte. However the Sunday, when there was nothing to offer the packed stadium but two dead rubbers, also, with hindsight, proved significant for McEnroe.

Mayer, who never had sufficient respect for the game he played with such natural skill, insulted the crowd by making no more than a token effort against Noah and lost 6–1, 6–0, dead rubbers being reduced to the best of three sets. There were those, I suppose, who might have expected McEnroe to be equally unconcerned by the duty of every public performer to treat the paying customer with respect. But, once again, they would have underestimated the man. McEnroe offered up a masterly exhibition of attacking clay court tennis to beat Leconte 6–2, 6–3. It earned him a standing ovation and saved his team from charges of disrespect towards their beaten opponents.

Few members of the USTA seemed to remember McEnroe's professionalism that day when the roof fell in on Ashe's team in Gothenburg two years later, but the French public didn't forget and there is little doubt that the love affair that now exists between McEnroe and followers of the game in France stems from that Sunday in Grenoble when a great player showed just how sincere he was about playing a serious game of tennis for a serious tennis audience.

In 1983 McEnroe made a brave attempt to lead a weakened team to do battle with Vilas and Clerc in Buenos Aires. But it was a hopeless task and the only consolation lay in the fact that the US drew Ireland in the relegation play-off round. So for the first time he had the chance to visit the land where all his grandparents were born.

But it was not until the final in 1984 that real disaster struck. Jimmy Connors had condescended to make himself available for the trip to Gothenburg and Ashe felt obliged to pick him. Frankly, I wouldn't have done. Quite apart from the fact that Connors had never won an important match on the slow European clay court the Swedes were preparing at the Scandinavium, Jimmy has never been a good team man and there would inevitably be resentment from the other squad members at the way he had elected to turn up for the big event after so much of the hard work had been done.

Ashe's problems were compounded when he failed to ensure that his two superstars arrived in good time. McEnroe had arranged exhibition matches earlier that same week and Connors was loathe to leave Patti, who was expecting a baby any minute. It is all very well saying that Arthur should have been stricter, but what are you supposed to do with a couple of individualistic millionaires who are only playing because they feel like it? Davis Cup spans four weeks of the year. The rest of the time they are free agents, able to play when and where they please. If Ashe had pressed them too hard both could have told him what to do with the Davis Cup and he would have had very little recourse. Because he cares, McEnroe would have been very unlikely to have walked out, but Connors, because he has shown so little sign of caring about anything other than the welfare of Connors and family, could have done anything. In retrospect, Ashe probably wishes he had never shown up at all. Win or lose, it would certainly have been better for McEnroe.

The team spirit was so bad that Connors actually left an abusive note for Jimmy Arias on court when he thought Arias had failed to turn up for a scheduled practice session. Arias, who had been hitting for hours earlier in the day with McEnroe and Peter Fleming, was waiting for Connors in the locker room – a perfectly reasonable place to be. But Connors arrived from his hotel already changed and didn't bother to look in the most obvious place. It was not a happy squad.

It became a great deal unhappier when Connors was run ragged by Mats Wilander in the opening rubber, and disgraced himself by arguing over calls and getting so worked up at one stage that he shook the umpire's chair with some violence. At the end he stormed off, omitting to shake hands with anyone except his opponent.

McEnroe didn't fare a great deal better against Henrik Sundstrom, a powerful baseliner who controlled the ball with a heavy top spin off both sides. Sundstrom made a brief and unsustained appearance in the world's top ten about that time and this was his finest hour. After a protracted battle in the first set, the Swede surged on to win 13–11, 6–4, 6–3 and put his country 2–0 ahead.

Importantly, in the light of what was to transpire, McEnroe did not behave badly during the match and made a big show at the end of shaking hands with everyone in sight, including the umpire, the opposing captain Hans Olsson and, of course, Sundstrom. Quite deliberately, I am sure, he was showing Connors how to lose.

Unfortunately for the States, he had to go through the whole act again the following day when he and Fleming suffered their first ever Davis Cup loss as a doubles team, going down 7–5, 5–7, 6–2, 7–5 to Anders Jarryd and the nineteen-year-old Stefan Edberg who poached brilliantly at the net. The American pair's behaviour was not impeccable but it wasn't bad, either, considering they had to carry the loss of the entire tie on their shoulders in front of 12,000 delirious, chanting Swedes.

There had been a great deal of behind-the-scenes activity the previous evening with the British referee Alan Mills weighing up the case against Connors. It was obvious he should be fined but should he be defaulted from the tie? That was the question the press was asking, as well as quite a few ITF officials who had been appalled by his behaviour. The decision was a momentous one because, were Mills to default Connors from the reverse singles, that would effectively have handed the Swedes the Cup even before the doubles was played. After his agent Donald Dell, himself one of the most successful American Davis Cup captains of the modern era, had gone to bat on Jimmy's behalf, Mills settled for a $2,000 fine. Many people thought he got off lightly. There was never, incidentally, any talk of fining McEnroe, even though some USTA officials were muttering about some unkind things he had said regarding the state of the court at the post-match press conference. As usual, McEnroe had been saying what needed saying simply because it was the truth. The court, laid in the vast stadium only four days before the tie began, was far from perfect. It was undiplomatic of him, perhaps, but McEnroe was far from being the first visiting player to criticize the conditions under which they were made to play. H. Roper Barrett, a proper English gentleman, did it after the very first Davis Cup tie ever played when Britain met the United States at the Longwood Cricket Club in Boston in 1900. And he was far ruder than McEnroe.

Later there were allegations from those patriotic souls watching back home on television in the American heartland that McEnroe and Connors had not paid sufficient respect to the flag during the playing of the national anthems, and had been seen smiling and maybe even cracking a joke. To accuse McEnroe of not being patriotic was like suggesting the Pope isn't Catholic. This was the man who, in defiance of his contract with Sergio Tacchini, wore his Davis Cup tracksuit top with 'USA' on the back virtually every time he walked on court in a Grand Prix tournament. This was the man who had always said there was no higher honour he could aspire to than playing Davis Cup for his country – and had proved it by six years of devotion to the cause.

Only McEnroe really knows how deeply the accusations that followed the Gothenburg defeat affected him, but I suspect that it was the beginning of his disillusionment with the game; the beginning of his feelings of paranoia about how the establishment were out to get him; and the first realization of the depth of his unpopularity.

Very slowly, for a man with such a quick mind, McEnroe began to realize just how repulsive his behaviour seemed to many who watched him play. But the virulence of the antagonism that came flooding forth as soon as defeat gave his detractors the chance to air their views shocked him.

He knew that the knives were flashing for sins committed at other times in other places, but the fact remained that McEnroe was virtually blameless for what happened in Gothenburg, apart, of course, from the fact that he lost. Had Ashe's team won, I guarantee the rumblings of discontent about behaviour would have been kept to a minimum. But defeat, as the gladiators found out in the Colosseum, brings its own penalties, and now Connors' disgraceful conduct had given certain factions within the USTA the opportunity to have McEnroe struck down as well.

Much of the impetus for the anti-McEnroe drive came from the American team sponsors, the Louisiana Pacific Corporation, which, ironically, was based in Seattle, the home town of Tom Gorman, who would succeed Ashe as Davis Cup captain. In a letter to the then USTA Vice-President Gordon Jorgensen, the President of Louisiana Pacific, Henry Merlo wrote: 'True, our team shines if one were to consider only the skills of the game. But we fail badly when it comes to living up to minimum standards on the court during award ceremonies and at other official Davis Cup events.'

Ashe, who was about to be replaced as captain and was starting to lose his influence, tried to point out that McEnroe was not to blame in Gothenburg, but it did little good. A large percentage of the USTA membership comes from those small American cities where Mom and apple pie and church on Sundays are still the guiding forces in one's life. Talk to them about New York and you might as well be talking about a different planet. They were ashamed of this particular New Yorker because he seemed to epitomize everything they resented about the image of The Ugly American. For them, McEnroe simply curdled the cream. He was beyond their comprehension.

As usual John did not help his cause. The USTA President at the time was an urbane and charming man called Hunter Delatour, who had made considerable efforts to understand his volatile young star. But few young bulls have become as enraged by the sight of a red cape as was McEnroe when presented with the badge and blazer of officialdom. It would take long sessions on the psychiatrist's couch to pluck out the deep-seated reasons for McEnroe's fear, hatred and total intolerance of authority which goes far beyond the normal rebelliousness of an adolescent. A long time later, at Flinders Park in January 1990, the remaining vestiges of that hatred came spitting out at Supervisor Ken Ferrar and resulted in his instant dismissal from the Australian Open. It erupted in personal abuse of the worst kind, but it was not Ferrar *the person* McEnroe was trying to insult. It was the blazer and everything it stood for.

It was this blind antagonism to those who might possibly sit in judgement over him that lost McEnroe an important ally in Hunter Delatour. Happily, I did not witness the actual scene which occurred when Delatour approached McEnroe at some function and tried to open up a line of communication. His efforts were rewarded with a stream of abuse. Delatour, a proud, sensitive man, has never been able to forgive McEnroe for that and I don't blame him.

So, almost inevitably, the Gothenburg fiasco resulted in some stringent conditions being placed on all potential Davis Cup players. Urged on by the sponsors, the USTA insisted that, in future, all players in line for selection would have to sign a good conduct pledge. Only people familiar with bureaucratic logic will understand what was to be gained by asking athletes to sign a piece of paper which said, in effect, 'I promise to be a good little boy'. But that was what the USTA demanded and that was what McEnroe refused to sign.

This was fine by Randy Gregson, the incoming USTA President

who was a far tougher and more ambitious character than Delatour. He saw himself in the role of the man who was to clean up American tennis and, as he felt he had the backing of a majority of his USTA constituents, he was perfectly happy to keep McEnroe off the Davis Cup team throughout his two-year term.

However, when he interviewed Tom Gorman for the captain's job, Gregson did not tell Ashe's potential successor that he would not be allowed to call on the services of the nation's No. 1 player.

'He made it clear he was not a fan of John's,' Gorman told me while he agonized over the problem later. 'But he never laid down rules about who I could or could not select for my teams. He wasn't straight with me.'

Gorman was not the only person who found Gregson a difficult man to deal with and his presidency was not a happy one for American tennis.

Throughout 1985 McEnroe, having refused to sign the good conduct pledge, was simply not a factor as far as the Davis Cup was concerned.

'I just can't face it,' he told me. 'I still have a very nasty taste in my mouth about the whole thing. After all I have tried to do for the team, it hurts to be treated this way.'

Looking at it from McEnroe's side of the net, it was a perfectly reasonable reaction. His contribution had been enormous; his loyalty and dedication unwavering. But he had insulted a few people and offended thousands. He was just starting to realize the limits of people's tolerance.

With Gorman in the captain's chair, the Davis Cup campaign of 1986 required the United States to play in Mexico City, never an easy assignment. McEnroe had intimated that he was ready to return to the fold, the good conduct pledge had gone the way of all stupid ideas, and Gorman, needless to say, was very keen to have this enormous talent back on his team. But Gregson said no. Gorman was shocked and angry. There was no further justification for keeping McEnroe off the team. More than a year had passed since Gothenburg. How long was Gregson's vendetta supposed to go on? The answer, of course, was for as long as Gregson felt it politically expedient.

The episode reminded me forcibly of what we had all been through with the ATP Wimbledon boycott of 1973 and the reasons for it. Total independence from the whims and prejudices of amateur officials is absolutely vital to a professional athlete and, to a large extent, the boycott achieved that end by releasing the players from the grip of the International Tennis Federation (ITF) forever. And even if the Davis Cup remained under the ITF's control, it was an annoyance rather than a catastrophe. The Gregsons of this world had no jurisdiction over whether or not a player could compete on the Grand Prix circuit.

But that did not help Gorman and he had to do without McEnroe until the more amenable and realistic Gordon Jorgensen succeeded Gregson as President of the USTA in 1987. Wisely, perhaps, Gorman did not try to force McEnroe onto the team right away because, that year, the Americans were drawn to play Paraguay in Asunción and the omens for a quiet tie were not good. It would have been testing McEnroe's nerves to the limit for him to make his comeback in front of some of the wildest crowds I have ever seen. It is just possible he could have prevented a Paraguayan victory. But with the drums beating and the cymbals clashing between every point and an atmosphere of barely contained hysteria, it is alarming to think what might have been the reaction of the armed body-guards surrounding the dictator Stroessner – now, happily, deposed – had McEnroe let the insults fly. Even without him, Gorman's squad was quite happy to get out alive.

But success in the first round for Victor Pecci and his colleagues who, it must be said, behaved impeccably throughout one of the most electrifying sporting confrontations I have ever witnessed, meant the United States had to play West Germany in a relegation battle in Hartford, Connecticut later in the year. This was more McEnroe's scene and, as I have related, he returned to the side to put up a heroic rearguard action against Boris Becker, before going down after a six-hour, twenty-minute battle that was an extra-ordinary feat of endurance for a man who was only just starting to take proper care of his body.

McEnroe's defeat meant an American defeat and the humiliation of the big drop down into the regional zones. Worse still, it meant that, after surviving a trip to Peru which was an ordeal in itself, they had to beat Argentina in Buenos Aires — something they had failed to do twice before, even with McEnroe on the team.

But the prospect of another visit did not daunt McEnroe. It was a challenge. 'I'll play,' he told Gorman. 'I just want to win one match in Buenos Aires before I die!'

And so, in 1988, with the startlingly flamboyant André Agassi as his singles colleague, McEnroe travelled south of the border yet again in America's cause. And once again the USTA, which makes money from the Davis Cup, provided the ties are important enough, found itself in their anti-hero's debt for hauling them back into the big time within twelve months. On the opening day McEnroe, ignoring the chanting crowds and determined to overcome the relentless persistency of Guillermo Perez-Roldan, a baseline clay court expert of the most obdurate kind, came through to beat the young Argentine in five sets and so realize his ambition. He had won in Buenos Aires and, when Agassi beat Martin Jaite, promotion back into the sixteen-nation World Group for the United States was virtually assured.

13

1984

In the whole of his career, there has never been a year like 1984 for John McEnroe. Maybe George Orwell, whose vision of the world that year didn't quite work out in global terms, might have predicted something strange would happen to precariously balanced talents and it did. 1984 produced the best and worst of McEnroe.

Looking back, he will rate his defeat of Jimmy Connors in the Wimbledon final as his greatest performance; the nearest his rage for perfection ever came to being fulfilled, while his loss to Ivan Lendl in the final of the French Open still haunts him to this day. It was the year he found the girl of his dreams and sullied his great Davis Cup record by losing both the singles and the doubles in the final against Sweden. It was a year of ecstasy and, occasionally, real agony.

The first moment of euphoria came early and was really a hangover from 1983. The Masters was always played in the January of the following year in those days – just to add to the confusion of a calendar that also included a truncated version of the old World Championship Tennis tour – and John reaped adequate revenge on Ivan Lendl for the straight set defeat he had suffered at the hands of the Czech at Madison Square Garden twelve months before by beating the man he liked least amongst his peers 6–3, 6–4, 6–4.

Ironically, in view of what was to transpire in Paris, Lendl became McEnroe's whipping boy for the first five months of the year. Within two weeks of winning his second Masters title, McEnroe was enjoying Marilyn Fernberger's hospitality at the Spectrum in Philadelphia while winning his third consecutive US Pro Indoor title, with Lendl his victim in the final.

In March it was the same story at the Belgian Indoors in Brussels, and even a switch in surface and conditions that should have suited Lendl – clay at Forest Hills in the Mercedes-Benz WCT Tournament of Champions – could not prevent a repeat of the same old story, McEnroe beating Lendl in the final for the fourth time that year.

But Lendl was not the only player having trouble with McEnroe in this kind of form. After winning WCT Richmond, McEnroe went on to collect his fourth WCT Dallas title by defeating Connors in the final at Reunion Arena. He was starting to look invincible. In the locker room players shook their heads and muttered about how impossible it was to return a serve from the ad court when you had to climb halfway into the stands to do it. The angle McEnroe was getting on his leftie serve was phenomenal. Left-handers have a natural advantage in this respect. For reasons that no one has been able to work out, they seem to be able to get a more acute angle when serving to the left-hand court than a right-hander can when serving to the right-hand court.

McEnroe was not the first player to demonstrate that this was so but, after studying McEnroe's extraordinary ability to curl first serves way out of an opponent's reach on the backhand, Ted Tinling, who has been studying great players since the days of Bill Tilden – against whom he actually played – decided that a change in rules was warranted.

'As left-handers do things back to front they should start serving the other way round, too,' said Tinling. 'It is not fair that a right-hander should have to face a left-hander's best serve on the big points all the time. At 40–30 up, or break point down, a left-hander always knows he has the chance of putting in an unplayable first serve to his opponent's backhand. So why not make the left-hander start serving to the left-hand court, which would mean that the 40–30 point would then be played in what we now call the deuce court when someone like McEnroe is serving.'

Ted has never been short of ideas and many people – with right-handers in the majority, I imagine! – felt this one was perfectly logical. But, to date, it has never come close to being passed into law.

So, with his body holding together, his temperament under

reasonable control and his talent flowing like pure gold, McEnroe, at the start of his twenty-fifth year, was in his prime as the early months of 1984 unfolded. Quite apart from his dominance in singles, he and Peter Fleming were picking up doubles titles wherever they went – Madison Square Garden (where they won the sixth of seven consecutive Masters titles), Philadelphia, Madrid and, later, Wimbledon. In Richmond, John had even helped his youngest brother, Patrick, to the first title of his young career. As a one-off it worked. Patrick was eighteen at the time and the brothers were able to go out and have fun. But, after Patrick left Stanford to join the tour as a full-time pro, the idea of the McEnroe Bros. turning into a regular partnership did not blossom in the way their father had hoped. They tried playing together at Forest Hills and in the Paris Open four years later and it was a disaster. Patrick, who was turning into a doubles expert of sufficient magnitude to win the French Open with Jim Grabb in 1989, was clearly nervous playing at his brother's side but, typically, John was not about to let him take all the blame.

'You think *he's* nervous!' John laughed when we talked about their defeat in Paris. 'How about me? I'm a wreck out there playing with my brother. There's just too much pressure.'

But in 1984 McEnroe was almost starting to forget what pressure was all about. He was producing a brand of tennis no one had ever seen before. His natural speed, coupled with the uncanny anticipation of the true ball player, seemed to shrink his side of the court in the eyes of a frustrated opponent. Just as so many players had found when trying to outwit Ken Rosewall, there was nowhere you could put the ball that would be out of his reach. And that was only the half of it.

The first serve was often unplayable; the second always deep and difficult. His back-court game was becoming steadier and the hands . . . ah, connoisseurs of the game were in raptures about his hands. Surely no one had ever had such sensitive hands. The ability to take a ball propelled towards him at speeds of nearly 100 mph and drop it back over the net with a deftness of touch that defied the eye, let alone physics, was a gift his peers could only marvel at.

But the sensitivity was not just in the hands. His whole body acted like a quivering aerial, sensitized to pick up the slightest noise or movement or change in atmospheric condition. The proverbial pin dropping falls like a hammer to McEnroe's ears. Blow your nose in row 14 and you might as well have stood up and waved a bed-sheet as far as he is concerned. Everything disturbs him. Yet his ability to be distracted one minute and locked into a state of vice-like concentration the next is something that drives his opponents mad and gives his critics all the ammunition they need to insist that every complaint is merely a premeditated attempt to upset his opponent. It would be stupid to suggest that McEnroe has never used a delaying tactic to suit his needs. But that is not the motivation for the majority of his blow-ups. They were spontaneous and, to a degree that finally began to worry him, uncontrollable.

People who might not have sat through as many of his matches as I have from start to finish often insist that McEnroe's tantrums always erupt when he is in trouble, or when his opponent is on the point of victory. This is very rarely the case. I can hardly remember an instance when McEnroe has acted up in the final stages of a match he was destined to lose. Most frequently, the anger and the vitriol has poured forth in the first or second sets when he has still not rid himself of the excess of nervous energy he takes on court with him. A tragic comparison could be made with the Avianca 707 that crashed a few hundred yards from the house he owns in Cove Neck, New York in January 1990. The plane did not catch fire when it came down because the tanks were dry. Had it crashed soon after take off from Bogota, it would have been engulfed in flames and no one would have survived. Towards the end of a match, McEnroe's tanks are running dry and he needs to conserve all the remnants of his nervous energy for his tennis.

But often it is not even as logical as that. Although most of the tantrums erupt when he is in a close match with an opponent he feels he should beat, there have been times when he has lost control of his temper when he has been in perfect control of the match – and lost out on both counts as a result. It is to be hoped, for his sake, there will be no more notorious example of this than the French Open Final of 1984.

Despite the brilliance of his early season form, there were still many experts who doubted his ability to claim a title that had remained, except in the case of the Argentine baseliner Guillermo Vilas, in European hands since Rod Laver won it in 1969 – the year of his second Grand Slam. Even the fact that he had beaten Lendl convincingly on clay in the Tournament of Champions at Forest Hills two weeks before was not sufficient evidence for the critics. And with fair reason. The grey Har-Tru clay used in America is faster than the so-called 'red' clay of Europe. Many Americans have been able to win on one but not the other, with McEnroe and Connors the prime examples. Considering the amount of tennis Connors plays from the back court it is amazing that, out of the 109 singles titles he has won during his career, not one has come on European clay. Yet winning on clay in places like Indianapolis, Washington DC and North Conway was not a problem for a man who was so versatile that he could win the US Open on three different surfaces – grass, Har-Tru and the cement-style Decoturf courts now used at Flushing Meadow. But the red clay of Europe always defeated Connors.

So McEnroe was under no illusions about the enormity of the task that faced him. He did, however, arrive in Paris, to be sequestered in some splendour at the Plaza Athenée, in a positive frame of mind. His experience the previous year, when he had swamped the reigning champion Mats Wilander 6–1 in the first set of their quarter-final with a brilliant serve and volley assault before allowing the Swede to wear him down in the next three to such an extent that he had lost the fourth set 6–0, had taught him a lesson. While priding himself on his ability to play from the back court, he knew that the best way to handle the red clay of Stade Roland Garros was to play one's natural game. He was an attacking player, so he should attack. Obviously one could not come charging in on everything, but caution should not be allowed to stifle one's strengths.

By the time he started to run into some really formidable clay court opposition in the fourth round, McEnroe was convinced he was on the right track. José Higueras, the former ball-boy from Barcelona who ended up marrying the daughter of the Mayor of Palm Springs, was one of those clay court experts who had hauled himself into the world's top ten by his boot straps. Charming off court, José was as obstinate as a mule in the heat of battle and no one ever beat him easily on clay.

But, hard as he fought, Higueras could never bridge the yawning gap that existed between McEnroe and himself in terms of pure ability. Even though José managed to win the fourth set, the New Yorker's greater array of shot-making carried him to a 6–4, 7–6, 3–6, 6–3 victory. Higueras never got further than the semi-finals in Paris as a player, but, typically, he refused to be satisfied with that and returned in 1989 as coach to a young lad called Michael Chang, who promptly created history by becoming the youngest player, at seventeen years, three months, ever to win a Grand Slam title. Higueras deserved that belated triumph.

For McEnroe, a victory over such a determined clay court opponent as Higueras was just the psychological boost he needed. While Wilander was reversing the result of the 1983 final by beating Yannick Noah in the quarters, McEnroe was making short work of Jimmy Arias, the youngster from Buffalo, New York whose powerfully top-spun forehand had lifted him to No. 6 in the world the previous year.

It is strange how McEnroe takes so much stick for this behaviour when Jimmy Connors was often getting away with things on court which were just as unpalatable, if not more so. There had been a good example of this in the quarter-final when Connors found himself struggling against the young Swede Henrik Sundstrom who, six weeks before, had rocketed to the forefront of the European game by beating Wilander in the final of the Monte Carlo Open. Sundstrom had a solid back-court game with heavy topspin off both flanks. He was tall, strong and could run all day. Connors, in his thirty-second year, did not like the look of this and decided that other means had to be employed to break down the Swedish defences. So he started imitating Sundstrom and taunting him verbally when Henrik complained. Sundstrom was a highly intelligent and highly-strung young man, whose temperament was a lot less solid than his game. Connors knew what he was doing. Sundstrom, visibly upset, went to pieces and Jimmy went through to the semi-final, 7–6, 6–1, 6–4.

No one needed to tell him he was not going to get away with that sort of stuff against McEnroe. The pair were not good friends but they respected each other as players, and the first set of their semi-final in front of a packed Centre Court crowd was a dogfight that pushed the younger man to the limit. McEnroe had to fend off two break points in the third game; two more in the fifth; and finally dropped his serve on a double fault to go 4–5 down. But when Connors served for the set, he was confronted by the full repertoire of McEnroe's virtuoso skills. A great forehand approach put Connors under pressure and an agile smash took the score to 15–40. Rashly, Connors came storming in and McEnroe's pin-point lob clinched the break back.

The match changed right there. Connors double faulted two games later, to lose a set he seemed to have under control, and the next two sets were no contest. With Lendl beating Wilander in straight sets in the other semi-final, McEnroe was exactly where he wanted to be – in the final of the French Open, facing an opponent he had been wiping off court all year.

The match was the talk of the city. In fact, for most of the fortnight it had been virtually impossible to dine anywhere in Paris without hearing a constant stream of debate about Roland Garros from neighbouring tables. A film producer friend of mine, who had a big desert epic called *Fort Saganne* with Gérard Depardieu showing on the Champs Elysées then, told me that all the major cinemas were reporting as much as a fifty per cent decrease in ticket sales since the tennis had started. People were sitting at home watching the highlights. Not only Paris but the whole of France was tennis mad. Philippe Chatrier and his expert staff had been responsible for refurbishment of the old Roland Garros complex and the revitalization of the Championships. Yannick Noah, of course, had played an enormous part in this the previous year by becoming the first Frenchman since Marcel Bernard in 1946 to win his native title. But, for reasons that I explain in the Davis Cup chapter, McEnroe's army of French fans was growing too. They knew how difficult it was for a non-European to come and win on the red clay and they respected anyone with the skill and nerve to try.

'A player like McEnroe puts his reputation on the line by coming here,' said Philippe Bouin of *L'Equipe*. 'It takes courage, and the French tennis fans respect him for that.'

Their respect was turning to awe by the time McEnroe had broken Lendl's serve three times to lead 6–3, 6–2. It had been a sublime exhibition of forceful clay-court tennis. Lendl, still without a Grand Slam title at that stage, kept hammering his huge forehand at McEnroe in a vain attempt to keep the American back, but it was no use. Lendl played in straight lines, as if his game was gauged to a railway track, while on the other side of the net McEnroe, like some dotty professor in geometry class, conjured up impossible angles that no sane man would have contemplated. After every game, the scarred court told its tale. Lendl's baseline was churned, the forecourt left almost unmarked. On McEnroe's side of the net, his constant sorties hither and thither, to the net and back, left a characteristic mosaic of genius at work.

And so it would have continued, with McEnroe coming in under fire to volley away balls at stupefying angles as Lendl glowered under the burning sun.

But Lendl could handle the sun and McEnroe couldn't. If there was one basic, uncomplicated reason for the change that came over the match, this was it. The sun burned down onto McEnroe's freckled forehead out of clear blue Parisian skies and sapped not only his strength but his sanity. With the match under control and the title he craved as good as in his pocket, he allowed himself to be distracted by nothing more than the crackle of a voice in a cameraman's earpiece at courtside. True, it was audible from the front row of the press box seats, so God knows what it must have sounded like to McEnroe's sensitive ears. But why allow himself to become upset by it? Why waste precious energy screaming into the earpiece with a ferocity that nearly blew the cameraman out of his harness when a polite request to umpire Jacques Dorfmann would have sufficed? McEnroe himself cannot answer that question coherently, so how is anyone else expected to? Even as one side of McEnroe's brain led him off, gesticulating, to do battle with a needless, unnecessary enemy, the other rational half would have told him it was pure folly.

'Double-think means the power of holding two contradictory beliefs in one's mind simultaneously and accepting both of them,' wrote George Orwell in 1984. And this was, after all, 1984. What kind of Big Brother was watching over him now? A malevolent one, to be sure, because it not only expended desperately needed energy and broke his concentration but it turned large sections of the crowd against him and gave Lendl heart. For the first time the coldly logical Czech, who has never suffered from the complication of having two thoughts at once, saw a lifeline and knew that, if he could clutch at it and hang on, simple resolve and sheer physical strength might earn him an improbable victory.

For Lendl would also have noted what Pierre Barthes, the former French No. 1, had also been quick to spot from his courtside box.

'Il est fatigué,' Barthes had said to the friends sitting next to him during the second game of the third set, long before anyone else in the crowd had noticed the subtle change in McEnroe's movement about court. It was just a couple of minutes before McEnroe, having allowed Lendl to pull back from 0–30 at 1–1, had charged off to yell in the cameraman's ear.

Barthes, who had known what kind of stamina is required to serve and volley on clay, was right. McEnroe was beginning to tire. To an extent, he had his lack of conditioning to blame for that. He had relied too long on his natural athleticism to get him through tough matches and, under normal conditions, it had often proved sufficient. Nobody could have come out a winner, as he had done after 6 hours, 22 minutes against Wilander in the Davis Cup two years before, without being passably fit. But that was indoors. Now he was facing a fitness fanatic who had changed his diet to rid himself of his own stamina problems, and in a concrete stadium packed with 17,000 people that was rapidly turning into a cauldron. It was ironic to think that the headband – his trademark for so long – which he had discarded a couple of years before, could have saved him now. It might well have protected him from what I believe was a touch of sunstroke.

McEnroe's fair Irish skin does not take kindly to the sun. It is why you will never find him playing at places like Grand Champions at Indian Wells in the Californian desert. It is why, ever since, he has tied silk scarves around his head whenever he has to play in excessive heat. But, in Paris in 1984, he had not learned that lesson,

JOHN MCENROE — TAMING THE TALENT

and he would learn it too late to save himself from the greatest disappointment of his career.

Afterwards, nothing irked McEnroe more than the knowledge that the match never changed so completely as to let Lendl gallop away with it. Even as the big Czech edged back into contention, McEnroe had chance after chance to put him away. Just two games after his screaming fit with the earpiece, he had Lendl 0–40 down and reached another break point in that same fifth game. On one of those points he fell flat trying to reach a cross-court return off the increasingly confident Lendl forehand. On another he let a backhand service return drift long. They were mistakes he could no longer afford.

In the next game, he dropped his own serve to allow Lendl to go ahead in a set for the first time, only to break back immediately, level at 4–4 and then drop serve again to lose the set 6–4 after Lendl had ripped a magnificent backhand service return down the line off a delivery that was beginning to lose its sting.

Again in the fourth set McEnroe had his chances, coming out ahead after a sequence of three consecutive breaks of serve. But Lendl, making McEnroe bend for his volleys now, fought back again, breaking serve twice to seize the set 7–5.

As the drama surged on into the fifth set, the crowd were working themselves into a Gallic frenzy. '*Allez*, McEnroe!' yelled the majority. But Lendl's support was growing as this knowledgeable gallery recognized his dogged courage. But McEnroe, visibly slower, wore his own red badge of courage on his glistening, scarlet forehead and refused to let the dream die. Once again he came agonizingly close to the decisive breakthrough. At 3–3, he pumped weary legs to race in and put away a tactically shrewd Lendl drop-shot and, a point later, reached 15–40 after his opponent had mishit a forehand. But just when he needed to pressure Lendl with accurate returns, McEnroe's own forehand let him down. Two errors – and the chance to serve for a 5–3 lead was gone.

Four more games came and went without the hint of a break until McEnroe served at 5–6. A forehand volley into the net and two short volleys that gave the Czech the opportunity to pass took Lendl to 15–40. Two match points. For the very first time in the entire match he was in front. A backhand cross-court volley saved the first match point, but saving the second was one desperate step too far for McEnroe.

If someone had handed McEnroe a gun, he may well have shot himself. Of all the defeats I have seen him suffer – and they all hurt – I have never seen him so crushed, so numbingly, heart-rendingly disappointed as this. Wimbledon and the US Open were his for the taking. He had won them before and he would win them again. But the French . . . the French Open was the ultimate test of his greatness as a tennis player. Only the likes of Hoad and Laver and Borg had been able to conquer Roland Garros on clay and Wimbledon on grass. And what tormented his thoughts in the hours and days that followed was the conviction that he was good enough to have joined that company. He had proved it in everything but the final deed. Had Lendl beaten him in straight sets, McEnroe would have said 'Too good', and gone away to work on his game. But the pain involved here was much greater than that. This was agony.

A few years before I had written a book on the psychology of competition with Dr Allen Fox, a former top American player who coaches Pepperdine University just down the road from where McEnroe lives in Malibu. It was called *If I'm The Better Player, Why Can't I Win?* It was a question McEnroe had not needed to ask himself very often. But he needed to now.

For Lendl it was the breakthrough he had been longing for. Another defeat in a Grand Slam final would have left him holding the bridesmaid's bouquet again, and that was not a very flattering image for such a macho man. Appropriately for a player who has had to toil for everything he has achieved in tennis, this victory came as a result of his bloody-minded determination to slug it out until the bitter end.

'I don't think I won it the easy way,' Lendl laughed. 'John was just playing great and all I could do was hang on. Actually, I tried different things as the match wore on. I moved the position when returning serve three times, going in close and then all the way back until I ended up halfway and that seemed to work best.'

McEnroe also came to press conference but, for once, was practically monosyllabic. 'I couldn't have asked for more chances,' he mumbled.

Less than twenty-four hours later I found him in the lounge at the Queen's Club in London where, the following day, he would have to eradicate Paris from his mind and switch his whole tactical game to the demands of grass. This is what the congested summer calendar asks of a player, and the extra week that will be gained between the French Open and Wimbledon when, in a couple of years, the All England Club moves forward its championships will offer all the top stars desperately needed respite.

In 1989 Stefan Edberg lost a very similar match in the final at Roland Garros, serving and volleying himself into a winning position against young Michael Chang before allowing himself to be worn down by some classic clay-court tactics. He, too, tried to make the switch directly onto grass in the Stella Artois championships at Queen's and lost in the first round to another teenager of promise, Venezuela's Nicolas Pereira.

Under the circumstances, it was a miracle that McEnroe did not suffer the same fate. There could have been no sterner test of the man's resilience than his survival of the early rounds at Queen's that year.

'Feel my forehead,' he said. He was still looking dazed, standing there by the bar, a heap of rackets with strings still smeared with traces of clay lying at his feet. 'It's like it's still on fire, man. That sun just scorched me.'

It was true. I realized then how close he had come to a severe case of sunstroke. Given the extent of the burn, it was amazing how competitive he had remained as the match against Lendl had entered its third hour.

Just as amazing was McEnroe's picking up of his fast court form as if the trauma of Roland Garros had never happened. Solid middle-ranked pros like Marty Davis, Van Winitsky, Steve Meister and Danie Visser were swept aside without the loss of a set and then, once again, it was Connors in the semi-final. Although Jimmy was still ranked No. 3 on the ATP computer at the time, the gulf between one and three seemed a great deal larger by the time

Top: You know you've made it when they paint your picture down the side of a twelve-storey building at the corner of Hollywood and Vine. Even Mickey Rooney never got a contract worth as much as Nike were paying McEnroe to wear their gear.

Above: Notoreity sells but McEnroe never got an endorsement out of Pepsi or the motel for this one.

Left: Happy family: John with Mum and Dad and the youngest brother Patrick after the ATP Player of the Year award at the Plaza Hotel in New York.

Right: Björn Borg was also honoured that night. Alan King, comedian and honorary life member of the ATP, brings together the two greatest players of the decade.

Left: Paris and a night on the Champs Elysées. John McEnroe and Martina Navratilova have been nominated as the No 1 players in the world by the ITF and celebrate with a dance at the Pavilion Gabriel.

Below: After a glass of wine, John feels sufficiently relaxed to ham it up with Virginia Wade.

Right: McEnroe doesn't make a noise about his charity work but here he was happy to have his photo taken with Vitas Gerulaitis and six-year-old Eddie Koller from Armonk, New York at the 1985 Forest Hills Pro Celebrity event in aid of Juvenile Diabetes.

PHOTO: RUSS ADAMS

Below: McEnroe, a typical sports fan, often has much more fun on the sidelines shouting the odds than he does on court. Here he watches a softball game with fellow American pros Marc Flur, Sammy Giammalva and Jimmy Arias.

Below: Over the years the Vitas Gerulaitis Youth Foundation has given away nearly 100,000 tennis rackets to children in deprived areas of New York. Here at the Sheraton Centre, 500 people paid $300 a plate to watch Björn Borg, Patrick and John McEnroe and Vitas play in a 'black tie' exhibition.

PHOTO: HOWARD J. RUBINSTEIN ASSOCIATES, INC.

Effort (top right), anguish (top left) and determination (bottom left) – the many faces of John McEnroe make for compulsive viewing.

PHOTO: JANET ZAGORIA

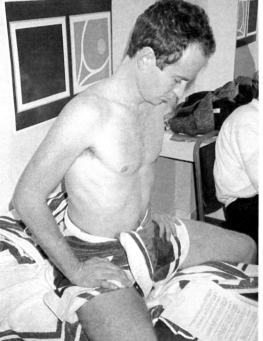

Above: John and Tatum in the players lounge at Wembley 1989.

Left: John in his dressing room at Wembley 1989

Above: A romantic
moment with Tatum at
the Champions dinner in
Paris in 1985.

Left: From left: Tatum,
Angelica Houston and
Jack Nicholson watch
John McEnroe play in Los
Angeles, 1986.

Right: Winning the 1989 WCT in Dallas.

Jakob Hlasek (left), the Czech-born Swiss No 1 seen here with another great doubles expert Guy Forget took his turn with McEnroe during the Silk Cut Championships at Wembley in 1989 where they won their second title of the year.

McEnroe had dispensed with his old foe 6–2, 6–2. And that was just a prelude for what was to come.

In the bottom half of the draw a good-looking twenty-four-year-old American called Leif Shiras became the unlikely pin-up boy of the week. He began by exposing Lendl's mobility to make the kind of rapid readjustment to surface speed that McEnroe managed by beating Ivan 7–5, 6–3 in the first round and then made it all the way through the final, beating former Australian Open champion Brian Teacher along the way. But Shiras was thrust into another spotlight that week as well. *Octopussy*, the James Bond movie in which Vijay Amritraj made his acting debut, was having its *première* at the Odeon in Leicester Square and, at Vijay's request, producer Cubby Broccoli had ensured that an entire row of seats was set aside for the tennis players. Then it was discovered that Grace Jones was without an escort.

Someone suggested Shiras would fill the bill and Leif was not slow to accept. They made a stunning couple, the jet-black singer with the red lips and the handsome tennis player with his flowing blond hair. Surprisingly, perhaps, the experience did not put Shiras off his stroke and he beat Rodney Harmon decisively in the semi-final to earn an unexpected meeting with McEnroe. Even that searching examination did not unnerve him and he won a set before going down 6–2 in the third. By that time McEnroe had allowed some of the bile that had been coursing inside him all week to spill out in an unpleasant tirade against the umpire, which included calling the official a moron and also an accusation that Shiras was trying to imitate him by practising backhands between points. An explanation from Leif that it was just a habit of his resulted in the pair enjoying a beer together in the locker room afterwards, but of course the public never saw that.

So instead of being acclaimed as a hero for having recovered from the depths of despair in Paris and risen to the not inconsiderable heights of coming through a tough 64-man draw on grass within seven days, McEnroe was being villified as a public menace by the press once again. To any rational human being it all seemed so unnecessary.

Yet, just two weeks later, the tabloids were more than happy to turn their villain into a hero. McEnroe had not only won Wimbledon for the third time but had done so with a dispositiot that, if not quite as sunny as the warm rays which beamed down on Wimbledon for most of the fortnight, was certainly free of the dark clouds and thunderclaps that so often punctuate the strokes of genius.

The way McEnroe behaved from the first ball of Wimbledon 1984 to the last was a revelation. When I spoke to him on the phone on the eve of his first-round match against Paul McNamee, he said, 'Don't worry, Richard. I'm going to be just like Björn out there tomorrow.'

As usual he was as good as his word. Not once, in singles or doubles, did he offer the officials anything more than the occasional glare. As was his intention, it made all those scribes who had been sharpening their quills in anticipation of more anti-McEnroe diatribes look slightly foolish.

And, of course, his unfamiliar behaviour was not the only thing to admire. The more familiar talent was back in its vein of gold, a twenty-four-carat package of brilliance that was far too rich for any of his opponents to handle. Only McNamee, who had beaten him in the French Open a couple of years earlier, took a set off him and, thereafter, only the teenage Australian prodigy Pat Cash, meeting him in the semi-finals, would come as close as a tie-break. In between, Harmon, Wally Masur, Bill Scanlon and John Sadri were all dismissed like actors with walk-on parts whose final cue was to exit stage, left.

But the man awaiting him in the final was far from being a member of the supporting cast. Once again, Jimmy Connors had defied the age gap which separated him from most of his opponents and proved that a shrewd tactical brain allied to gritty resolve could win through. Two of the younger Americans with big serves, Tim Mayotte and Paul Annacone – the latter an unseeded quarter-finalist – had both looked menacing until Connors' searing service returns cut them to smithereens.

To his credit, Lendl had masked his deficiencies on grass well enough to reach the semis after beating his tireless compatriot Tomas Smid in the previous round but, after winning a good tie-break in the first set, the efforts of Paris seemed to drain him and Connors finished looking far stronger than the strapping twenty-four-year-old opponent seven years his junior.

So despite the defeats in Paris and at the Queen's Club, Connors, on this form, was expected to give McEnroe some sort of a match. Some hope. The score was 6–1, 6–1, 6–2. McEnroe dismissed the man who revelled in the big occasion, who never knew when he was beaten, who had won more singles titles than any other player in history as if he was some kind of upstart who had strayed onto the Centre Court by mistake.

That description would have fitted Chris Lewis better than Connors, but the worthy New Zealander, who had deserved his day in the sun, actually did rather better than the great Jimbo against McEnroe in the previous year's final, winning six games to Connors' four. More extraordinary still, the player with the finest service return in the game never came close to breaking the McEnroe serve and won only eleven points off it in the entire match.

In the end McEnroe's mastery was so complete that he was playing the occasion, not the man. For once the old adage, that you only play as well as your opponent makes you play, didn't apply. McEnroe was very conscious of the fact that this was a Wimbledon final; very conscious of history. Always his ambition had been to play the perfect tennis match – an impossibility because the game is undoubtedly too difficult – but he came as close as he has ever done to achieving it here. He knew he had the perfect stage and, on the day, the perfect opponent. Connors couldn't hurt him any more as he had done in the 1982 final. By concentrating furiously he eliminated all but the rarest error.

Not only did seventy-two per cent of his first serves find their mark, but he came up with such a bewildering variety of deliveries that Connors, who has faced that serve more than anyone else, was continually fooled by their varying pace and direction. The ultimate piece of wizardry came at 4–1 in the second set. John was actually flat on his back near the net on the left-hand side of the court as Connors pulled back his racket to return a desperate McEnroe volley. Yet, by the time Connors' cross-court shot landed precisely where he wanted it to land, McEnroe was not only on his feet but had found time to race across the court to put away a deep and perfectly placed winner. Even the slow-motion replay made one blink.

Not since Fred Perry beat the German ace Baron Gottfried Von Cramm in 1936 had there been a more one-sided final. That day Perry had won his third consecutive title 6–1, 6–1, 6–0. In the modern era one could pick Lew Hoad's 1957 defeat of Ashley Cooper by 6–2, 6–1, 6–2; Rod Laver's comparable annihilation of Marty Mulligan in 1962; and John Newcombe's crushing 6–3, 6–1, 6–1 victory over another German, Wilhelm Bungert, in 1967 as victories of similar magnitude. But with due respect to Cooper, Mulligan and Bungert, they were not in Connors' league. McEnroe had destroyed one of the legends of the game. Ironically, only Connors himself had done something similar when he relinquished only six games to Ken Rosewall in the Wimbledon final exactly ten years before.

Since then I can think of only one occasion when a great player has produced such a near-perfect demonstration of serve and volley tennis against an opponent of similar class. That occurred quite recently, in the semi-final of the Australian Open at Flinders Park in 1990, when Stefan Edberg hardly put his racket wrong in overwhelming Mats Wilander 6–1, 6–1, 6–2.

With McEnroe in such supreme form it was almost a foregone conclusion that he and Peter Fleming would win the doubles but, in the end, they had to work for it as the new combination of Paul McNamee and Pat Cash pushed them to five sets in the final. It was the fourth Wimbledon title for McEnroe and his often underestimated partner. Since the Doherty brothers in the early days of tennis championships, only John Newcombe and Tony Roche, achieving five, have won more as a pair.

Few could have guessed at the time that it would be the last Grand Slam doubles title McEnroe and Fleming would ever win, and that McEnroe himself would have to wait until 1989 before he could claim another. By then he had found a red-headed Australian left-hander called Mark Woodforde to help him win the US Open doubles for the fourth time. 'It's good. Woody makes me think I'm playing with Rod Laver,' McEnroe quipped. Five years on, John was capable of having a bit of fun on a doubles court. But, in 1984, despite the enormous satisfaction he derived from his twin triumph, tennis was still too tense a business for him to allow frivolity to creep into his working hours.

Gene Scott, writing in his magazine *Tennis Week*, alluded to this in his Wimbledon report. 'McEnroe may not look like he is having fun but he should be,' Scott wrote, 'because his game is so playful. He has hiding places for the ball that the other little boys cannot possibly find. His angles are the apotheosis of hide-and-seek – with no seek currently available for his rivals . . . McEnroe's virtuosity simply left no room for anyone else on stage. If Eric Clapton were McEnroe that day and Connors Pete Townshend, Townshend would simply have unplugged himself and listened.'

McEnroe was certainly making better music, as far as the All England Club were concerned, than he had done during his first tempestuous year as champion in 1981. Then, all the nonsense about not being properly invited to the Champions' dinner at the Savoy, and the withholding of the honorary membership normally afforded all singles title-winners, left a very bad taste in the mouth. Much of it had been washed away when he had reclaimed the title in 1983 but now, with the eruption during his match with Shiras at Queen's forgotten, the men wearing the mauve and green tie could really start to feel proud of their champion. And for all his apparently rebellious nature, McEnroe was only too pleased to be accepted.

'There are lots of British ways of doing things that get on my nerves,' he told me. 'But people are really trying to be nice this year and I appreciate that.'

Soon after the final was over I had taken my turn in the queue of television and radio personnel waiting to interview him. With an All England Club official in attendance, as is the custom, I led him into the little cubicle reserved for BBC Radio next to the main press conference beneath the No. 1 dressing-room. I waited for producer Dave Gordon to pass the word through to our presenter Peter Jones that I had McEnroe with me, and then waited for Peter to give me the cue to go live.

After talking about how well he had played we came, inevitably, to the subject of his behaviour.

'I am really glad I was able to win the way people wanted me to win,' he said. 'I was only sorry that I could not prove to everyone that I could play like that in a tight match. I'm glad I won as I did, but if I had been in a losing position and still behaved that way it would have been even more satisfying.'

As McEnroe is almost incapable of making an insincere statement, I'm sure this was exactly the way he felt. It was hardly, therefore, the sentiment of a man who deliberately uses temper tantrums to put off his opponents – no matter what he might say all those years later after his default at the Australian Open. But more of that later.

Before and after the US Open, McEnroe's year continued on its successful path. In August he won the Canadian Open in Toronto and in late September the TransAmerica Open at the old Cow Palace in San Francisco – two tournaments to which he remained constantly loyal throughout the eighties. It was his fourth TransAmerican title but, strangely, his first in Canada.

By the time we trekked out to Flushing Meadow again for the 1984 US Open, it was also hard to believe that McEnroe had not won his native title since 1981. For the previous two years Connors, whose vanity is stoked by the bonfires of Tom Wolfe's raucous city, had proved that nowhere is he more difficult to beat than in New York, New York. But McEnroe was the native New Yorker, and he did not like the idea of Connors being the crowd's darling while they frequently booed the kid who grew up down the road in Douglaston. And this year he was in the mood to do something about it.

After knocking off the likes of Bob Green, now a leading figure in the organization of the new ATP Tour, and Gene Mayer without dropping a set, McEnroe was primed and ready for what became known as Super Saturday. For reasons that have everything to do with the demands of CBS Television and absolutely nothing to do with the welfare of the players, the men's semi-finals at the US Open are played on the Saturday with the women's final sandwiched in between. At all the other Grand Slams, where television has not yet been allowed to dictate its own terms, the men's semi-finals are played on the Friday, so as to give the winners a suitable length of time in which to recover and prepare for one of the biggest matches of their lives.

On this particular occasion, the unnecessary feast of tennis laid before a public that has too short an attention span to enjoy it all actually turned out to be rather memorable. For sheer excess it was all very New York. Beginning at 11.00 a.m. with Stan Smith beating John Newcombe in the Over 35 final – as if we needed a curtain-raiser on a day like this – the entire programme did not finish until 11.13 p.m. that night. All three of the matches that followed were fine contests, but it was Lendl's victory over Cash that left everyone emotionally exhausted with only half the programme completed. The young Australian got as far as match point against the No. 2 seed before a misjudgement on a high backhand volley allowed Lendl to escape with another blood and guts victory, 3–6, 6–3, 6–4, 6–7, 7–6.

Martina Navratilova then appeared on the stadium court to continue her career-long rivalry with Chris Evert, and eventually prevailed after a tough three-set duel. The lights were on by the time McEnroe faced Connors and, of course, this time Jimmy refused to roll over. Working the crowd, revelling in the cries of 'Come on, Jimbo' and strutting about court in his usual hyped-up manner, Connors snarled and fought before McEnroe could prise the title from his grasp 6–3 in the fifth set.

The only good thing about the CBS-orchestrated schedule was that the men's final did not start until 4.00 p.m. on the Sunday, so that the network could make a few extra million with their precious gridiron football. (And if the football overran, you could be sure the tennis had to wait.) But, in this instance, the late start at least gave McEnroe a couple of extra hours in which to recover. Even then it was absurd that one player should have the evening off while his opponent was struggling back to bed at one o'clock in the morning. But just such a handicap had worked in Manolo Orantes' favour when the US Open was played at Forest Hills in 1975. The Spaniard was caught in a late match with Guillermo Vilas and returned next day to beat none other than a defending champion called Jimmy Connors. And it was to work now for McEnroe.

In an exhibition of controlled genius that took only one hour, forty minutes, McEnroe wrought partial revenge on Lendl for that nightmare in Paris by beating the Czech 6–3, 6–4, 6–1. In his book *Game, Set and Match*, Rex Bellamy wrote: 'Both had been physically drained by awfully strenuous semi-finals. Lendl looked stiff – in body and mind, technique and tactics. Lendl wrote humdrum prose while McEnroe wrote poetry; unfussy, but so carefully constructed that every word hit the mark.'

It was McEnroe's seventh Grand Slam singles title and, it seems, his last.

In November McEnroe claimed his eleventh title of the year in the Stockholm Open, but by then another dark period was approaching. Fines, levied under the stricter rules of the Men's Tennis Council – rules that, McEnroe insisted with some degree of accuracy, were rewritten especially for him – were catching up with him. One thousand here, five hundred there, fines for crimes like shouting at a linesman or bouncing his racket had accumulated past the statutory $7,500 mark and, immediately after returning from Sweden, he was suspended.

As a result, he had only a couple of exhibition matches with which to prepare himself for the débâcle that awaited the United States Davis Cup team in Gothenburg in December. But he was not about to offer that as an excuse. Excuses are not his style.

So it was not until he had spent his first Christmas with the girl he had met in Hollywood three months before, Tatum O'Neal, that McEnroe was able to return to the level of brilliance that had illuminated so much of 1984. The Masters at Madison Square Garden in January belonged to 1984 as far as the tennis world was concerned, and McEnroe was determined to finish it with a flourish.

The Masters was in its straight knockout phase at the time and, after a first round bye, McEnroe dropped a set to Anders Jarryd before cutting Mats Wilander's game to ribbons 6–1, 6–1 in the semi-final. Once again that left him with Lendl in a best of five sets final. On that particular Sunday in New York, McEnroe was awesome. The score was 7–5, 6–0, 6–4 and the closeness of the first and third sets shows how well Lendl was playing on the medium-paced, low bouncing Supreme carpet that he had come to favour above any other. But the middle set also tells its story. There was a spellbinding sequence in the match in which McEnroe won eleven straight games; eleven games against the strongest and most resilient of opponents; eleven games when McEnroe not only served like a dream but did eye-popping things to Lendl's delivery. I was sitting in the first row of press seats at courtside, watching this muscular man from Ostrava pound down serves that would have done the coalminers' work for them at the pit face on the Czech–Polish border. They were the sort of serves that players normally take a step back to receive. McEnroe took two steps forward. Not only that but, taking the ball on the rise, he would glide straight in behind it and then angle away the sweetest of volleys to a sector of the court that Lendl had never even thought of visiting. And these were first serves; serves travelling well over 120 mph. Lendl did well to stay in the match as long as he did.

As had been the case twelve months before, when poor Ivan had once before been the stooge for the maestro's skills, everyone was wanting to crowd round the Master in the little player's ante-room backstage at the Garden. But, after accepting a few congratulations from his family and friends, the rest had to wait. He wanted to attend to a very special visitor.

Ever since the Association's inception in 1972, the ATP had adopted Cystic Fibrosis, the incurable respiratory disease, as its official charity. McEnroe had done some promotional work on behalf of CF and, in the process, had met the CF poster child. It was this boy who had come to see him now.

'They wouldn't let me in at first,' the youngster told McEnroe. 'They didn't believe I knew you!'

'Really?' replied John, laughing. 'Well, look, I have to play a doubles now, but you come back and see me afterwards when we'll have more time to talk. And don't let them stop you!'

They chatted briefly for a couple of minutes and the boy went off, his eyes shining, bright with happiness. McEnroe's expression changed as he turned to talk to me.

'That kid's not going to be with us much longer. Isn't that unbelievable? When you meet him like that, he looks so healthy.'

People stood aside to let McEnroe back into the locker room to change for the doubles. When he re-emerged with Peter Fleming, ready to make their seventh successful assault on the Masters title, the public face was back in place and the voice that could talk with such sensitivity to a sick child would soon be saying something unpleasant to a linesman. It is hardly surprising he is misunderstood.

for the loneliness that was building up inside him. Without doubt there were moments when he missed Stella.

But by the time he had conquered Flushing Meadow, this native New Yorker thought that maybe the moment had come to follow the well-trodden path and go west, young man. So, after winning the Barry MacKay's TransAmerica Open in San Francisco for the fourth time in six years, he decided to go back to Los Angeles and, with his worldly-wise pal Vitas Gerulaitis to lead him around, explore the Hollywood scene.

It is Vitas who must take the credit for bringing John and Tatum together; Vitas the party man; Vitas the nearly-man of tennis, skidding over the surface of life, almost beating Björn Borg in one of the great Wimbledon semi-finals, almost finding the girl of his dreams, almost making his idea of a Harry Hopman-style Florida tennis camp work. Almost. Vitas, too, is a good guy with a dubious image but, unlike John, he is still searching.

To a large extent, the searching stopped for McEnroe the night he walked into a party at the Hollywood home of record producer Richard Perry and saw Tatum O'Neal sitting on the couch.

'Vitas said we should go that evening because Richard Perry was a nice guy and gave great parties,' McEnroe recalled. 'Richard's produced some big hits with Carly Simon and Barbra Streisand and throws the kind of parties that are real Hollywood. It's all a question of who's going to be there. In LA people need to be convinced of someone's status by the number of famous faces sitting in their living room. I'd never been into that sort of thing, but Vitas said it would be good for me to branch out a little. Maybe he was right!'

It was the 'Who's going to be there?' syndrome that snared Tatum. 'I wasn't thinking of going out that night but, when a friend told me that John McEnroe was going to be there, I thought "why not?" I was already a fan of his.' Tatum lit up our conversation with one of her brilliant smiles. 'Within twenty minutes of our meeting he was flirting with me.'

But not, apparently, with a great deal of confidence. 'After just a few minutes talking with her I remember feeling, this is a girl I could marry,' McEnroe admitted. 'But somehow I didn't think the odds were too favourable. My life-style on the circuit doesn't help and I just thought, what would she want with me? But we met again the following night at another party, and then I had to go off to play in the Stockholm Open, after which I got suspended because of an accumulation of fines. So although I ended up back in New York quite soon after, I just thought I'd let the relationship cool for a while. Or maybe it was just a question of not getting my nerve up. I still wasn't sure she was interested. But then she phoned and said she was coming to New York and I thought, hey, maybe I have another chance.'

When Tatum saw John again in New York she was invited to visit his apartment on Central Park West. It surprised her.

'He just said "Come and see this little place I've got on Central Park. It isn't decorated properly yet." When we got there, we kept on walking up one set of stairs after another. There were four floors to this apartment in one of the most expensive blocks in the city and I remember thinking, how can a 25-year-old afford all this? Then we spent the rest of the evening just sitting there on the floor watching Johnny Carson, eating pretzels and drinking ginger ale.'

Although Tatum realized even then that she felt a particular fascination for this strange young man, even she could not have envisaged her future lover buying a house from the man on the screen – Johnny Carson himself, no less – for a little over a million dollars, plus, at Carson's own request, a few private tennis lessons.

'After I flew back to the coast, I decided to call him to say I was missing him. I just felt I had to take the initiative. If we'd played the normal boy-girl thing I doubt if we would ever have made it. His travel schedule was just ridiculous and still is, really.'

Taum's call was all the encouragement McEnroe needed. After a few days fidgeting and pottering around New York, he got on a plane and flew to Los Angeles – and that was it. There was no looking back. The electrical wires had crossed; the sparks were flying and the current of attraction was too strong. In no way was it going to be an easy relationship, but it was destined to be a powerful and lasting one.

'I knew something was up when he flew out to see me two days earlier than he said he would,' Tatum continued. 'I thought that signified something. But, you know, even after we had seen each other half a dozen times, he still hadn't taken me out to dinner. Getting him out of the house was like pulling teeth. He was just so uneasy in public. I'm a shy person, but not nearly as shy as John. Even after we had Kevin, just getting him to come with me when I took the baby for a walk down the street in New York was a major operation. It was the "hat pulled down and the dark glasses" bit, as if that helped. Now he's better and has come to realize it is actually quite nice to go outside once in a while!'

Tatum and I had slipped into one of the hospitality areas at Flushing Meadow during the 1989 US Open. We had never really talked before. She, like John, guards her privacy as much as is possible for anyone living in the constant glare of publicity.

About a year after they were married, they decided, following some discussion in between phone calls from London, to turn down an offer of $100,000 from a British tabloid for a half-hour interview and some pictures. John was tempted for a moment because he wanted to buy Tatum a nice Christmas present. But the temptation was resisted.

I had met the future Mrs McEnroe for the first time over dinner in Antwerp, during the European Community Championships that the former French No. 1 Pierre Darmon has built into such a gigantic success. Late dinners, usually at some Italian restaurant hand-picked by Sergio Palmieri, have become the custom for McEnroe and his immediate friends while on tour in Europe. As long as he is in company he trusts, he is quite happy eating out.

I found Tatum much younger than I had expected. Like most people I had seen pictures of her in the newspapers, all dolled up for Hollywood parties in high-heeled shoes at the age of eleven. I had assumed that this aura of sophistication was an extension of her personality and that she would have grown up to be a worldly-wise and even cynical young woman. This was not the case. She was obviously shy and obviously younger in spirit as well as age than John. There was a reserve and a certain touchiness which made her difficult to get to know.

This, as Tatum confirmed during our talk, was largely due to the unease she felt initially about her new nomadic surroundings.

Joining the travelling caravan of players, wives, girlfriends and coaches that jet around the globe on a non-stop basis is not easy unless you happen to have a very outgoing and trusting personality.

'I found the first year very hard,' Tatum admitted. 'It took me two or three years to start feeling comfortable with everyone. To begin with I found people very unfriendly. That changed after I had Kevin because all the wives wanted to talk about babies. That's fine up to a point, but I'm not that outgoing and I'm just not into shopping expeditions. Basically, I suppose I'm more comfortable in male company.'

The fact that as a child Tatum spent a lot of time with her father, Ryan O'Neal, would account for that. From what one can tell, she grew used to male behaviour and male responses through those stormy adolescent years spent with O'Neal; years that were full of fun, full of love and full of hurt. Since Tatum went from one Irish-American superstar with a hot temper to another, the explanation suggests itself that she was merely looking for a Daddy substitute. But that is too simple. Ryan O'Neal is a macho man with something to prove, while John McEnroe is not. No one is clearer about the differences between her father and her husband than Tatum herself.

'John is more direct and more sensitive,' she says. 'My father is much more temperamental. If someone told him to be quiet in a movie house, you never knew how he would react. Going out with him in the evening was what you might call an exciting experience because you never knew how the evening would end. He was quite capable of getting into a brawl which John would never do.

'I suppose you could call my father a bully. He likes to assert his authority and flaunt his fame. There again, that is quite the opposite of John, who goes out of his way to make sure people do not feel uneasy in his company just because he is famous.'

Do not imagine, however, that this harsh assessment means that Tatum does not love her father.

'Sure, she still loves him,' McEnroe told me later. 'No matter what happens between them, she always will. Blood really is thicker than water.'

But that love was put on the back burner when the couple decided to get married – a ceremony that was postponed until after the birth of Kevin in May 1986, so that Tatum would not look pregnant when she walked down the aisle. But Tatum also decided something else. The man walking down the aisle to give her away would not be her father.

'Originally, Ryan was going to put on the wedding. But they probably had a row because she wouldn't play racket-ball with him, or something – I still don't know the full story to this day – and she banned him from the wedding. It was entirely her decision. You wouldn't exactly call Ryan and me close – in fact, we virtually never see each other although his house is only about a mile away from ours in Malibu – but we have never had a blazing row or anything. In fact, we have never even raised our voices to each other. We just keep out of each other's way.'

There was one occasion, however, when McEnroe, allowing his foolhardy pride to get the better of him, agreed to put on a pair of boxing-gloves and spar with Ryan O'Neal.

'It could have been a big mistake,' McEnroe laughed. 'He could have let one go and I would have been out like a light. He sparred with Joe Frazier once. He's probably an inch shorter than I am, but he's very strong in the upper body and he knows a lot about boxing. He probably wishes he was a fighter. He certainly knows a lot about it. But it's just not my scene, man. I don't care for it at all.'

A general aversion to boxing did not stop McEnroe climbing into a proper ring at a charity evening at the Berkeley Court Hotel in Dublin precisely one week before the start of Wimbledon 1988. He and Mats Wilander, all decked out like prize fighters with big red gloves and attended by a referee, boxed for three rounds with only a gentleman's agreement between them to stop the blood from flowing. Wilander's coach, John-Anders Sjögren, who was watching at ringside with the organizers – Matt Doyle, the Irish Davis Cup player and John O'Shea, a journalist heavily involved with charity work in Africa – was very happy they were not trying to knock each other out. Watching McEnroe's left hand peppering Mats' peek-a-boo defence, Sjögren muttered, 'That's a pretty quick left hand John's got. He could do a lot of damage with that!'

For the sake of family harmony, it is to be hoped that it is never sent snaking towards the handsomely boyish features of his father-in-law. The response and the consequences could be dire.

But, as McEnroe himself points out, that is most unlikely to happen, firstly because he only fights with his tongue and his racket and has never thrown a naked fist at anyone in his life, and, secondly, because they keep out of each other's way.

'In our case the distance we put between ourselves might be somewhat accentuated, but in another sense it is just the natural way of things,' he says. 'When you get married and have your own family it just happens that way. I love my parents very much, but I don't get to see them that much any more. I certainly don't avoid them but it is just the way things work out.'

Things worked out between John and Tatum for a whole variety of reasons that included an instant physical chemistry; a shared experience of being naturally shy people who had to learn how to deal with the unrelenting glare of public scrutiny; Celtic blood that came quickly to the boil; and matching intellects.

Although he can be disparaging about women's ability to play tennis, McEnroe is a long way from being your average male chauvinist jock. His mother is a strong woman and he wanted a strong wife. 'I could never be interested in someone who could just be happy to have my kids and wash my socks,' he told me. 'I needed someone to stand up to me and teach me things.'

In Tatum O'Neal he found just such a woman. She may be shy and she may have seemed younger than her years, but the very fact of banning her own father from her wedding reveals a woman who is not afraid of taking tough decisions. This independent streak was born in her at an early age.

'My life with my father made me independent long before I met John,' she told me. 'Independent, that is, within my own world. I was very sheltered in a way. I didn't go to school. I was always on location somewhere, having to take care of myself in an adult world that often left me to my own devices. If I gave the impression of precocious sophistication by going to all those Hollywood parties, it was wrong. I was just playing at dressing-up; just a little girl having fun.'

If McEnroe had to learn how to deal with the intrusion of a press conference and a television interview at the age of seventeen, little Miss O'Neal was a veteran at it by that age. Starring roles in movies like *Paper Moon* had made her a child celebrity, and she was able to pass on what she had learned about how to deal with the press to a husband who was still snarling at photographers by the time they were married.

'Tatum taught me a lot in that respect,' John admits. 'She's been through it from such a young age. She forced me to straighten up my act a little.'

And the educational process continues to a far greater extent than people imagine.

'I demand a lot of him,' said Tatum firmly. 'I don't settle for second-best. He had the choice. He could have gone for a demure little wife, but he chose me and he knew I wasn't going to shut up. I was determined to make him aware of the consequences of his behaviour; to understand the results of years of shitting on people. When we went to England I saw how crushed he was by some of the things that were written about him. I may have had a bad press occasionally but never anything like that. He's regretting it now – all that time when he couldn't appreciate the winning and the success; all those negative responses like "I'm going to win because the crowd hate me, people hate me; I've got to beat the crowd, beat the officials." He makes life so difficult for himself.

'After Wimbledon last year I said I wasn't going to go with him to Grand Slam tournaments any more. There was too much pain for me. I couldn't face going through that gut-wrenching unhappiness any more. I know it's all wrapped up in some sort of tortured genius thing with him, but I felt he would do better just to close himself off and concentrate on his tennis.'

Ironically, Tatum decided to take the two boys and be with him throughout his extended stay in Australia beginning the day after Christmas in 1989. Right up to the infamous moment of default in the Australian Open at Flinders Park, it had all worked like a dream. But with 'the genius thing'; with a temperament like that, there is simply no knowing when the volcano will erupt.

Tatum, however, is far too determined a person to give up. Her vision of the life they could lead has been infiltrating McEnroe's consciousness for some time now, and anyone attending his press conferences has been able to pick up snippets of his new thinking. Mainly it has manifested itself in his oft-repeated feelings of responsibility as a husband and a father, and of the need to set a proper example. But it was only after talking to Tatum that I realized the degree to which she was influencing him.

'As a couple we have to think about a higher level,' she said. 'That does not mean getting away from tennis, but just seeing the bigger world and getting things in perspective. We are two of the luckiest people on the planet right now. We are two young people with so many material things and we have the good fortune to be able to influence not only our own children but the way other people think, too. We have a public voice that can be used in so many ways. We can urge people to think about the environment; to pick up bottles and re-cycle cans, things that a lot of people still don't consider important. We should dwell on the positive and enjoy our own lives while trying to make lives better for others, too.'

There is no question that McEnroe is responsive to this kind of thinking. As an Aquarius, concern for other people is simply part of his nature and is quite divorced from that dark side of his character which enables him to treat some people on some specific occasions with appalling disregard for human decency. But trying to convince anyone that he cares while he continues to get thrown off tennis courts is a battle that may take a long time to win.

Nor is Tatum content with merely trying to change the public perception of her man. Domestically, she gives him a rough ride, too.

'We have homes to run that don't run themselves,' she pointed out. 'I make him pick up his clothes and try to stop him walking out of a room when I'm talking to him. He'll tell me I'm good at telling him the same things I need to do myself, but that's all right. If we're tough on each other, we'll both get better. It may sound hard but I'm still his biggest supporter. I'm so proud of him because he wants to do better, he wants to improve – not just as a tennis player, but as a person. And he's getting there. He dotes on the children and has tremendous fun with them and, as for myself, the two little kids must be our prime concern. I have a lot of ambition but not necessarily in the acting field. I've never been crazy about being an actress. And anyway, if I made a film right now I'd be on location somewhere and John would be in Timbuctoo, and where would the kids be? I'm making a commitment to them for their stability and I'm quite happy about that. With a bit of luck we've got it all before us. We're really very lucky and I think John is beginning to understand that.'

Tatum surprised me. There's a lot more going on behind that attractive, if prickly, exterior than she lets on through casual acquaintance. She obviously sees her marriage as a challenge and is undaunted. Demanding, difficult men do not frighten her. Before the real match, she had lots of childhood practice.

15

The Decline

John McEnroe won eight singles titles in 1985 and had a terrible year. Even players ranked in the top ten would consider a tally of eight tournament wins terrific. But for McEnroe it was a disaster because none of the victories came in the Grand Slam events, and when Brad Gilbert, who did not rank in his list of great players, beat him in the first round of the Masters the following January, McEnroe had, in his own estimation, touched rock bottom.

The misery was accentuated, partly because the previous year had been such a triumph but also because everything about McEnroe's life is accentuated. The pace at which he lives, and the reputation he had built for himself as a scowling, short-fused genius, ensured that every gesture was scrutinized and every remark magnified out of all proportion. That is just as true today as it was in the mid-eighties. After his default in Australia, there were reports on the wire services, published in papers all over the world, that McEnroe made a few complaints about line calls when he played a doubles match with Jakob Hlasek in the Stella Artois Championships in Milan. A few complaints! Is this news? There is no older story in sport than McEnroe complaining about a line call.

With the odd exception, like the indefensible outburst at Flinders Park, McEnroe has his method of complaining under control now. But that was not the case in 1985, and his inability to police his emotions was a major factor in leaving him, at the start of the following year, as close to becoming a psychological disaster area as he has ever been. He had realized by then that he had a major problem. The temper was running out of control and he didn't knew what to do about it.

'Having people remember me because of my behaviour is not

what I want,' he told me during the course of one of our frequent conversations. 'I want to be remembered for my tennis. Despite everything, I think I have brought a new dimension to the game as a player. I think I have been a positive influence. Maybe people have not liked how I have gone about it, but I think I have helped raise the standard of officiating and *that*, whatever people may think, has always been my aim. I am hard on them but I am hard on myself, too.'

All this was true, but deep down McEnroe knew that he had to get to grips with the tantrum factor; that he had to find a way of taming the talent.

'I know I've got a problem,' he told me. 'When I walk out there on court I become a maniac. I'm capable of saying anything. I suppose I didn't care about what I said for so long that now I want to change I can't. Something comes over me, man. It's weird.'

The thought of seeking psychiatric help was anathema to McEnroe. He couldn't see what a stranger could tell him about himself that he didn't know already. Psychoanalysts across the length and breadth of America will be happy that millions of McEnroe's compatriots don't share that view, but to this bright, perceptive man it seemed obvious. He felt quite sure that lying on a couch talking about himself was not going to make him any happier about whether a call was in or out.

Later, under Tatum's influence, he did get into yoga and other relaxing activities that Californians tend to indulge in more than do New Yorkers but, by the end of 1985, there did not seem to be any solutions in sight for what was building up into a major crisis of confidence about his ability to continue playing tennis.

On court, fleeting moments of success in places like Philadelphia, Chicago, Milan and Montreal were interspersed with major setbacks at the Grand Slam championships. Strangely, he did far better at the French Open than at Wimbledon. Fighting his way through a five-set quarter-final against such an elegant clay-court specialist as Joakim Nystrom at Roland Garros was a triumph in itself, but Nystrom's great pal Mats Wilander was quick to avenge the defeat in the semis, beating McEnroe 6–1, 7–5, 7–5. Nevertheless, a semi-final showing on clay was a great deal more bearable than the stunning 6–2, 6–2, 6–4 thrashing he received at the hands of Kevin Curren, the South African-born American, in the quarter-final at Wimbledon. Curren's huge serve carried him all the way to the final that year, where he lost to the seventeen-year-old sensation Boris Becker. But the fact that Curren had a big serve was not accepted by the defending champion as an excuse for his defeat. It was his own game and his own state of mind that McEnroe lambasted in such typically uncompromising style.

That he had gone into the tournament on edge was amply demonstrated by an incident which fuelled the conversation in the Queen's Club bar for many an evening that summer. As a loyal supporter of the Stella Artois tournament, which had done very nicely out of all the publicity McEnroe's presence had given the event over the years, John was always offered practice facilities during the week before Wimbledon. One afternoon, as he fretted away at a serve that was not working to his required level of perfection, a lady member of Queen's arrived to claim the court that she had booked after McEnroe's time expired.

Vitas Gerulaitis, who had just come off court after practising with McEnroe, saw that the woman was not taking kindly to being kept waiting and that, equally, McEnroe was showing no immediate signs of wanting to vacate the court.

'I recognized a potential problem looming,' Vitas told me the next day. 'So I went over to the lady and explained that John was pretty uptight about his game and that it would be great if she could give him another ten minutes. But she started going on about members' rights and I took one look at John and I thought, "I'm not getting in the middle of this. I'm getting out of here."'

So Gerulaitis walked back to the clubhouse and sure enough the woman pressed her case and just as surely McEnroe told her to fuck off. It was, of course, an indefensible reaction on his part and both he and the club paid dearly for it in the ensuing years. The matter was taken up in committee and the offended member insisted on taking a stand and making the whole thing public. She wanted a written apology. McEnroe, who was prepared to *say* he was sorry, was not about to commit anything to paper. Despite all the mediating efforts of tournament director Clive Bernstein, who had built up a very good working relationship with McEnroe over the years, the net result of this needless affair was that McEnroe has not been seen at Queen's since.

McEnroe was, of course, completely in the wrong to have spoken to the woman in that manner, but there are some people, myself included, who would be thrilled to find the reigning Wimbledon champion practising on my court. Rather than trying to get him off, I would have begged him to stay so that I could sit and watch. But, in my experience, members of tennis clubs are rarely broadminded enough to take that attitude. When the US Open was played at Forest Hills, the members often made the pros feel as if they were trespassing, and there were moments when it was not much better at Kooyong before the Australian Open moved to the splendour of Flinders Park.

At any rate, McEnroe's reputation had taken another battering and the year did not get a lot better. One of the main problems was his body. Neglected throughout his entire career as far as proper training was concerned, various bits of it were now starting to rebel. A hip and lower back problem began flaring up with increasing frequency, and the fact that he had decided to play fewer doubles did not help. Regular doubles play had acted as substitute training sessions over the years and kept him from stiffening up in between singles. Now the pulls and strains were becoming more frequent.

He managed to go one stage better at Flushing Meadow than he had in Paris, coincidentally beating Nystrom again in the quarters, and then, on the Decoturf court that favoured his game so much more than clay, he got past Wilander in five sets. But McEnroe knew he was playing well below the form of the previous year and despite a great start against Lendl in the final, which took him to a 5–2 lead in the first set, he was quite unable to maintain the momentum against the Czech machine and lost his crown 7–6, 6–3, 6–4.

Somehow he managed to retain his Stockholm Open title, but a decision to take another crack at the Australian Open, where Wilander had beaten him on Kooyong's grass in 1983, did not turn out to be a wise one. Completely nonplussed by the slight incline up towards the net that is a feature of the Stadium Court at Kooyong, McEnroe came as near as he has ever done to giving up when he lost

6–0 in the fifth set to the hulking Slobodan Zivojinovic, who not only had a big enough serve to keep McEnroe at bay but also had a big enough personality to make fun of the Great Complainer whenever John started an argument. This was not appreciated.

McEnroe's fragile frame of mind led to another fracas, trivial enough if it had happened to a less newsworthy personality but which turned out to be just the kind of grist the Australian press needed for their anti-McEnroe mill. Walking through the lobby of Melbourne's Regency Hotel, McEnroe found himself besieged by reporters and he reacted by laying a finger on one of them for the only time in his life. It was, almost literally, just a finger, and it toppled the man back into the not inconsiderable comfort of a large armchair.

'McEnroe assaults reporter!' screamed the headlines. It sold a few newspapers.

It also added fuel to the theory that McEnroe was getting into more arguments and unsavoury incidents than even he could handle. By the time he had gone down 5–7, 6–4, 6–1 to Brad Gilbert in the first round of the Masters the following January, he realized that it might be time to take a breather.

He had driven in from the new house he had bought at Cove Neck, not very far from the original family home in Douglaston, and, after another self-critical press conference, I followed him out into the night. 'Want a ride?' he asked as he flung his gear into the boot of his old Mercedes. He needed to talk. The match had been a disaster and, for John playing in front of so many friends at the Garden, an embarrassment. Gilbert, who, a couple of years later, was to become a much better player than McEnroe or anyone else imagined, had been allowed to dictate the play from the back court, passing with his usual fluency against a man who could no longer dominate the net.

'I've got to take time off,' he said as we set off up Eighth Avenue. 'My hip's hurting, my mind's not there. This relationship with Tatum is great, but we take so much out of each other, you can't believe it. It's just so intense, man. By the time I get on court I'm emotionally drained. I just find myself drifting out of matches. That's not me. That's not the way I play tennis.'

We talked about his need to take better care of his body and he promised that, during the weeks he was intending to take off from the tour, he would start a proper training routine. But although he knew it was necessary, the idea still irked him. The challenge of doing things the hard way, of bucking the odds, was still what set the pulse racing and gave him the ultimate satisfaction.

'Hey, but I did it for eight years, didn't I?' he exclaimed suddenly as he pulled up in front of Essex House, where I had a room that year. 'I stayed in the top two in the world all that time without training. That wasn't bad, was it?'

I had to laugh. The man is quite incorrigible. For McEnroe, the easy way is boring. There must never be a dull day. If life gets too simple, make it complicated.

But, despite the sudden spark of bravado that night, he knew he was reaching the end of his tether. Deep inside he was worried that, if he did not step back and reflect for a little while, he might do something on court that he would regret in a big way. Somehow he had to learn to deal with his monkey – not a monkey on his back, as some people were trying to make out, but the devilish monkey that lurked inside an otherwise intelligent and caring human being and took over, unbidden, with explosive results.

Having a monkey on your back used to be the expression for a man with a drug problem in the days when Frank Sinatra was making *The Man with the Golden Arm*. But, to the best of my knowledge, McEnroe never had a drug problem. I know several frequenters of jet-set parties in New York and Los Angeles who will laugh at that assertion. But I am certainly not about to pass judgement on someone regarding so sensitive an issue without evidence. And I have no evidence.

There has been just one occasion, one only, when I have seen McEnroe use drugs of any kind. It was back in the early eighties. One evening in Miami, after he had spent the entire day signing autographs and going through the motions of being Mr Celebrity at Harold Solomon's charity exhibition for the World Hunger Project, we went out to dinner and, in the car back to the hotel, we shared a spliff of marijuana.

I mention this not as a 'McEnroe smokes pot!' revelation,

because it is no longer an offence in most states of America to possess a small quantity of marijuana for one's personal use, and well over fifty per cent of the people I know have tried it at one time or another. I mention it simply to come clean as to the full extent of my first-hand knowledge about McEnroe and drugs. And I do so because there is no use trying to hide the fact that, during those months he spent with Tatum at Malibu, all sorts of rumours were flying around about 'McEnroe's drug problem'.

Eventually, it got as far as reports appearing in the press to the effect that McEnroe had admitted himself to the Betty Ford drug clinic in Palm Springs for a cure.

'That's crap,' John said privately and repeated it for the benefit of the doubting world at large. 'I was seen all over the place in Malibu and LA during the time I was supposed to have been in Palm Springs. I can't be in two places at once.'

Cocaine was supposed to have been McEnroe's problem. Rumours that he was a heavy user were inevitable, I suppose, because some of his friends were and even a couple of players on the tour had to seek help at one stage. It would have been virtually impossible for him not to come into contact with the stuff, as most smart parties in those days offered guests the tantalizing sight of lines of the little white powder on the drawing-room table. And no matter how much McEnroe did or did not use, he only had to be in the room to set the tongues wagging. Good gossip does not survive on stories of what boring socialites get up to. It needs star names to add the spice and, by 1986, few names were bigger than John McEnroe.

As I don't get much of a thrill from having a numb nose, I tended to avoid that scene, which makes me a very bad source of information on the subject. But I have spent quite enough time in McEnroe's company over the years to know that no one with a so-called problem could have concealed it so effectively.

Before we move on to more pertinent topics, it is worthwhile pointing out that McEnroe, during his period as Vice President of the ATP, was on the Board of Directors that voted for voluntary drug testing in 1986 – making tennis the first sport to take the step of policing itself over the use of social drugs. (Testing for steroids has only been adopted in the last year.)

Typically, McEnroe thought long and hard over whether to vote in favour of testing. 'My original thought was that we did not want to draw attention to the issue in such a dramatic way, because it would make it appear tennis has a major drug problem, which it doesn't,' he told me. 'But then I thought it would set a good example for other sports to follow and I think we made the right decision.'

Back in Malibu, McEnroe was trying to make a few correct decisions about his career as he and Tatum waited for the birth of their first child in May 1986.

In the event, McEnroe stayed away from the circuit rather longer than he had originally intended. He missed the French Open and Wimbledon, and the All England Club, in particular, seemed a little strange without the three-time former champion who had made his presence felt in every imaginable way for the previous nine years. But many people considered his absence a relief. It was, for them, a chance to return to the old-fashioned values of demure sportsmanship and civilized behaviour.

'Judging from the silence, I guess not too many people are missing me,' he said, trying to laugh it off, when I called him in the middle of the championships.

But, in truth, the realization that his absence was being welcomed in many circles hurt him and made him more acutely aware than ever before just how much he had offended large segments of the tennis community. When he returned, it was something of which he would be very conscious.

A first-round defeat in the US Open was not the best way to make his return to the tour, but everything suddenly snapped back into place when the New Yorker returned to his new home in the West. In quick succession he won the Volvo title at the UCLA Tennis Center in Los Angeles; the TransAmerica for the fifth time in San Francisco; and then a relatively new Grand Prix event at Scottsdale outside Phoenix. It was almost as if he could play again.

Almost. He was still not quite ready, even though there seemed to be moments in 1987 when he was on the right track. But they were fleeting moments and it turned out to be the only year between 1978 and 1989 in which he did not win a title.

The best thing that happened to him resulted from his decision to play in the Italian Open for the first time. Despite numerous appearances at the Milan Indoors and a frequently stated love for Italy and just about anything Italian – especially the food – McEnroe had never dared pit his volcanic temperament against the equally volatile crowds at the Foro Italico. But Tatum wanted to see Rome and then do some shopping in Florence, one of her favourite cities where John was intending to play in the doubles of the Grand Prix tournament at the pretty Club de Circolo.

The first part of the plan worked quite well. From the moment McEnroe walked out onto the Centre Court at the Foro Italico, raising his arm in a Roman salute to the packed evening gallery, the crowd fell in love with him. Here was an emotional showman after their own heart; someone with hot blood in his veins, fire in his belly and, if a little craziness in the head . . . bella! What fun! This was entertainment.

Both McEnroe and the crowd got more than they bargained for that night. He was drawn against an unknown seventeen-year-old Argentine called Franco Davin who refused to be overawed by the occasion and was heading for what might well have been a rather rapid victory until the lights went out.

'What a happy coincidence,' grinned Cino Marchese mischievously. I would not want to suggest that Cino, Mark McCormack's man in Rome who has done so much to revitalize interest in the Italian Open, would have done anything so naughty as to pull the switch. But the twenty-minute delay certainly allowed McEnroe to gather his wits and, after another power failure which might well have been to his disadvantage, scrape together a none too impressive victory.

Until he lost to Mats Wilander in the semi-final, McEnroe continued to illuminate the week with the glow of the love affair he had developed with the crowds. It was a happy experience for him – a novel one, in fact, to find himself cheered at every turn. Had fate not taken a hand, a triumphal journey up the peninsular to Florence should have put him in the best possible frame of mind for the French Open and could well have affected his whole year.

But a phone call changed all that. A phone call from, of all people, Jimmy Connors.

'Jimmy wants me to play with him in the World Team Cup in Düsseldorf,' McEnroe had told me soon after receiving the call a couple of weeks before. 'We'd make a pretty strong team. Maybe I ought to play.'

Even though Connors had never been one of his favourite people, McEnroe was strangely flattered by the proposal. Connors, as the highest ranked American entered in the ATP-affiliated team competition, had the right to choose the other team members. Not for the first time the call of the Stars and Stripes proved irresistible to McEnroe. So plans were changed at the last minute and Tatum, who had set her heart on Florence, decided to drive up there anyway to do some shopping with a girlfriend and join John in Düsseldorf at the weekend in time for Kevin's first birthday. McEnroe, meanwhile, would charter a plane to take himself, Kevin, the nanny and coach, Tony Palafox, who was travelling with him for the first time, to Düsseldorf.

But, as we have seen, nothing is simple with McEnroe. What followed was a McEnroesque drama of gross and giddy dimensions.

With Tatum disappearing up the autostrada, McEnroe gets to the airport to discover that he does not have Kevin's passport. It is with Tatum in the car.

'But he's my son. I can take him where I like!' says McEnroe indignantly when the immigration officer begins to indicate that baby Kevin, a McEnroe or not, is to stay put in Italy. After a few well chosen McEnroe epithets showed no signs of changing the officer's mind, Sergio Palmieri, already in Florence where he is in charge of the tournament, gets a frantic phone call. After listening to the sorry tale, Sergio tells John that the only solution is to fly up to Florence.

'It's your plane,' he says. 'You're paying a fortune for it. You can fly it anywhere you want. As soon as Tatum arrives, I'll get the passport from her and bring it to you at the airport.'

So the pilot, who thought he was flying to Düsseldorf, now finds he is going to Florence. No problem. Not, at least, until they reach the airspace over Tuscany and find themselves in the middle of a nasty storm. The pilot makes one rather hair-raising attempt to put the little plane down, overshoots the runway – and announces adamantly that he has no intention of trying again.

'I will take you to Bologna,' he says.

Once they are safely on the ground in Bologna, Palmieri gets another phone call.

'It's OK,' he says. 'Tatum, she just arrive, and I have the passport.'

'Great,' says McEnroe, 'but I'm not in Florence. We landed at Bologna.'

'Oh, shit,' says Sergio.

If you drive as fast as Palmieri, it takes about two hours to get from Florence to Bologna and it was a very tired and irritable little group he found at the airport. With a tournament to run the next day and a long drive back in the middle of the night, Sergio wasn't in the best frame of mind either.

With Kevin McEnroe sufficiently well-documented to be allowed to leave Italy, the plane eventually got the party to Düsseldorf, where things continued to go from bad to worse. First of all Connors, having lured McEnroe into the whole deal, decided to pull one of his great 'no show' acts, and withdrew with some injury or other. McEnroe, landed with the captaincy of a team that included Brad Gilbert, found the irony almost too much to bear.

Then it rained and tournament director Horst Klosterkemper asked McEnroe if he would mind playing Argentina on an indoor court. McEnroe agreed, only to read in the papers the next day that he had been the one member of either team to object. In fact, it was the Argentines who had not wanted to play indoors.

Despite various other hiccups, the United States managed to make it through to the final against Czechoslovakia. Then real disaster struck. Aggravated, inevitably, by a line call and some other umpiring decisions, McEnroe was warned and then docked a penalty point during his match against Miloslav Mecir. Suddenly he picked up his gear and walked off court. He didn't even shout much. He just left.

'I felt it was the only thing I could do at the time,' he told me when

I found him practising in the Bois de Boulogne the next day, as he tried to get his head together in time to compete in the French Open. 'If I had stayed on that court another second, I might have done something really terrible. It was much better for all concerned that I left.'

Officialdom, of course, did not see it quite that way. There were more fines; more finger wagging; more criticism in the media. And on top of that, injuries started to crop up again. After a first-round loss in Paris, McEnroe decided to give Wimbledon a miss for the second successive year and, when Lendl wiped him off court in the quarter-final of the US Open 6–3, 6–3, 6–4, the year was as good as finished as far as he was concerned. A series of clashes with officials on court had led to another accumulation of $7,500 in fines, which brought an automatic two-month suspension plus another $10,000 fine for being suspended! Pocket money, do I hear someone say? Throw the man out! Ban him for life! Yes, there were plenty of people around screaming for McEnroe's blood – some of them decent sports lovers who genuinely believe that tennis players should give opponents points after bad calls and that batsmen should walk. But there were also many, I suspect, who demanded a very high standard of behaviour from McEnroe and then, back at the office, cheated a business associate out of a deal, yelled at their secretary, or maybe even went home and beat up their wife. It is so much easier when one can give vent to the bad traits in one's character behind closed doors. Everything bad about McEnroe happens in public. There is not too much wrong with the private man.

After another seven months away from the game, scepticism about McEnroe's ability to get back to the top was rife. Those who did not actually expect him to follow Björn Borg into retirement were convinced he could never again challenge the best players in the world. Even a surprise victory in the Suntory Japan Open at the new Ariake Stadium in Tokyo, where he beat Stefan Edberg in the final, was not enough evidence of resurging ability for the critics. It was, after all, his very first Grand Prix tournament since the 1987 US Open seven months before. Ah, but Edberg was carrying an injury, they said.

His results in the next two Grand Slams were not convincing, either. Despite a brilliant spell against Lendl in the fourth round in Paris, a bad line call (upheld on the TV replay but not by the umpire), failing light which forced overnight postponement and a very heavy court the following day all worked against McEnroe's small chances of causing an upset. On his reappearance at Wimbledon, Wally Masur beat him in the second round and McEnroe said nothing in press conference afterwards about the food poisoning he had been suffering from during the previous twenty-four hours.

'He looked like death in the locker room before his match,' John Lloyd told me.

A second-round defeat at the US Open only confirmed the pessimistic viewpoint. At twenty-nine, it was all over for John P. McEnroe. But as his performances in the European Community Championships in Antwerp and a Grand Prix event in Detroit at the end of the year showed, there were a few people who didn't agree with that assessment, the most important of whom was the man himself.

16

Default

By the time the McEnroe family arrived in Perth for the Hopman Cup two days after Christmas 1989, the old decade was fading into a far rosier sunset than John could have dared hope for twelve months before. The ATP ranked him as the fourth best player in the world and, earlier in December, results at the last ever Nabisco Masters confirmed it as he and the three players ranked above him – Lendl, Becker and Edberg – opened up a clear gap between themselves and the supporting cast by reaching the semi-finals.

The ranking, his highest since 1985 and an improvement of seven places on the year before, came as a result of near-vintage performances in winning Grand Prix events at Lyon, where promoter Gilles Moretton deserved to have a superstar of McEnroe's status adorn his excellent new event; Indianapolis, where tournament director Mark Miles had switched the former clay-court championship to Decoturf; and the last Dallas Finals that a shrinking World Championship Tennis would be promoting at Reunion Arena. The victory in Dallas was particularly satisfying because it enabled him to grab a much prized victory over Lendl, who had beaten him decisively in the quarter-final of the Australian Open when McEnroe had made his debut at Flinders Park three months before. He then went on to defeat Brad Gilbert in the final. It had been a long and glittering road that Lamar Hunt had opened when he put up $50,000 for the winner back in 1970. Ken Rosewall had won it then and now it was fitting that another legend should be holding the famous WCT trophy aloft for the last time.

But, from a psychological point of view, nothing was as significant as the fact that McEnroe proved he could win five matches in a

Grand Slam event by reaching the semi-final at Wimbledon, something he had not achieved since the 1985 French Open. He had to work for it, too, battling back from a two set to love deficit for the very first time to beat Australia's Darren Cahill in the first round. Having closed that one 8–6 in the fifth set, McEnroe got past Richey Reneberg and Jim Pugh before winning an acrimonious clash with John Fitzgerald 6–4 in the fourth. Fitzgerald is one of those honest, straightforward Aussies who have absolutely no comprehension of what McEnroe is all about and no tolerance for his antics. When the New Yorker started complaining about some line calls, Fitzgerald responded like a farm lad from South Australia and told him to cut out the bullshit. McEnroe reacted badly and the word 'tantrum' was back in the headlines. Everyone started talking about how to control McEnroe and what should be done if he let loose again in his next match. But, twenty-four hours after they happen, McEnroe's outbursts are as old as yesterday's newspapers, and while listening to Peter Jones, Fred Perry and Christine Janes discuss what was likely to happen as they chatted on air in our BBC Radio studio next to No. 1 Court I remember thinking, 'Nothing will happen. He has got it all out of his system now.'

Part of that prediction was based on the fact that McEnroe's quarter-final opponent was to be Mats Wilander, whom he respected and liked, which always has a bearing on how he behaves. Sure enough there was no problem as McEnroe, suddenly remembering what it was like to play sublime tennis in the world's most wonderful tennis arena, surged away from the Swede to win 7–6, 3–6, 6–3, 6–4, offering the Centre Court crowd as lovely an exhibition of tennis artistry as had been seen all fortnight.

On grass, Edberg was a much more difficult proposition, however, and McEnroe was always a point or two away from the breakthrough he needed as the Swede won a tough three-setter 7–5, 7–6, 7–6. Nevertheless McEnroe was encouraged and, apart from one blemish, his play maintained a very high standard for the rest of the year.

The blemish was a bad one. He had a perfect draw stretching before him at the US Open, with Aaron Krickstein the only seed standing between him and a semi-final meeting with Becker once

Wilander fell in the second round to the promising Californian Pete Sampras. But, in possibly one of his worst displays ever from a technical point of view, the former four-time champion at Flushing Meadow lost to a largely unknown Dutchman called Paul Haarhuis 7–5 in the fourth set. It is true that Haarhuis played exceptionally well and showed no signs of choking when the opportunity to serve out for a storybook victory presented itself. But McEnroe had no business losing to a player ranked 136 in the world on a court that should have suited him so perfectly.

He had, after all, virtually owned that Stadium Court at Flushing Meadow in the early eighties and, even under lights, when conditions tended to be more taxing, he had been able to draw energy from the electricity generated by the crowd, though a good percentage of them were against him. But that was no longer the case. A combination of circumstances that had to do with living in California, revelling in the really appreciative crowds that flocked to see him in Europe and the mere fact of growing older had unplugged him from the New York scene. Instead of being able to draw inspiration from the chaos that always accompanies a big match on the Stadium Court, with people constantly on the move and hecklers in the corporate boxes behaving like the worst of the yuppie generation, he found it had become a distraction. Amazingly, New York was no longer his kind of town. The man who had spoken with surprising eloquence and feeling about the beauty of Paris, when we had dined near the Plaza Athenée one night a year before, was beginning to appreciate a different set of values. A lack of patience more than anything contributed to his loss against Haarhuis, and it made him sick when he realized what he had thrown away.

Despite all the success of the summer, the defeat was severe enough and shocking enough for him to consider, momentarily, whether there was any point in going on.

'If I play like that I should stop,' he told a group of players who had gathered around him in the competitors' lounge at Flushing Meadow a couple of days later. 'I can't go on embarrassing myself like that. It's a joke.'

Considering the animosity he creates on court, it may be

imagined that his peers would be only too pleased to see the back of such a dangerous rival. But Vijay Amritraj, Jakob Hlasek, Jimmy Arias, Richey Reneberg and a few others in that circle offered nothing but support and encouragement. 'Put it out of your mind,' they told him. 'Just forget it. You're playing far too well to quit now.'

Nothing helped him forget it quicker than his decision to enter the doubles with Mark Woodforde. Having to return to Flushing Meadow the very next day was the kind of therapy a rider needs when he falls off a horse. 'Woody' is just the sort of cheerful, upbeat character John wanted to have at his side in such circumstances and they were soon playing with sufficient harmony to win their first Grand Slam title together by beating the tough pair of Ken Flach and Robert Seguso in the final.

Ever since his return to full-time competition, McEnroe had spoken of his desire to enjoy his tennis more. Enjoyment was something he felt he dare not flirt with during his years as No. 1 in the world. The strain and the striving for that unattainable goal of perfection had been too intense. Now, with a real effort being made to get life in perspective, aided enormously by the responsibilities of a family, the possibilities of taming the wilder edges of his talent was within his grasp. Perfection in that respect, too, was still a long way off. But he would have been a strange man indeed had he not responded to the previously unrealized joy of popularity. With it, the last lingering remnants of that early shyness were falling away and he was learning, albeit belatedly, to respond to the clamour of the crowd and rouse them to even greater heights of adulation. The arm raised in acknowledgment was becoming a hallmark, but there had been moments too when the sheer fervour of his supporters still embarrassed him.

The extent to which he had become a cult figure in certain countries, notably France and Italy, was brought home to him most forcibly at the French Open in 1988 when he had appeared at the back of the players' enclosure on the Centre Court to take a quick look at the quarter-final in which Henri Leconte, a Frenchman after all, was in the process of beating Boris Becker. It was a riveting encounter and one which should have had the crowd's undivided attention. But as soon as McEnroe appeared, a murmur started from those seated nearest to where he was standing. He wasn't trying to make a spectacle of himself. In fact, dressed in a black raincoat and surrounded by other players, he could hardly have been more inconspicuous as he chatted to his Davis Cup captain, Tom Gorman. But the word spread and, at the next changeover, the chant started, 'McEnroe, McEnroe . . .' Then, even as Leconte and Becker returned to the court, a Frenchman called out in heavily accented English: 'We love you, McEnroe!' It was extraordinary. Realizing that he was in danger of disrupting the match simply by standing there, McEnroe withdrew.

This was a level of popularity he had never dreamed of. The great anti-hero was learning what it was like to be loved. Some of the calluses that had grown on the outer edges of his personality as a defence against the public wrath, and which had contributed to his becoming a more cynical and suspicious character, were being massaged away.

'It's definitely more enjoyable this way,' he told me after he had received another tumultuous welcome at the Paris Open. 'It gives you the incentive to go on playing.'

Obviously, it also offered the incentive to go where he was wanted – and that meant Europe. It was no coincidence that, after dispensing with the services of Advantage International who had looked after his affairs for many years, he should choose Sergio Palmieri, an Italian promoter and former Davis Cup player, as his agent. Palmieri was able to organize exhibitions in between tournaments all over the Continent and generally smooth McEnroe's path in countries where he could not speak the language. He had come to accept Sergio's presence at his side, whereas the constant proximity of others while he was on the road was something he could never tolerate for long. Being surrounded by an entourage had never been his style, but he realized now that it was impossible to travel alone.

And the travelling did not stop. The lure of Europe led him to committing himself to a six-week European tour in the autumn of 1989, longer than he had ever undertaken before at that time of year. It began with Ion Tiriac's special event in Stuttgart and ended at a venue of much previous triumph and disaster, the old Wembley

Arena, where he spent time between matches at the Silk Cut Championships feeding his two boys huge helpings of ice cream and chocolate cake as they sat on his knee in the competitors' lounge. Out on court he was in an equally extravagant mood, leading the crowd in a passably tuneful rendition of 'Happy Birthday, dear Jakob' after he and his Swiss partner had won the doubles title on Jakob Hlasek's birthday. Finally he was learning how to enjoy himself.

Even during matches he was proving himself capable of a little sardonic humour. When 'Cyclops', the electronic eye which calls the service line, had come up with a few dubious, mostly anti-McEnroe decisions during his match with Michael Chang at the Masters a couple of weeks later, he turned to Vitas Gerulaitis, Ilie Nastase and a few other friends sitting at courtside and said, 'I don't want to sound paranoid, but this machine knows who I am!' Nastase, who had once got down on his hands and knees and tried to remonstrate with the thing, knew exactly how he felt.

In the ever-changing political areas of the game, McEnroe's voice was being heard with increasing frequency. Having criticized the structure of the new ATP Tour with typical candour when it was first announced twelve months before, it was gratifying to learn that the former ATP Vice-President had taken part in discussions with Executive Director Hamilton Jordan aimed at reducing the work-load that was being placed on the top-ranked ticket sellers, who every tournament was anxious to coerce into an even greater playing commitment than had been the case under the Men's Tennis Council. After further talks with Player Council President Vijay Amritraj at the Paris Open, McEnroe was prepared to throw his weight behind the new venture.

Certainly McEnroe was unequivocal in his reaction to the amazing counterattack launched by the International Tennis Federation in the form of a six-million-dollar Grand Slam Cup, originally intended for eight players, that would offer two million dollars to the winner. As the event was to be played in West Germany two weeks after the new ATP Finals in Frankfurt, where the total prize money would be 'only' two million dollars, it was hard to view it as anything other than a blatant attempt to undermine the players' own circuit by throwing vast sums of money at players who didn't need it.

McEnroe, who joined Boris Becker in denouncing the Grand Slam Cup as inflationary and unnecessary, did not, as usual, bother to mince his words.

'They are trying to turn us into money whores,' he said. 'It's obscene. None of us should play unless a large percentage of the prize money is donated to charity.' So much for the myth of money-grabbing tennis players.

In the light of all this – the new-found enjoyment, the remarkable return to form on court, and the high moral standards he was setting off it – the happenings in the 1990 Australian Open were a tragic setback for McEnroe. To become the first player to be defaulted out of a Grand Slam Championship in the Open era was the last thing he wanted, the last thing he needed, and, given his exemplary start to the tournament, the last thing anyone expected. But, as he was the first to admit, he only had himself to blame.

His behaviour, admittedly, had been far from perfect while partnering Pam Shriver in the Hopman Cup, a team competition devised and promoted with considerable success by the former Wimbledon doubles champion Paul McNamee.

'John was great to play with in the mixed,' Pam told me. 'He was always a very supportive partner, but some of the stuff he pulled in the singles wasn't too good.'

The United States team lost in Perth when McEnroe went down to Spain's Emilio Sanchez, but he quickly put that behind him and was in a much calmer frame of mind the following week when he beat Stefan Edberg to win the final of the Rio Challenge in Adelaide after being match point down.

Having moved Tatum and the kids into an apartment at Gordon Place in Melbourne, McEnroe embarked on his smoothest and most impressive start to a Grand Slam event since the US Open in 1984. After beating the Frenchman Thierry Tulasne 6–2, 6–1, 6–1 in the opening round at Flinders Park, he dismissed the rugged Austrian Alex Antonitsch with equally unruffled flair 6–1, 6–2, 6–1. Dan Goldie, a former star of McEnroe's alma mater at Stanford, was the next victim of the No. 4 seed's overpowering form and went down

6–3, 6–2, 6–2. Ivan Lendl wasn't admitting anything but, as the high seed in McEnroe's half, Ivan must have been viewing this kind of progress with increasing alarm.

'It's too early to start talking about winning the tournament,' a relaxed and affable McEnroe told us in press conference. 'But I feel good about myself and my game. I've spent a long time in Australia so as to prepare properly for the event this year, but having my family with me has made it so much easier. Everybody's been really nice and helpful and we're all having a good time.'

The good time ended abruptly after he had won the first set with deceptive ease, 6–1, against the pugnacious little Swede Mikael Pernfors. For the first time that week, McEnroe was feeling out of sorts with himself. The game wasn't flowing; the timing wasn't there. So, lulled into a state of false security by the absence of confrontation in the earlier rounds, McEnroe began falling back into a behavioural pattern that had become second nature: niggling complaints over line calls, repeated requests for spectators to stop using flash on their cameras – all the usual things that irritate McEnroe when the temperament is racing and the mind unsure. It was nothing terrible. There was no screaming or carrying on in the manner of the demented teenage prodigy with the red headband. We were way past that. But, nevertheless, this was McEnroe on edge and when Pernfors, who had attacked brilliantly from the baseline against Henri Leconte in the previous round, took the second set 6–4, the sense of anxiety only increased.

The worst of it from McEnroe's point of view was the ease with which Pernfors started to break his serve. There was a spell at the start of the third set when seven consecutive games went against serve and it was then, at 2–1, that McEnroe, annoyed at another highly dubious call, walked up to the lineswoman in question and stared at her from a range of about three feet. In the chair, British umpire Gerry Armstrong quite rightly decided that this was intimidation and gave McEnroe a code of conduct warning.

Under the old Men's Tennis Council (MTC) rules which governed the now defunct Grand Prix circuit, that would have been the first step in what was a four-step route to default. The next would have been the loss of a point; then a game; then default. What

McEnroe insisted he did not realize was that the Grand Slam tournaments had hurriedly adopted new and stricter rules brought in by the players themselves for their own ATP Tour. One was to cut the length of time allowed between serves from thirty seconds to twenty-five, and the other was to shorten the default process to three steps by eliminating the game penalty.

Strangely, it had only been two days before that Armstrong and I had been discussing the new rules which the umpires had been at great pains to explain to the players before every match started in the New South Wales Open the previous week.

'But it can all happen very fast now,' Armstrong warned me. 'Before long, some player is going to find himself defaulted just because the procedure is so much shorter.'

Armstrong, one of the best of a strong contingent of young umpires who had been trained as professionals under Marshall Happer's regime at the MTC, could not have been more prescient. The fact that McEnroe had not played in the New South Wales Open was not, of course, any excuse for being ignorant of the rules (they were posted on the walls of the locker room at Flinders Park), although it must be said that, as late as the Friday of the previous week, neither Vijay Amritraj nor his ATP Vice-President Larry Scott had had time to read the new ITF rules which had only just been handed to them. The breakaway tour had created a great deal of revisionist work in the backrooms of the game and there were a lot of people who did not know everything that was going on.

Nevertheless, McEnroe had no excuses. If anyone should have been wary of possible rule changes, it was he. So, when he bounced his racket in frustration at 2–3 in the fourth set, a harmless gesture that Armstrong might possibly have let pass but didn't, McEnroe was one step away from being thrown off court. That, obviously, did not cross his mind as he walked over to the chair and demanded to see the Supervisor to complain about the umpire's decision which had deprived him of a game (the next step following the earlier warning), thus making the score 4–2 to Pernfors.

Again, he did not scream at Supervisor Ken Ferrar or the referee Peter Bellenger when they appeared on court. He merely pointed out that, although the racket was slightly cracked, he had every intention of continuing to play with it and therefore it could not be deemed broken. It was pure McEnroe, that argument, and, not surprisingly, Ferrar would not fall for it. Although slightly harsh, Armstrong's decision was perfectly correct and Ferrar was much too conscious of the need to back up his umpires to question their judgement.

That should have been the end of it. McEnroe, although 2–4 down, was still two sets to one up, having taken the third 7–5, and, as Pernfors has no reputation as a great fifth-set player, there should not have been too much of a problem about McEnroe winning the match. But that was the logical viewpoint.

Remember what McEnroe had said to me? 'I become a maniac out there. I am capable of saying anything.'

And so, reaching again into the past, he spat out a residue of venom that had been lingering deep inside him. Although it came out as personal abuse of the worst kind, there was nothing personal about it. He does not hate Ferrar or Bellenger. He simply hates what they represent. They are the jailers of his talent; the men who try to handcuff his genius. It took him three seconds to say what he said. Three seconds that destroyed months of preparation, ruined his chances of winning a Grand Slam title that was starting to look as if it was within his grasp, and gave all his critics every excuse in the world to pour out the abuse that they, too, had been bottling up inside them for years.

As soon as Ferrar heard McEnroe's vicious retort, he turned round and walked back to the umpire's chair. Armstrong nodded agreement with what Ferrar said and then announced, 'Default, Mr McEnroe. Game, set and match, Mr Pernfors.'

The words pierced McEnroe's brain and you could see the look of shock and pain express itself in his eyes. Then he smiled the wry smile of a condemned man, walked quietly over to his chair and seemingly did not notice Pernfors' attempts to offer his condolences.

While the vast majority of the crowd leapt to their feet and started to shout 'We want McEnroe!', Pernfors appeared in the interview room looking mildly shell-shocked which, depending on his hairstyle of the moment, is not unusual for him.

'Yes, I was surprised it happened,' he said. 'It is not the way I would have wanted to win, but the players made these new rules and we should stick to them.'

If there is a small spark of light in all this darkness, it serves to illuminate another myth about tennis players. The Grand Slam Cup episode had proved that not all of them would sell their souls for a pot of gold, and now the second most frequent charge one heard when the ATP Tour was announced – that the players could never be trusted to police themselves – had also been proved wrong.

Although this was a Grand Slam event, run under the auspices of the ITF, the stricter default rule was an ATP Tour creation and the umpire in the chair was an ATP Tour umpire. Nor was Armstrong, who is paid by the ATP Tour, afraid to state his case afterwards.

'If Ken had not heard what McEnroe said, I would have defaulted him anyway because I heard it,' said Armstrong. 'Abuse of that kind should be an immediate default offence.'

Armstrong is absolutely right on that point. I have been one of the severest critics of overzealous, interfering umpires over the years because on innumerable occasions they have been the instigators of the trouble that has followed. But, equally, they have been too lenient in clamping down on abuse, which should not be tolerated under any circumstances. At least that has now been established beyond reasonable doubt.

When he eventually appeared in the press conference room – again, those who don't know better had expected him to duck it, which he never does, come rain or come shine – McEnroe seemed almost resigned to what had happened.

'This is a long story that culminates in me being defaulted in a big tournament. It was bound to happen. I don't feel good about it, but I can't say I'm totally surprised.'

Then McEnroe, stupidly, went on to give his critics all the ammunition they were looking for.

'If I'd known the rules I probably would have bounced my racket, but I probably wouldn't have said what I said to the guy.'

Several Australian commentators who had been calling him puerile and infantile for years could now call him the one name they had been dying to use for years. Cheat.

He had proved it, hadn't he? they argued. He had proved that everything he did on court was done purely as a method of upsetting his opponent. If he was so much in control that he could stop himself one step short of default, it was all premeditated. That was a perfectly logical conclusion to draw from what he said, even though he was struggling to offer a rational explanation for a traumatic and highly embarrassing occurrence that had happened just thirty minutes before. Murderers get months in which to prepare their case and have a highly trained lawyer to help them do it. McEnroe has never been afforded such luxuries.

The facts, as I see them, are these. McEnroe is perfectly correct in suggesting that he would have controlled himself had he known he was so close to being defaulted. He has always had a sixth sense that warned him of impending danger – a sense that totally failed him here, just as all senses begin to fail when you get older.

But being able to grab the handbrake as the car starts sliding down the hill does not mean that you were in control of the vehicle in the first place. In the vast majority of instances McEnroe does *not want* to blow up on court and does *not* do so as a deliberate act of intimidation. He may not care very much whether the end result is intimidating, but that is not the motivation for behaving in the way he does. In fact, there is no motivation at all. It is simply an explosion of pure anger at what he sees as an injustice.

I can state this as an absolute certainty on two counts. Firstly, I have watched more of McEnroe's matches than virtually anyone alive and, secondly, I was born under the same Aquarian sign. I suffer from exactly the same kind of reaction to perceived wrongs, even if they might seem trivial to someone else. I get angry. Often I wish I didn't, but at least I don't have to show my fury in front of 15,000 people and a worldwide television audience.

McEnroe does and McEnroe pays for it. Those types who are the first to throw stones want him to pay more; want him out of the game for good. They are entitled to their point of view. But I simply don't agree with them. What I do agree with are the first two paragraphs of John Roberts' report from Flinders Park for *The Independent*. It read:

'By showing John McEnroe the door at the Australian Open here yesterday, tennis began the new decade as it ought to have started the old one. The turbulent New Yorker's disqualification was nine years overdue.

'If there had been a similar response to McEnroe's appalling behaviour at Wimbledon in 1981, the sport, and its most talented player, might have avoided years of acute embarrassment.'

All that is undeniable and the last person to try to refute it would be McEnroe himself. It may still not be too late to do him some good.

Dennis Ralston was in Melbourne and a heavy dose of discipline had done him no harm early in his own career when he was known as the bad boy of American tennis. Ralston, who is now enjoying considerable success as Yannick Noah's coach, was suspended just before the US Championships at Forest Hills in the early sixties. 'I was mad as hell at the time,' Dennis told me as little clusters of people gathered in the passageways of the players' area at Flinders Park, talking in shocked tones about the day's events. 'But I have no doubt at all that it did me good. I needed straightening out and I am sure John would have benefited from a much stricter discipline right at the start of his career.'

Like Ralston, Noah is one of those people who have taken the trouble to look past the public pout and discover what McEnroe is really like. They are good enough friends for Noah to have been able to tease McEnroe gently in the locker room afterwards and say how happy he was to see him defaulted as now they wouldn't be able to meet in the quarter-finals.

'John usually kicks my ass, so I am happy in that respect,' Noah said. 'But obviously I am sorry for John. He is a friend of mine and I don't like to see that happening to him. But he shouldn't have said whatever it was he said.'

Pat Cash and Mark Woodforde were others who sprang to McEnroe's defence, but it would be wrong to suggest that the locker room was awash with tears. There were many players who felt he had it coming to him and that it was long overdue.

There have, of course, been other players who have behaved far worse than McEnroe in those good old days when everyone, perceived through those timelessly rose-coloured spectacles, was supposed to be such a gentleman. But none of them were nearly as talented as McEnroe and so have faded into history. As far as one can remember, there have been just two instances of players being defaulted out of Grand Slam Championships prior to the Open era. In the fifties a wild American called Earl Cochell was thrown out of Forest Hills for punching the referee on the nose, and in 1963 the crafty Colombian Willie Alvarez, who now coaches the very well-mannered Sanchez brothers, went a little too far when he entered into a wrestling match with his opponent. Or maybe it was the umpire, who happened to be a young Australian not well versed in Latin American etiquette. The exact details fail me but I distinctly remember seeing Alvarez, whose bottom stuck out rather alarmingly even in those days, rolling around in the clay on Court 4 at Stade Roland Garros, his hands around his adversary's throat. The referee was most displeased.

So Gerry Armstrong and his colleagues can be thankful they live in such a well-disciplined age for, quite seriously, the behaviour of the vast majority of tennis professionals today is remarkably good. Of the various distortions Australia's Channel Nine news team perpetrated during its coverage of the Australian Open, none was more stupid than the attempt to make it appear that McEnroe's default had hauled the tour back from the brink of anarchy. This particular piece of fiction gave Channel Nine the excuse to air grainy film clips of McEnroe, Connors and Nastase yelling and screaming at umpires ten or twelve years before. It would have been impossible for them to show anything of more recent vintage because there has been no such material. Trying to suggest that McEnroe's behaviour somehow suggests the norm as far as behaviour on the tennis circuit is concerned is akin to offering up *Private Eye* as an example of a commonplace newspaper.

'Fines for bad behaviour have been falling steadily for the past five years,' said the senior ATP road manager Weller Evans, who is in the best position of anyone to monitor such things. 'Considering the kind of pressure they are under week after week, following a lifestyle that is a lot more stressful than people think, the young players, in particular, maintain a very high standard of discipline.'

So where is the generation of screaming banshees that McEnroe's behaviour was supposed to have fostered? Some parents of young tennis players may tell you that little Willie wanted to ape Big John in everything he did, but surely it was up to the parents to ensure that he didn't?

'McEnroe has always been the player I admired most,' David Wheaton, a charming twenty-year-old from Minnesota, told us after he had reached the quarter-finals at Flinders Park. 'But there was no chance of my being allowed to behave like he did. My parents would have put a stop to that very quickly.'

We can stack up the positives and the negatives of McEnroe's influence on the game according to our own attitudes. Those who see only the bad aspects in his personality are, in my opinion, taking a very blinkered view of the demands of the world in which we live. People are increasingly bored with the commonplace and McEnroe, through his exceptional skills as well as his frequently outrageous behaviour have ensured that pro tennis continues to be compulsive viewing for millions around the world. Professional sport should remain, first and foremost, sport by firmly adhering to all the rules and constrictions that finally stopped McEnroe dead in his tracks at the Australian Open. But it is also show business – and those who believe otherwise are deluding themselves.

What the future holds for McEnroe as I write is unclear. He was climbing the wall, literally and to some extent figuratively, when Vijay Amritraj and I drove out to see him at Malibu in March. After being ushered into the beach-front house by Tatum's brother Grif, we found two of the McEnroes with sweat pouring off them in the little gymnasium that has been equipped with all the latest fitness machines. Patrick, fresh from appearing in the Newsweek Cup doubles final at Indian Wells with Jim Grabb, was on the treadmill while John was working the wall climber, arms and legs pumping and his heart beat monitored by an electrode clamped to his chest. It was steady at 152.

'If it hits 200 I either stop or drop dead,' he grinned. 'Actually I can manage this OK but I can't serve or hit a backhand. I did something to my shoulder warming up against Tim Mayotte in Milan and it got worse.'

McEnroe had not been a happy fellow since his default. Even though he reached the semi-final in Milan, the loss to Mayotte did nothing to improve his humour and by the time he reached the semis again in Toronto the following week, he was decidedly tetchy. A first round loss to Richey Reneberg in Philadelphia told him all he needed to know about his state of mind, and he pulled out of Memphis the following week, muttering about his ridiculous schedule.

When he climbed down off the wall, McEnroe led us through to the brightly decorated living room and unburdened himself.

'I'm seriously thinking about quitting for good,' he said. 'I never contemplated that seriously before, not even when I stopped back in '86. But I just don't know whether I can go on like this. I'm worried about what I might do on court. It's obvious I have a problem and I need help. I've been trying to clean up my act for 12 years now and I just can't seem to control myself. I never thought a psychiatrist would do any good, but maybe I should try to find one now.'

Well, he never did beat about the bush. He is always pretty forthright in public but everything is stripped bare when he is amongst friends and this was much clearer evidence than anything he had said in those agonising moments after the Pernfors match about his attempts to reform — attempts that he recognised had failed.

He went on to explain the strangely destructive workings of his mind that led to disaster in Melbourne. 'My attitude changed the day before I played Pernfors. Everything had been going so well and I had been feeling so completely in control on court that I realised I was going to get through to the semis against Lendl. Then the thought of having to rush home and leave almost immediately for Milan and another four weeks on the road hit me. The pressure suddenly built up and I was in a nervous state again by the time I played Pernfors. I used an obscenity at the end because I have allowed that sort of talk to creep into my everyday conversation. I never used to talk like that even when I was mad. I've got to cut it out.'

He was equally critical of the way he allowed himself to be persuaded to play tournaments just to earn money he didn't need.

'I don't know how I am going to be feeling in a few weeks but let's go and have a look at my schedule. You tell me where I should play.'

We went upstairs to his second floor study where a large pop art sketch of Tatum and himself – one of the last painted by Andy Warhol before he died – hung behind the desk. For the first time he was planning to play Nice and Monte Carlo in an attempt to give himself some serious clay court play before Rome and Paris.

'It should be OK, I've had some good times in the South of France. And maybe it's time I played Queens again. Clive Bernstein has cleared up that problem with the committee. But can I handle it all? I don't know . . .'

After the conversation had turned to the problems facing the new ATP Tour, of which McEnroe was highly critical, we drove down the road to the Malibu Deli and munched on huge sandwiches until Gary Muller, the South African touring pro who had been practising nearby, joined us. Amritraj, who had just been elected to the Tour Board, tried to get John to spell out his grievances which, as usual, were based partially on a genuine desire to make the game better for everybody but also on the persecution complex that lies at the heart of so many of McEnroe's problems.

Still at odds with the demands his extraordinary talent places on him; still searching for ways to tame that talent, McEnroe has never been able to come to terms with an imperfect world any more than he has been able to tolerate his own shortcomings.

When we left him in the parking lot, an unlikely-looking millionaire in baggy track suit trousers and crumpled T-shirt, the road ahead was strewn with uncertainty. Only his place in the Valhalla of sporting superstars was secure.

John McEnroe Career Statistics to January 1990

Name: JOHN MCENROE
Born: Wiesbaden, West Germany
Date of birth: 16.2.1959
Height: 5' 11"/1m 80
Weight: 165lbs/74kg
Plays: L

Prize Money Career (US dollars):
10,887,456
Best Career Rank: 1
Current Rank: 4
Doubles Rank: 8

Wife: Tatum O'Neal (married 8/1/86)
Sons: Kevin (5/23/86) & Sean (9/23/87)

Grand Slam singles titles: Wimbledon 1984/83/81; US Open 1984/81/80/79
Grand Slam doubles titles: Wimbledon 1984/83/81/79; US Open
1983/81/79 (w/Fleming) 1989 (w/Woodforde)

Singles titles: 75, as follows:

1989–(3) Lyon, WCT/Dallas Finals, Indianapolis
1988–(2) Japan Open, Detroit
1986–(3) Los Angeles, San Francisco, Scottsdale
1985–(8) Philadelphia, Houston, Milan, Chicago, Atlanta, Stratton
Mountain, Montreal, Stockholm
1984–(13) Philadelphia, Richmond, Madrid, Brussels, WCT/Dallas, Forest
Hills-TOC, Queen's, Wimbledon, Toronto, US Open, San Francisco,
Stockholm, Masters (Jan. '85)
1983–(7) Philadelphia, WCT/Dallas, Forest Hills-TOC, Wimbledon,
Sydney Indoor, Wembley, Masters (Jan. '84)
1982–(5) Philadelphia, San Francisco, Sydney/NSW, Tokyo Indoor,
Wembley
1981–(10) Boca West, Milan, Frankfurt, Los Angeles, WCT/Dallas,
Queen's, Wimbledon, Cincinnati, US Open, Sydney/NSW
1980–(9) Richmond, Memphis, Milan, Queen's, US Open, Brisbane, Sydney
Indoor, Wembley, Montreal-WCT Challenge Cup
1979–(10) WCT/Dallas, New Orleans, Milan, San Jose, Queen's, South
Orange, US Open, San Francisco, Stockholm, Wembley
1978–(5) Hartford, San Francisco, Stockholm, Wembley, Masters (Jan. '79)

Doubles titles: 74, as follows (57 with Fleming is a Grand Prix record):

1989–(3) Milan, Wembley (w/Hlasek), US Open (w/Woodforde)
1988–(2) Los Angeles, San Francisco (w/Woodforde)
1986–(4) Stratton Mountain, San Francisco, Paris Indoor, Wembley
(w/Fleming)

1985–(1)Houston (w/Fleming)
1984–(7) Richmond (w/P. McEnroe), Philadelphia, Madrid, Wimbledon,
Toronto, San Francisco, Masters (Jan. '85) (w/Fleming)
1983–(6) Los Angeles, Wimbledon, US Open, San Francisco, Wembley,
Masters (Jan. '84 (w/Fleming)
1982–(6) Queen's, Sydney Indoor (w/Rennert), Philadelphia, Cincinnati,
Wembley, Masters (Jan. '83) (w/Fleming)
1981–(9) Los Angeles, Cincinnati (w/Taygan), Las Vegas, Forest
Hills-TOC, Wimbledon, US Open, San Francisco, Sydney Indoor, Masters
(Jan. '82) (w/Fleming)
1980–(11) Memphis (w/Gottfried), South Orange (w/Maze), Brisbane
(w/Mitchell) Philadelphia, Milan, Forest Hills-TOC, San Francisco, Maui,
Sydney Indoor, Wembley, Masters (Jan. '81) (w/Fleming)
1979–(17) Richmond (w/Gottfried), Indianapolis (w/G. Mayer), London
Doubles, New Orleans, Milan, Rotterdam, San Jose, Wimbledon, Forest
Hills, South Orange, Toronto, US Open, San Francisco, Stockholm,
Wembley, Bologna, Masters (Jan. '80) (w/Fleming)
1978–(8) Hartford (w/Maze), Basle (w/Fibak), South Orange, San Francisco,
Cologne, Wembley, Bologna, Masters (Jan. '79) (w/Fleming)

Year-by-Year Highlights:

1989–Runner-up at Montreal (1. Lendl), Toulouse (1. Connors);
Semifinalist at Milan, Japan Open, Wimbledon, Paris Ind., Wembley,
Masters; Doubles Runner-up at Lyon (w/Hlasek); Doubles S F at Aust. Open,
Paris Indoor (w/Woodforde) Toulouse (w/Nargiso); Doubles Q F at Forest
Hills-TOC (w/P. McEnroe).
1988–Runner up at Indianapolis (1. Becker); Semifinalist at Los Angeles, San
Francisco; Quarterfinalist at Toronto, Paris Indoor; R D 16 at French Open.
1987–Runner-up at Philadelphia, Rotterdam, Brussels, WCT/Dallas;
Semifinalist at Roma; Quarterfinalist at Montreal, US Open; Led Lendl 7–6,
1–4 in Stratton Mountain final but was cancelled due to rain.
1986–Semifinalist at Stratton Mountain; Quarterfinalist at Paris Indoor.

Holds the record for most US Davis Cup wins (39–8 singles, 15–1
doubles)

Held the year-end No. 1 singles ATP computer ranking from 1981–84
and No. 1 in doubles from 1979–83.

He is No. 2 on the all-time prize money list with more than $10 million
surpassed the mark in February 1989 at Lyon. He led the tour in prize money
in 1984 ($2,026,109), 1981 ($991,000) and 1980 ($972,369.

He won 98 matches in 1979 (16 losses), but in 1984 he had a .965
winning percentage with an 82–3 match record. It is the highest winning
percentage in Grand Prix history.

He entered the computer rankings in August 1976 with a first round win
South Orange, NJ. He cracked the top 100 in the ranking after the 1977

Wimbledon where he qualified and reached the semifinals (jumped to No. 71 from 233).

He was elected Vice-President of the ATP in August 1984 (one-year term) and was elected a member of the ATP Board in June 1984 (two-year term). He was active in the fund raising efforts for the Cystic Fibrosis Foundation, the ATP's official charity, and he won the 1982 CF Humanitarian Award.

Has earned nine ATP awards: Newcomer of the Year and Most Improved Player 1982; Player of the Year, 1984/83/81; and Doubles Team of the Year, 1984/83/81/79 (w/Fleming).

He has won both the singles and doubles titles in the same tournament 29 times, more than double the total of any other player in the Open Era. His total of 149 singles and doubles titles is a career Grand Prix record.

Earned a career-high $2,026,109 and 13 singles titles in 1984.

Information courtesy of ATP, Florida.

Career Scores Against Major Opponents to January 1990

CONNORS VS. MCENROE — MCENROE 19–13

	TOURN-NAME	SURF	RND	WINNER	SCORES			
77	WIMBLEDON	GRASS	S	CONNORS	63	63	46	64
77	BOSTON	CLAY	R32	CONNORS	57	62	75	
78	INDIANAPOLIS	CLAY	Q	CONNORS	36	61	61	
78	US OPEN	HARD	S	CONNORS	62	62	75	
78	MASTERS	CARPET	R1	MCENROE	75	30		RET
79	LAS VEGAS	HARD	S	CONNORS	75	64		
79	WCT DALLAS	CARPET	S	MCENROE	61	64	64	
79	US OPEN	HARD	S	MCENROE	63	63	75	
80	PHILADELPHIA	CARPET	F	CONNORS	63	26	63	36 64
80	MEMPHIS	CARPET	F	MCENROE	76	76		
80	WCT DALLAS	CARPET	F	CONNORS	26	76	61	62
80	WIMBLEDON	GRASS	S	MCENROE	63	36	63	64
80	US OPEN	HARD	S	MCENROE	64	57	06	63 76
81	WEMBLEY	CARPET	F	CONNORS	36	26	63	64 62
81	MASTERS	CARPET	R2	MCENROE	62	75		
82	PHILADELPHIA	CARPET	F	MCENROE	63	63	61	
82	QUEEN'S	GRASS	F	CONNORS	75	63		
82	WIMBLEDON	GRASS	F	CONNORS	36	63	67	76 64
82	SAN FRANCISCO	CARPET	F	MCENROE	61	63		
83	QUEEN'S	GRASS	F	CONNORS	63	63		
83	CINCINNATI	HARD	S	MCENROE	67	61	64	
83	WEMBLEY	CARPET	F	MCENROE	75	61	64	
84	WCT DALLAS	CARPET	F	MCENROE	61	62	63	
84	FRENCH OPEN	CLAY	S	MCENROE	75	61	62	
84	QUEEN'S	GRASS	S	MCENROE	62	62		
84	WIMBLEDON	GRASS	F	MCENROE	61	61	62	
84	CANADIAN OPEN	HARD	S	MCENROE	26	62	63	
84	US OPEN	HARD	S	MCENROE	64	46	75	46 63
85	CANADIAN OPEN	HARD	S	MCENROE	62	63		
86	SAN FRANCISCO	CARPET	F	MCENROE	76	63		
87	CANADIAN OPEN	HARD	Q	CONNORS	63	36	63	
89	TOULOUSE	HARD	F	CONNORS	63	63		

BORG VS. MCENROE — 7–7

	TOURN-NAME	SURF	RND	WINNER	SCORES	
78	STOCKHOLM	HARD	S	MCENROE	63	64

	TOURN-NAME	SURF	RND	WINNER	SCORES				
79	RICHMOND,VA	CARPET	S	BORG	46	76	63		
79	NEW ORLEANS	CARPET	S	MCENROE	57	61	76		
79	ROTTERDAM	CARPET	F	BORG	64	62			
79	WCT DALLAS	CARPET	F	MCENROE	75	46	62	76	
79	CANADIAN OPEN	HARD	F	BORG	63	63			
79	MASTERS	CARPET	S	BORG	67	63	76		
80	WIMBLEDON	GRASS	F	BORG	16	75	63	67	86
80	US OPEN	HARD	F	MCENROE	76	61	67	57	64
80	STOCKHOLM	CARPET	F	BORG	63	64			
80	MASTERS	CARPET	R1	BORG	64	67	76		
81	MILAN	CARPET	F	MCENROE	76	64			
81	WIMBLEDON	GRASS	F	MCENROE	46	76	76	64	
81	US OPEN	HARD	F	MCENROE	46	62	64	63	

LENDL VS. MCENROE   LENDL 17–15

	TOURN-NAME	SURF	RND	WINNER	SCORES				
80	MILAN	CARPET	S	MCENROE	63	16	62		
80	US OPEN	HARD	Q	MCENROE	46	63	62	75	
81	FRENCH OPEN	CLAY	Q	LENDL	64	64	75		
81	USA V CZH QF	HARD	R1	LENDL	64	1412	75		
81	MASTERS	CARPET	S	LENDL	64	62			
82	WCT DALLAS	CARPET	F	LENDL	62	36	63	63	
82	CANADIAN OPEN	HARD	S	LENDL	64	64			
82	US OPEN	HARD	S	LENDL	64	64	76		
82	MASTERS	CARPET	F	LENDL	64	64	62		
83	PHILADELPHIA	CARPET	F	MCENROE	46	76	64	63	
83	WCT DALLAS	CARPET	F	MCENROE	62	46	63	67	76
83	WIMBLEDON	GRASS	S	MCENROE	76	64	64		
83	SAN FRANCISCO	CARPET	F	LENDL	36	76	64		
83	MASTERS	CARPET	F	MCENROE	63	64	64		
84	PHILADELPHIA	CARPET	F	MCENROE	63	36	63	76	
84	BRUSSELS	CARPET	F	MCENROE	61	63			
84	TOC-NY	CLAY	F	MCENROE	64	62			
84	WORLD TEAM CUP	CLAY	F	MCENROE	63	62			
84	FRENCH OPEN	CLAY	F	LENDL	36	26	64	75	75
84	US OPEN	HARD	F	MCENROE	63	64	61		
84	MASTERS	CARPET	F	MCENROE	75	60	64		
85	TOC-NY	CLAY	F	LENDL	63	63			
85	WORLD TEAM CUP	CLAY	F	LENDL	67	76	63		
85	STRATTON MT	HARD	F	MCENROE	76	62			

	TOURN-NAME	SURF	RND	WINNER	SCORES			
85	CANADIAN OPEN	HARD	F	MCENROE	75	63		
85	US OPEN	HARD	F	LENDL	76	63	64	
87	US OPEN	HARD	Q	LENDL	63	63	64	
88	FRENCH OPEN	CLAY	R16	LENDL	67	76	64	64
89	AUSTRALIAN OP	HARD	Q	LENDL	76	62	76	
89	WCT DALLAS	CARPET	S	MCENROE	67	76	62	75
89	CANADIAN OPEN	HARD	F	LENDL	61	63		
89	MASTERS SNGLS	CARPET	R1	LENDL	63	63		

BECKER VS. MCENROE BECKER 6–1

	TOURN-NAME	SURF	RND	WINNER	SCORES					
85	MILAN	CARPET	R32	MCENROE	64	63				
85	STRATTON MT	HARD	S	BECKER	36	75	76			
87	GRM v USA WGPO	CARPET	R2	BECKER	46	1513	810	62	62	
88	INDIANAPOLIS	HARD	F	BECKER	64	62				
89	MILAN	CARPET	S	BECKER	62	63				
89	PARIS INDOOR	CARPET	S	BECKER	76	36	63			
89	MASTERS SNGLS	CARPET	S	BECKER	64	64				

WILANDER VS. MCENROE MCENROE 7–6

	TOURN-NAME	SURF	RND	WINNER	SCORES					
82	USA v SWD QF	CARPET	R5	MCENROE	97	62	1517	36	86	
83	FRENCH OPEN	CLAY	Q	WILANDER	16	62	64	60		
83	CINCINNATI	HARD	F	WILANDER	64	64				
83	AUSTRALIAN OP	GRASS	S	WILANDER	46	63	64	63		
83	MASTERS	CARPET	S	MCENROE	62	64				
84	STOCKHOLM	HARD	F	MCENROE	62	36	62			
84	SWD v USA F	CLAY	R4	MCENROE	63	57	63			
84	MASTERS	CARPET	S	MCENROE	61	61				
85	FRENCH OPEN	CLAY	S	WILANDER	61	75	75			
85	US OPEN	HARD	S	MCENROE	36	64	46	63	63	
87	BRUSSELS	CARPET	F	WILANDER	63	64				
87	ROME	CLAY	S	WILANDER	61	63				
89	WIMBLEDON	GRASS	Q	MCENROE	76	36	63	64		

EDBERG VS. MCENROE MCENROE 7–3

	TOURN-NAME	SURF	RND	WINNER	SCORES		
84	RICHMOND, VA	CARPET	Q	MCENROE	62	63	
84	US OPEN	HARD	R64	MCENROE	61	60	62
85	STOCKHOLM	HARD	S	MCENROE	63	75	

TOURN-NAME	SURF	RND	WINNER	SCORES		
86 LOS ANGELES	HARD	F	MCENROE	62	63	
86 SAN FRANCISCO	CARPET	S	MCENROE	75	62	
87 ROTTERDAM	CARPET	F	EDBERG	36	63	61
87 WCT DALLAS	CARPET	S	MCENROE	76 67	76 64	
88 JAPAN OPEN	HARD	F	MCENROE	62	62	
89 JAPAN OPEN	HARD	S	EDBERG	64	63	
88 WIMBLEDON	GRASS	S	EDBERG	75	76	75

GILBERT VS. MCENROE   MCENROE 12–1

TOURN-NAME	SURF	RND	WINNER	SCORES		
83 WIMBLEDON	GRASS	R32	MCENROE	62	62	62
83 SAN FRANCISCO	CARPET	R32	MCENROE	64	61	
83 SYDNEY INDOOR	HARD	R16	MCENROE	62	60	
84 SAN FRANCISCO	CARPET	F	MCENROE	64	64	
85 PHILADELPHIA	CARPET	R16	MCENROE	61	62	
85 HOUSTON	CARPET	Q	MCENROE	63	63	
85 LOS ANGELES	HARD	Q	MCENROE	46	60	63
86 MASTERS	CARPET	R16	GILBERT	57	64	61
86 LOS ANGELES	HARD	S	MCENROE	61	36	63
87 STRATTON MT	HARD	Q	MCENROE	63	62	
88 JAPAN OPEN	HARD	S	MCENROE	63	06	64
88 WCT DALLAS	CARPET	F	MCENROE	63	63	76
89 JAPAN OPEN	HARD	Q	MCENROE	26	64	61

AGASSI VS. MCENROE   MCENROE 2–1

TOURN-NAME	SURF	RND	WINNER	SCORES		
86 STRATTON MT	HARD	Q	MCENROE	63	63	
88 LOS ANGELES	HARD	S	AGASSI	64 06	64	
89 WCT DALLAS	CARPET	Q	MCENROE	46	30	RET

CHANG VS. MCENROE   MCENROE 4–0

TOURN-NAME	SURF	RND	WINNER	SCORES		
88 FRENCH OPEN	CLAY	R32	MCENROE	60	63	61
88 LOS ANGELES	HARD	R16	MCENROE	62	64	
89 PARIS INDOOR	CARPET	Q	MCENROE	64	63	
89 MASTERS SNGLS	CARPET	R1	MCENROE	62	57	64

Information courtesy of ATP, Florida.

INDEX